RECLAIMING **42**

RECLAIMING
42

Public Memory and the Reframing of
Jackie Robinson's Radical Legacy

DAVID NAZE

University of Nebraska Press • LINCOLN

Chapter 4, "Jackie Robinson Day: The Contemporary
Legacy," originally appeared in *Out of Bounds: Racism
and the Black Athlete*, 135–58 (Santa Barbara: Praeger,
2014). Used with permission.

Library of Congress Cataloging-in-Publication Data
Names: Naze, David, author.
Title: Reclaiming 42: public memory and the
reframing of Jackie Robinson's radical legacy /
David Naze.
Other titles: Reclaiming forty-two
Description: Lincoln: University of Nebraska Press,
[2019] |Includes bibliographical references and index.
Identifiers: LCCN 2018048120
ISBN 9780803290822 (hardback: alk. paper)
ISBN 9781496214942 (epub)
ISBN 9781496214959 (mobi)
ISBN 9781496214966 (pdf)
Subjects: LCSH: Robinson, Jackie, 1919–1972. |
African American baseball players—Biography.
| Baseball players—United States—Biography. |
Collective memory—United States. | Racism in
sports—United States. | Political activists—United
States—Biography | Major League Baseball—
History. | BISAC: SPORTS & RECREATION / Baseball /
History. | SOCIAL SCIENCE / Ethnic Studies / African
American Studies.
Classification: LCC GV865.R6 N39 2019 | DDC
796.357092 [B]—dc23 LC record available at
https://lccn.loc.gov/2018048120

Set in Scala OT by E. Cuddy.

In memory of Ed Wilson and Andrew Muldowney. Thank you for helping shape my sports world.

Contents

Preface

On April 15, 1947, the racial landscape of America changed. Not because of crisis, chaos, or confusion, but because of a political vision. That is, a vision shared by members of numerous communities and organizations. A vision not without disagreement or controversy. A vision that required colossal ambition and strategy. A vision that endured years of disappointment. A vision that was met with heavy resistance as well as anticipated approval. It was on this day that Jack Roosevelt Robinson broke baseball's modern-day color barrier, forever changing the ways in which Americans viewed, and experienced, their favorite pastime. No longer would baseball stand as a mere outlet for or escape from our quotidian routine, but baseball would forever become a microcosm of how communities embrace or reject cultural change. Mainstream America was seeing something new on the baseball field, literally, which consequently has forced us to consider the following question: Did Jackie Robinson's breaking of baseball's color barrier capture our national imagination, or does our memory of Jackie Robinson illuminate our own desires for what Barack Obama refers to as "racial reconciliation on the cheap"?[1]

Either way we answer that question, there is no mistaking that Jackie Robinson was a radical. And by *radical* I mean in the most robust way possible. That is, Robinson was an individual whose mere presence in a white-dominated space posed a racial, political, and cultural threat beyond the periphery, a threat that posed a challenge for even those who supported racial change on a national level. This book is written through the lens of a rhetorical scholar who comes from an admittedly privileged, white, male perspective, who is specifically interested in how Jackie Robinson's legacy has been constructed by a mainstream, white, and male perspective. Robinson's identity as a radical should be clear after seven decades since his breaking of baseball's color barrier. In fact, not only should it be clear, but it should also be celebrated, if for no other reason than Robinson's legacy has forced us to reconsider what racial reconciliation truly looks like in today's mainstream America. But Robinson's identity as a radical is not celebrated, at least not in the ways by which we typically celebrate his legacy. We can pretty much agree that Jackie Robinson was pivotal in the way America began talking about racial injustice. We can pretty much agree that Jackie Robinson was a unique baseball player with a skill set unseen by many mainstream baseball fans in the 1940s. And we can pretty much agree that Jackie Robinson is an American hero and icon, deserving of every accolade and celebration of his impact on American culture. But there appears to be something missing from those sentiments, something that hasn't quite been identified in the mainstream narrative when talking about Jackie Robinson's legacy. In fact, there is a lot missing. Case in point: When we hear the name Jackie Robinson, what images and thoughts do we immediately conjure about the man? It would be a safe bet to assume that most of us would immediately think about his integrity, his perseverance, his personal character, his maturity, and, perhaps most of all, his courage. It would likely be just as safe of a bet that we don't think about his political aspirations, his postbaseball career, his harsh critiques of Major League Baseball (MLB), or his clashes with fellow members of the civil rights movement. Those details, the details that came to define the man more privately than publicly, have been forgotten, or more likely never been taught to the general public. Consequently, those details have been forgotten or neglected because it has been easy to forget or neglect them. And this should not come as a surprise to us as a society. Often we forget the details of one person's legacy, either because of the passage of time or because we were never really taught about those details in the first place. That is what this book is attempting to do: to reclaim at least some of the details of Jackie Robinson's life, the details that have been too easily washed away in a culture that seems to be satisfied with the idea that we live in a postracial society.

Generations never saw Robinson play, and that allows numerous overly reductive and simplistic narratives to survive. Knowing the depths of Jackie Robinson the player and political agent would take hard work that most are unwilling to begin. The ease with which we have chosen to remember Jackie Robinson in a general sense makes it a convenient legacy. In fact, Michael G. Long's recovery of Robinson's documented civil rights discourse has allowed us access to a Robinson not typically conveyed in mainstream recollections of his legacy. Long's book *First Class Citizenship: The Civil Rights Letters of Jackie Robinson* addresses how problematic it is to reduce Robinson's memory and legacy to an oversimplified account of convenience. As Long proclaims:

> Perhaps it has been safe and convenient for us to picture Robinson as the tolerant, clean-cut ballplayer who gently helped to integrate professional sports in the United States. But however comfortable it may be, our collective focus on the first part of his baseball career is utterly unfair to the Jackie Robinson who loudly criticized the practices and policies of racist America, devoted countless hours to civil rights fundraising and rallies, twisted the arms of politicians hungry for black votes and yet fearful of a white backlash, and encouraged young African Americans who have since become well-known veterans in the ongoing battle for civil rights.[2]

Long is right. It is utterly unfair to reduce Robinson's legacy solely to the beginning of his baseball career. Building on Long's work, this book aims to move beyond Robinson the baseball player.

Perhaps the most compelling, maybe even the most obvious, historical parallel we can draw from Robinson's legacy is that of Martin Luther King Jr. Both were pivotal characters in the genesis of the modern American civil rights movement; both drew the ire of members in both white and black communities as each man attempted to balance the racial tensions found within and across racial lines; both have been celebrated as the most important figures in their respective spaces; both have been praised for being subservient when it was deemed necessary and criticized for being outspoken when it was deemed inappropriate; both were skilled at their respective crafts but perhaps praised, at least from a mainstream perspective, more for their personal character and courage than their celebrated skill set; and both, sadly, have had the details of their legacies oversimplified, commodified, and forgotten. The parallel is so similar in fact that when Michael Eric Dyson exclaimed in his book *I May Not Get There with You: The True Martin Luther King, Jr.* that we have failed Martin Luther King's racial memory, I couldn't help but immediately think about our same failure on behalf of Jackie Robinson. The following passage from Dyson's biocriticism provides a basis for understanding the critical importance of reexamining the commemorative legacies of agents of social change such as MLK and others:

> Since his death, we have made three mistakes in treating King's legacy. First, we have sanitized his *ideas*. . . . Second, we have twisted his *identity*. . . . Finally, we have ceded control of his *image*. . . . King becomes a convenient icon shaped in our own distorted political images. He is fashioned to deflect our fears and fulfill our fantasies. King has been made into a metaphor of our hunger for heroes who cheer us up more than they challenge or change us.
>
> Using King in this way harms our nation's racial memory. Indeed, it feeds the national amnesia on which we desperately depend to deny the troubles we face, troubles that grow from our unwillingness to tell the truth about where we have come from and where

we are headed. . . . Reducing King's brilliantly disturbing rhetoric to sound bites lets us off the hook. It even causes us to forget his challenging ideas. . . . Ironically, King's friends sometimes short-change his challenging legacy by forgetting that he made America better by disagreeing with it when it was wrong. . . . When King was suddenly crowned the Negro of choice within the white press, some blacks became suspicious of his authentic connection to the needs and interests of ordinary black folk.[3]

While Dyson's proclamation focuses specifically on King, we cannot ignore the similarities to how we have made significant mistakes in treating Robinson's legacy. The fact that King owned a gun, for example, is seldom, if ever, mentioned during our conversations of Martin Luther King Day because we have so flattened our remembrances of him. In terms of Robinson, we too have sanitized Robinson's ideas, we have twisted his identity, we have ceded control of his image, and we have used his legacy to fulfill our oversimplified racial reconciliation fantasies. Consequently, Robinson too has become a convenient icon, and such a convenience also harms our nation's racial memory. Furthermore, the role that the white press played in cultivating Robinson's mainstream cultural ethos made many folks in the black community feel betrayed at worst and skeptical at best. Evidence of these parallels will be provided throughout this book. Mainstream America's version of Robinson's story, like King's, makes it okay not to remember the multiple layers to Robinson's political legacy. Such a cultural and racial amnesia feels good. In other words, ignorance is bliss. As King might say, the way we remember Jackie Robinson cements the "tranquilizing drug of gradualism" that mainstream American audiences crave.

As this book began, it focused more broadly on African Americans in sport, but then moved to an examination of the Negro Leagues, then to a more specific emphasis on Jackie Robinson. However, the choice between an examination of the Negro Leagues or an analysis of Jackie Robinson led to the realization that a separation of the two would not be as productive as a critical assessment of not only how the two go hand in hand but also how Jackie Robinson *and* the Negro Leagues inform one another. Furthermore, the political ramifications of baseball's racial landscape could not be ignored, as the Negro Leagues as an institution and Jackie Robinson as both a player and a political advocate were, and still remain, rooted in racial politics.

As an academic scholar, I am trained in rhetorical studies, and that is the lens through which I write this book. However, my targeted audience is not merely those trained in or familiar with a rhetorical studies background. That is, my purpose is to appeal to a broader audience interested in baseball history and culture more broadly and Jackie Robinson and the Negro Leagues specifically. With that said, it should be noted to the reader that I plan to use some rhetorical studies vocabulary throughout the book. The intention is not to make this book inaccessible or foreign to those without academic or rhetorical interests, but to in fact make accessible some of the rhetorical concepts with which broader audiences may not be familiar. Ultimately, this book offers an examination into what political work baseball does in order to manage its own narrative of power. My charge, both as a rhetorical scholar and frankly as a baseball fan, is to broaden that narrow focus and, if nothing else, to offer an analysis that examines the complexities of Robinson's political persona and dissects the ways in which his legacy is more relevant today than ever before. Through my research, I have come to the realization that the institution of Major League Baseball has become a space in which controversy is often silenced for the purpose of perpetuating a palatable narrative that celebrates a racially inclusive tone. Despite the desire of Major League Baseball to rejoice in its contemporary racially tolerant policies, the institution of baseball has merely perpetuated a self-congratulatory narrative that praises itself for its willingness to include participants of any race. That type of narrative may seem fine on the surface, but as we will see throughout this book, it becomes problematic, even dangerous, when the narrative simply stops there. After all, as documentarian Ken Burns proclaims, "The baseball story, let's be honest, is written by white guys. . . . We want to feel good about ourselves, so we tend to select the information we make, and we don't do anybody, not ourselves nor Jackie, any service by not painting a fuller picture."[4]

Acknowledgments

The conceptualization, creation, and completion of this book would not have been possible without the help of many advisers, colleagues, peers, friends, and loved ones. A special debt of gratitude goes first to Robert Terrill. His guidance and encouragement made me believe that this is a project worth pursuing and worthy of giving it a voice. The Department of Communication and Culture at Indiana University was the incubating space whereupon this project began. Without the existence of that graduate department, this book would not have happened. It is also important to recognize my mentors and advisers who helped me begin this journey at Indiana University, Northern Illinois University (IU, NIU), Prairie State College, and elsewhere: John Butler, Brad Manley, Elighie Wilson, Ed Schwarz, Michael Butterworth, Jon Cavallero, Byron Craig, Korryn Mozisek, Jeff Motter, Bob Ivie, Phaedra Pezzullo, and Carolyn Calloway-Thomas, among others. A special thanks goes to Bob Betts and Judy Santacaterina, who introduced me to the disciplines of communication and rhetorical studies and showed me how they can shape my worldview. My family deserves special recognition, as it has been their encouragement and support that has made this book complete. Thank you to my father, Richard Naze, whose love for sports has helped shape my worldview on and off the playing field. Thank you to my mother, Susan Fletcher, whose talent for writing eloquent prose has permeated throughout my academic life. Thank you to Mary Ellen Naze, Rita Naze, Loretta and Kenneth Turner, Tricia Kitelinger, and Teri Lesniewski, whose constant praise and encouragement will never be forgotten. I would be remiss to not mention my students, faculty, and administrative colleagues at IU, NIU, and Prairie State College who have indulged me in my research pursuits. My colleagues at Joliet Junior College have offered encouragement and excitement through this process as well. Thank you to Rob Taylor and his editing team at the University of Nebraska Press, who championed this project from day one and walked me through my maiden voyage into the world of manuscript publication. And certainly to my wife, Katie, whose knack for knowing when to challenge me with this project and when to let me walk away from it and refresh has allowed me to give this project a voice and make it what it is. And most of all to Jackie Robinson himself, who demonstrated that sport is a wonderful endeavor but civic responsibility is an absolute democratic necessity.

RECLAIMING 42

Introduction

Have We Failed Jackie Robinson's Legacy?

When Jackie Robinson broke Major League Baseball's color barrier more than seven decades ago, the American landscape experienced the beginning of a cultural shift. This cultural shift required colossal ambition and strategy and was met with heavy resistance as well as anticipated approval. This shift forever altered the ways in which Americans viewed their favorite pastime. In the spring of 1947 Jackie Robinson captured the national imagination, making the people's favorite pastime no longer just playful but political.

The topic of baseball's color barrier has long been discussed, researched, and published, and Jackie Robinson is, not surprisingly, typically the prologue to most conversations about such a topic. The notion of another project or historical examination of arguably baseball's most iconic figure may leave us wondering, what else could be said about Jackie Robinson? If prompted to do so, most Americans could, at the very least, paint the broad strokes of Robinson's legacy. We would most likely not be surprised to find that a discussion on Jackie Robinson would include a familiarity with his athletic prowess, baseball accolades, and of course his status as the first black baseball player to play in the Major Leagues in the modern-day era. Yet most Americans have lost sight of the scope of Robinson's legacy. America's craving of nostalgia has resulted in our remembering Robinson's legacy in primarily oversimplified ways. Our culture's longing for nostalgia, which ultimately stems from an opposition to or critique of the present state of affairs, allows us to delight in losing ourselves within the Jackie Robinson narrative. Rooted in public memory studies, this book argues that the institution of Major League Baseball is hegemonic, meaning that it is a space in which controversy is often silenced for the purpose of perpetuating a palatable narrative that celebrates a racially inclusive tone.

Major League Baseball's construction of Robinson's legacy is less about Jackie Robinson and more about how a hegemonic institution, like Major League Baseball, controls the narrative and the numerous power dynamics involved. By looking at the commemorative discourse and other elements that Major League Baseball includes in its celebration of Robinson's legacy, it is equally as important to examine the elements that Major League Baseball excludes from its celebration, leaving us as critical consumers with a better opportunity to investigate which controversial components are silenced and why they are left out. I examine Robinson's legacy as it is presented by Major League Baseball in the present day and critique the limitations of that portrayal by comparing the presentation of Robinson in the National Baseball Hall of Fame and Negro Leagues museums and analyzing Robinson's public clashes with Paul Robeson and Malcolm X. In the end, this project is a more nuanced understanding of white power that uses baseball as a way to manage white supremacy.

In contemporary, mainstream America, Robinson is often remembered as a black man who endured many obstacles on and off the baseball field. In short, Robinson is remembered as a baseball player. Granted, he is remembered as a very significant baseball player, but his identity, and therefore his memory, has been relegated to the boundaries of a baseball diamond and to the context of a sport. As years pass, he is remembered more and more as an icon of civility. Frankly, this is where we have failed Jackie Robinson. We celebrate, correctly, Robinson's social impact, we praise his pioneering spirit, we admire his ambition, and we revere his reticence in the most tumultuous of times. What we fail to do, as a culture, is call attention to his political voice during and after his playing career, and we certainly do not call attention to the negative repercussions that his inclusion in Major League Baseball had on many factions within the black community. Understandably, many Robinson admirers are not completely comfortable with an emphasis on Robinson's controversial and political endeavors during and after his baseball career. That lack of comfort will become clear throughout this book. After seventy years of celebrating Robinson's inclusion in baseball and forty-seven years of remembering his life, it is easy to forget the details of one individual's legacy. Unfortunately, it is even easier to construct a memory that depicts the positive attributes we want highlighted and to leave out the negative attributes we want forgotten, such as his willingness to challenge the very institution—Major League Baseball—that gave him access to mainstream society that was otherwise denied to people of color. To reiterate, the ease with which we have chosen to remember Jackie Robinson in a general sense makes it a convenient legacy. Robinson's memory should be anything but convenient. That convenience is a point of contention throughout this book.

Jackie Robinson Today

In 1969 sociologist Harry Edwards argued that the black athlete was in revolt, arising from "his new awareness of his responsibilities in an increasingly more desperate, violent, and unstable America." Edwards made this declaration at a time when America was experiencing particularly turbulent racial animosity, in an era that saw sports provide a public platform for social protest. Whether it was Muhammad Ali, Bill Russell, Lew Alcindor, Tommie Smith, or John Carlos, the black athlete was seizing an opportunity to speak out against social injustice. As Edwards argued,

> The revolt of the black athlete in America as a phase of the overall black liberation movement is as legitimate as the sit-ins, the freedom rides, or any other manifestation of Afro-American efforts to gain

freedom. The goals of the revolt likewise are the same as those of any other legitimate phase of the movement—equality, justice, the regaining of black dignity lost during three hundred years of abject slavery, and the attainment of the basic human and civil rights guaranteed by the United States Constitution and the concept of American democracy. It was inevitable that this revolt should develop.[1]

While Edwards provided scholars and sports enthusiasts alike an introduction to the rise of the activist athlete fifty years ago, scholar Abraham Khan has recently introduced that same audience to the decline of the activist athlete. Focusing on the role that former Major Leaguer Curt Flood played in the rise of professional sports free agency, Khan sheds light on how today's professional athletes are often perceived, rightly or wrongly, as focused more on financial and celebrity status than taking public stances against social injustices. Khan asks us to consider if idealizing outspoken athletes of the past is an endeavor that might provide us a compass for how we view today's athlete. As Khan suggests, "Contemporary accusations of deliberate ignorance urge critical reflection on the historical details of the black athlete as a revolutionary subject. One wonders if that familiar pantheon of lost heroes has not somewhere been corrupted from within. . . . So it is easy and perhaps even worthwhile to idealize Jackie Robinson and Muhammad Ali and John Carlos and Tommie Smith and cobble them together into a bygone civic ethos, the memory of which might recuperate sport's civic spirit."[2] That recuperation of "sport's civic spirit" is at the forefront of mainstream society's ideal version of Jackie Robinson's memory.

More than seventy years after breaking baseball's color line, the memory of Jackie Robinson's legacy has had a contemporary resurgence of sorts. Granted, the topic of Jackie Robinson has never truly been absent from America's national or racial memory. However, Robinson's legacy has been in the spotlight the past several years on a national stage, perhaps on a more notable platform than what we have seen in the past decade or more. Since Robinson emerged on the national stage in 1947, there have been countless books, articles, films, documentaries, and commemorations, among other media, that have taken measure of his life and legacy. But perhaps more than ever, the American public has looked to Jackie Robinson's life in the past several years to assign some semblance of definitive meaning to his national, cultural, racial, and sports legacy.

Several national events have, predictably, been compared to Robinson's breaking of baseball's color barrier because of the groundbreaking implications that have come along with them. Specifically, I argue that there have been six prominent events in the past decade that have contributed to discussions about Jackie Robinson's legacy and its subsequent contemporary resurgence: the election of President Barack Obama in 2008; the release of the major motion picture 42 in 2013; the first openly gay National Basketball Association (NBA) player, Jason Collins, coming out in a 2013 *Sports Illustrated* cover story; the drafting of college football's first openly gay player, Michael Sam, into the National Football League (NFL) in 2014; the controversy surrounding former San Francisco 49er Colin Kaepernick's refusal to stand for the national anthem before NFL games during the 2016 season; and the release of Ken Burns's 2016 documentary, *Jackie Robinson*.

When Barack Obama was running for president of the United States in 2008, immediate comparisons between Obama and Robinson were, predictably, at the fore of mainstream public discussions about race and the breaking of a monumental color barrier. Prior to the general election, *Politico* published an editorial titled, "Obama = Jackie Robinson?" The opening line of the editorial made a direct comparison to the two African American pioneers and their approach to breaking a historical racial barrier:

> Barack Obama is like baseball pioneer Jackie Robinson—enduring jeers without the ability to hit back. . . . "Barack Obama has the capacity to hit," (Jesse) Jackson (Jr.) said at a breakfast panel just before the opening of the Democratic National Convention. "But he is in the

situation where he can't hit back, which Jackie Robinson could not do. . . . He had to be able to run the bases, even though the crowd was jeering the first African-American on the field." Jackson, son of the civil rights leader, said Obama is in the same situation: "He has to keep smiling, because no one wants an angry African-American man in the White House."[3]

Jackson's reference to "an angry African-American man in the White House" is a direct comparison to Dodgers general manager Branch Rickey's insistence that Robinson, or whomever was to be chosen to integrate Major League Baseball, must have the "courage not to fight back" in the midst of the racial vitriol that was surely to be directed toward Major League Baseball's first African American player.

Similarly, Mike Jones of the *St. Louis American* made a similar comparison in his editorial titled "Barack Obama Is the Jackie Robinson of American Politics." As Jones argued:

In November 2008, America broke the ultimate political color barrier: It elected a man who was not white to be president of the United States, Barack Obama. . . . Because of Barack Obama, America is at the beginning stage of changes that will be of epic proportions. It is impossible to imagine the changes in the future course of America because of one black man. In fact, we've been here before, though you'd have to be over 90 years old to have witnessed it. The last time America underwent a social change with this kind of seismic implications was 1947. Before there was Montgomery, before there was Selma, before there was a March on Washington, there was Jackie Robinson. Today baseball is a game played by overpaid marginal athletes, but in the first 60-plus years of the 20th century baseball was much more. Then, it was said, if you understand baseball, you understand America. And no man of color, no matter how skilled, was allowed to play Major League Baseball. It represented everything that white America considered American, and it could only be played by white men—a lot like presidential politics before 2008. Jackie Robinson and Barack Obama share important historical similarities.[4]

Jones's explanation that "we've been here before" through the endeavors of Jackie Robinson in 1947 makes the comparison hard to ignore. Harvey Wasserman offered an almost identical question as the one put forth by Jones in his article titled "Can Barack Obama Become the Jackie Robinson of the American Presidency?" As Wasserman stated, "Sixty-one years ago, a truly great athlete broke the color line in America's 'National Pastime,' which still resides near the core of our culture. Now the question of whether Barack Obama can do the same for the American presidency has moved to center stage."[5] The reminders of Jackie Robinson via Barack Obama's presidency continued with Michael Dowd of the *Huffington Post*:

> Watching Barack Obama on the stump and particularly in the debates reminds me of Jackie Robinson, the man who broke the color barrier in Major League Baseball. When Branch Rickey brought Robinson to the majors, he had to be more than a great player to make my beloved Brooklyn Dodgers. He promised Rickey, the Dodgers General Manager, that he would endure the expected wave of racism that would wash over him. From the beginning, Jackie Robinson endured all manner of insult and affronts with a poise that was extraordinary. His inner strength was needed as much as his ability and talent on the diamond. His Herculean effort changed baseball and society. Senator Obama came out of political nowhere to the United States Senate and an improbable run for the Presidency. Many of us were aware of his intellect and the soaring oratory inspiring people in a way that wasn't heard of for decades. . . . I saw another great man who had that extra something that the great Jackie Robinson had.[6]

Again, the correlation between Robinson's ability to endure the "expected wave of racism" and Obama's poise on the national stage during the 2008 presidential debates is made explicit. The title of Frank Palacio's 2016 book about Robinson and Obama made a similar explicit comparison to the two men: *Obama, the Jackie Robinson President*. As Bonnie Sierlecki points out, "Moreover, media narratives consistently portrayed barrier-breaking black athletes—such as Jackie Robinson, Arthur Ashe, Muhammad Ali, Michael Jordan, and Tiger Woods—as 'paving the way' for Obama's victory. Reinforcing the idea that sport has been a 'saving grace' for black citizens, Obama's campaign 'used' sports imagery to build a positive image for the candidate, yet it also may have deflected attention from the persistence of racial discrimination and inequality in the U.S. For some, the election of the first African-American president would come to symbolize the end of racism in America." Shaun Powell of *Newsday* drew a direct connection between Barack Obama's election and the sports pioneers that came before him, stating, "Joe Louis, Arthur Ashe and especially Jackie Robinson helped put Barack Obama on the ballot."[7] The desire to imagine a postracial America with Barack Obama's election draws similar comparisons to that same desire to imagine a postracial Major League Baseball, and America, with Robinson's integration sixty years earlier.

The comparisons to Barack Obama are plentiful, and such comparisons served as the first catalyst for Robinson's contemporary resurgence. In 2013, sixty-six years after Robinson's Major League debut, the major motion picture *42* was released, a biopic that characterized Jackie Robinson's first year in the Major Leagues in 1947. Starring Chadwick Boseman as Jackie Robinson and Harrison Ford as Dodgers general manager Branch Rickey, *42* was the first major motion picture to focus on Robinson and the 1947 season. However, there were initial plans in 1995 for the major production of a Jackie Robinson biopic. It was originally planned to have Spike Lee direct and Hollywood A-lister Denzel Washington play the role of Robinson. The original plans included a 1997 release date to "coincide with the 50th anniversary of Robinson's achievement."[8] The film, however, never came to fruition. The 2013 film made quite a splash on the American movie scene, with reviews ranging from high praise to mixed reactions that many critics described as having missed the mark for a potentially bolder take on Robinson's volatile experience during the 1947 season. The *New York Times* suggested that the film *42* found itself somewhere in between such a needed bolder approach but settled for the safer method instead, arguing that the film "gestures toward the complicated and painful history in which its subject was embroiled. . . . [Instead] it is blunt, simple and sentimental, using time-tested methods to teach a clear and rousing lesson." Overall, the reviews were primarily positive. Of historical note was the film's domestic box-office revenue. *Forbes* reported that 42 broke records for an opening weekend for any baseball movie ever produced, bringing in $27.3 million. When adjusted for inflation, it's also the most of any baseball-themed opening weekend. The film would go on to gross more than $95 million domestically.[9]

While the nation's first election of a black man as president and a major motion picture biopic set the wheels in motion for prominent Jackie Robinson discussion in popular culture circles, perhaps nothing generated more Robinson discussion than three national controversies. Most notably, the controversies surrounding three athletes catalyzed a quest for a cultural resolution of some kind in the last five years: Jason Collins, Michael Sam, and Colin Kaepernick. Collins, Sam, and Kaepernick, while not the focus of this study on a larger scale, offer a point of comparison to Jackie Robinson that appeared to be irresistible to the mainstream American public and media when their respective controversies emerged into the public spotlight.

Jason Collins, a now-retired thirteen-year NBA veteran, came out publicly in an April 29, 2013, cover story in *Sports Illustrated*. The media comparisons to Jackie Robinson were immediate and consistent in a plethora of publications. The *Washington Post* could not resist the comparison in their article titled "Is Jason Collins the Jackie Robinson of 2013?"[10] William Cobb of ESPN.com delved into the comparison in his article "The Parable of Jackie Robinson." As Cobb expressed,

> Somewhere in the zeitgeist just after Jason Collins became a hashtag but not yet a hero, we seized on the idea that this was our 21st century Jackie Robinson moment. Seeking to contextualize Collins: Gay-American, African-American, of late Celtic- and Wizard-American,

the Dodgers second baseman became seemingly the instant referent of choice by cable news announcers, half-attentive observers and the truest authority in such matters: Twitter. Captured in broad strokes, the story of Jason Collins' emergence as the first openly gay athlete in the NBA made the comparison easy: a lone figure doing battle with calcified prejudices; a quiet man who is unwillingly reborn as a metaphor, an individual whose very presence changes the contours of a sport and therefore a nation. When you've got the president of the NAACP [National Association for the Advancement of Colored People] tweeting that "98" is the new "42" and the U.S. president phoning his support, there's a good chance you've made the moral all-star squad.[11]

Cobb points to what he basically describes as the predictability, the borderline laziness, involved with the quick comparison of Collins to Robinson in mainstream and social media. Cobb's point is echoed in Marc Tracy's article on Collins in the *New Republic*: "Upon hearing that Jason Collins, the journeyman National Basketball Association center, just became the first active male major-league athlete to announce publicly that he is gay, the mind involuntarily compares him to a previous sports trailblazer. When he donned a Brooklyn Dodgers uniform in 1947 . . . Jackie Robinson became the first black man to play Major League Baseball or any other professional sport." The national sentiments that Cobb and Tracy describe are evidenced in a *USA Today* article, whose headline provides a common correlation between the two athletes: "Jason Collins Walks in Robinson's Path." In the article David Person furthered the connection in his subheading: "First Openly Gay Active Male Athlete in a Major Sport Can Confront Backlash Like Number 42." The comparison is more explicit as the article offers the following assessment:

At a moment when baseball Hall-of-Famer Jackie Robinson is being celebrated in the popular biopic *42*, another professional athlete has taken a step that will break down social barriers. Jason Collins, a free-agent center in the NBA, announced that he is gay in an essay that was published on the *Sports Illustrated* website on Monday. As the first openly gay active male U.S. athlete in a major sport, Collins, 34, a 12-year veteran, is entering uncharted territory just as Robinson did 66 years ago. And though a lot has changed since the hostile Jim Crow-era in which Robinson entered the Major Leagues as the first African-American baseball player, the 21st century has not been very welcoming to lesbian, gay, bisexual and transgender (LGBT) people.

Whether it's caustic, profane insults or biblical denunciations, Collins would do well to use Robinson as his role model once he signs a new NBA contract and plays next season. Just like No. 42, if Collins has the guts not to dignify bigotry with an angry or equally offensive response, he will empower other LGBT athletes who yearn to come out—and their straight allies who want to support them.[12]

Person's suggestion that Collins "would do well to use Robinson as his role model" points to the public's need to immediately frame Robinson as the definitive standard by which any sports-related social endeavor should be measured. Prominent sports columnist Jason Whitlock ended his FoxSports.com article on the Jason Collins *Sports Illustrated* story with a reference to Robinson's arrival in Major League Baseball. As Whitlock opined, "This is a chance for basketball to be as important as baseball in 1947."[13] As noted above, the comparisons between Jason Collins and Jackie Robinson came quickly and rather predictably in the mainstream media spotlight. One year later, a similar narrative found its way into the national consciousness.

Michael Sam, college football's first openly gay player to enter the NFL draft in 2014, drew immediate comparisons to Robinson because of his potential as a sports trailblazer in the hypermasculine and heteronormative space of American football. Sam, a defensive end from the University of Missouri, was a consensus All-American and voted Defensive Player of the Year in the Southeastern Conference during his senior season. Sam publicly announced that he is "an openly, proud gay man" during an interview on ESPN's *Outside the Lines* in a February 9, 2014, episode. The announcement came two months prior to the NFL draft. Similar to Collins, the media comparisons to Jackie Robinson came quickly. Emma Margolin of MSNBC.com asked the question of comparison in the title of her article "Is Michael Sam the Gay Jackie Robinson?"[14] The USA Today's Jarrett Bell offered the sentiments he's received regarding the Sam and Robinson comparison:

> When Michael Sam checks in at the NFL scouting combine Friday as the first openly gay draft prospect in league history, the Missouri defensive end will be further distinguished by the standard combine gear emblazoned with his essential ID tag for the week. Sam is DL42.
>
> What a coincidence. Since Sam disclosed his sexual orientation 11 days ago, I've heard and read so many cases where people have been quick to compare him to Jackie Robinson, who broke Major League Baseball's color barrier in 1947. Now Sam's combine wardrobe—sweats, T-shirts, workout shorts, etc., with the numbers assigned by alphabetical order within the different position groups—will bear No. 42.
>
> Robinson, of course, wore No. 42.[15]

The observation that Sam's jersey number was the same as Robinson's for the NFL combine workouts made the comparison that much more germane to the Sam-Robinson discussion. Former NFL linebacker Brendan Ayanbadejo made a civil rights comparison in a CBSSports.com article. As Ayanbadejo argued, "We were there to celebrate his ground-breaking voyage that in many ways is similar to those of Jackie Robinson and Rosa Parks—extraordinary moments in the push for equality." The *Atlantic* offered a headline that touched on the explicit comparison between the two men: "Michael Sam, Jackie Robinson, and Why the Bigots Always Lose." Buster Olney of ESPN.com expressed the following comparison: "Some of the questions being asked in regards to Sam—will he be accepted in the locker room; how will others feel about sharing a community shower with him?—are in the same vein as those that were asked about Jackie Robinson at the outset of his time with the Brooklyn Dodgers, in 1947."[16]

Despite the comparisons, one glaring difference was the level of success the two men experienced at the professional level. Robinson was a Hall of Famer who earned Rookie of the Year honors and a Most Valuable Player (MVP) award during his career, whereas Sam, drafted by the St. Louis Rams in the seventh round of the NFL draft, never played an NFL game. The Rams released Sam in August 2014, a few weeks before the NFL season began. Following his release by the Rams, Sam joined the Dallas Cowboys practice squad but was released in October and never played in a regular-season game. When Sam was no longer in the NFL after the 2014 season, he joined the Montreal Alouettes of the Canadian Football League in 2015, making him the first openly gay football player in the CFL.[17] Despite Sam's lack of NFL success, the Robinson comparisons still shone after his shift to the CFL. As Dave Zirin expressed,

> When it was announced that free agent linebacker Michael Sam was signing with the Canadian Football League's Montreal Alouettes, many people's thoughts turned to Jackie Robinson. Robinson famously spent a year playing for the minor league Montreal Royals before making his way to the Brooklyn Dodgers. It was believed by Dodgers General Manager Branch Rickey, quite simply, that Montreal was less bigoted than the United States. Jackie Robinson would have the experience of playing without the weight of a dominant culture casually putting his humanity on trial with every at-bat. . . . The connection between Michael Sam and Jackie Robinson is even more illustrative. . . . The differences are real, but the similarities however have been too glaring to ignore. Michael Sam was going to have the burden of being "a first."[18]

Despite hopes for professional football success, even in the Canadian Football League, Sam left the CFL, and professional football entirely, after just one game with Montreal. As Abraham Kahn argues, "Given the media environment in which Sam finds himself, and the rhetorics of social change available to him and his advocates, Sam's embrace of Robinson's example makes good strategic sense. Our culture and social order, however, might be better served if the civil rights frame established through Robinson were less urgently applied, if we were provided space to elaborate the rethinking of intimacy incipient in Sam's unique social location."[19] Kahn's assertion that the social order would benefit from not rushing to a Jackie Robinson framework allows us to tap the brakes on so often asking the question that has become rather predictable, "What would Jackie Robinson say?"

While Jason Collins and Michael Sam shared a similar narrative within the context of Robinson comparisons, the controversy surrounding Colin Kaepernick in 2016 offered a Robinson comparison in a different vein. Colin Kaepernick, the former San Francisco 49ers quarterback who refused to stand for the national anthem before football games during the 2016 NFL season as a statement about police violence targeting the African American community, drew a less direct comparison to Robinson as Collins and Sam did but definitely sparked much public discussion about how his stance catalyzed amateur and professional athletes to push for social change through their respective sports platforms, not unlike Robinson.[20]

The *Sporting News* made it a point to defend any Kaepernick criticism through its recognition that the comparisons to Jackie Robinson are ill-fitting, albeit prominent, in their headline "Colin Kaepernick Is No Jackie Robinson and Shouldn't Have to Be."[21]

Craig Calcaterra of NBCSports.com invoked a famous passage from Robinson's autobiography, *I Never Had It Made*. As Calcaterra argued,

> One more bit of baseball via which we may reflect on the Colin Kaepernick controversy. In 1972 Jackie Robinson wrote his autobiography. In it he reflected on how he felt about his historical legacy as a baseball player, a businessman and as a political activist. . . . [Robinson wrote] "As I write this twenty years later, I cannot stand and sing the anthem. I cannot salute the flag; I know that I am a black man in a white world. In 1972, in 1947, at my birth in 1919, I know that I never had it made." Colin Kaepernick is not Jackie Robinson and America in 2016 is not the same as America in 1919, 1947 or 1972. But it does not take one of Jackie Robinson's stature

or experience to see and take issue with injustice and inequality which manifestly still exists.[22]

Yahoo! Sports contributor Mike Oz asked the question in his editorial headline "What Would Jackie Robinson Think about Colin Kaepernick's Protest?" The article goes on to make reference to the same Robinson autobiographical reference about his resistance to "stand for the anthem." As Oz states, "The world has changed a lot since 1972—maybe not enough for Colin Kaepernick's liking—but enough that no one can say for sure that Robinson would, 44 years later, agree with Kaepernick's stance. Though it is clear that at this point in his life, Robinson definitely knew the place from which Kaepernick is coming."[23] The references to Robinson's autobiography didn't stop there. Kirsten West Savali made similar references to Robinson's stance on saluting the American flag, comparing Kaepernick's and Robinson's refusal to stand for the national anthem:

> Jackie Robinson, in his 1972 autobiography, *I Never Had It Made,* described the moment when he realized that he could not "stand and sing the anthem," nor "salute the flag," which calls to mind recent statements made by San Francisco 49ers quarterback Colin Kaepernick. . . . In 1947 Jackie Robinson felt the beautiful burden of blackness as "The Star-Spangled Banner" played. His dual consciousness, something that even during the last year of his life he could not quite explain, is evident in each word of his book. The gravitational pull of racism at odds with the euphoric pull of patriotic possibilities is what continues to keep many people of color off-balance, slipping and sliding on streets filled with the blood of our children and the tears of those who love them.[24]

In Shaun King's editorial for the *New York Daily News,* the article's headline makes a bold pronouncement: "If You Hate Colin Kaepernick, You Must Hate Jackie Robinson." King offers his take on the comparison between the two men: "Jackie Robinson the World War II vet, Jackie Robinson the barrier-breaking baseball legend said, 'I cannot stand and sing the anthem. I cannot salute the flag.' I call that inconvenient history. Now, as every talking head in America piles on football player Colin Kaepernick for refusing to stand up for the national anthem, I must ask them this question. Was Jackie Robinson wrong? Do you hate him the way you seem to hate Colin Kaepernick?"[25] As these references to Robinson's autobiography note, the comparison between Robinson and Kaepernick was very much a part of public dialogue on athletes and social protest in a contemporary setting.

The resurgence of discussions regarding Jackie Robinson's legacy has been offered to this point through President Obama, the film *42*, Jason Collins, Michael Sam, and Colin Kaepernick. Finally, in 2016, acclaimed documentarian and social critic Ken Burns released his documentary *Jackie Robinson*. The four-hour film, which aired on PBS as a two-part series, chronicles the life of Robinson, both on and off the field. The *Los Angeles Times* lauded the film, describing its design to go beyond the baseball diamond: "Narrated by Keith David, with Jamie Foxx reading Robinson's words, it's a lump-in-the-throat trip, inspiring and exciting, through a life that has often been viewed only within the confines of the game he played; Burns widens the view to take in the husband, father, activist, columnist, businessman and political figure, for better and worse (but mostly for the better) an expression of the man." The film explores all areas of Robinson's life prior to, throughout, and following his Major League Baseball career. Topics include Robinson's military service, his time spent in the Negro Leagues, his marriage to Rachel Robinson, the relationships with his teammates, his business endeavors, his political presence after his playing career, his social justice endeavors, and his criticism of both Major League Baseball and his place as a black man in a white America.[26]

Burns's approach to the documentary was celebrated for his willingness to provide a depiction of Robinson in a comprehensive fashion, contrasted from the typical Robinson treatment of identifying Robinson as a patient and silent participant in the endeavor to break baseball's color barrier. As one publication expressed,

He has been celebrated many times before, most recently in *42*, a 2013 movie starring Chadwick Boseman. Robinson is also honored each April 15—the anniversary of his major league debut—when every player and coach on every team wears his jersey number. And he certainly will be remembered fondly for generations to come, in recognition of his pioneering legacy that transcends sports. But thanks to a new documentary from noted filmmaker Ken Burns, we're able to see and appreciate Robinson in an entirely different light. This is no fictionalized script, such as in *42* or *The Jackie Robinson Story*, a 1950 movie starring the player as himself and Ruby Dee as his wife. In *Jackie Robinson*, a two-part film that airs Monday and Tuesday on PBS, Burns delivers the unvarnished truth that Hollywood treatments often whitewash.[27]

ESPN.com offered similar praise in the headline of its documentary review, "Ken Burns' New *Jackie Robinson* Documentary Kills Myths of Civil Rights Legend." *Time* dissects the documentary's efforts to debunk aspects of the Jackie Robinson mythology.[28]

Within the context of the recent, massive, and prominent social protest related to police violence in the African American community, Burns explained that the documentary is relevant not only to fans of baseball but to broader American culture as a whole. According to *Mother Jones*, "Burns said his take on the Brooklyn Dodgers star will deconstruct the 'mythologized' version of him as a rule-abider, focusing instead on the broader spectrum of racial politics that he helped unsettle—one that has resonance in modern America." The documentary, Burns explained, is the result of two primary driving forces: his 1994 documentary, *Baseball*, and Robinson's widow, Rachel. While the film explores Robinson's life on the field, Burns attempts to "go beyond mythology to reveal more about the complicated life of a pioneering ballplayer." As Burns stated in a *Mother Jones* interview on the mythology of Robinson:

We felt that once you're free from the barnacles of that sentimentality, once you've liberated them from the mythology, then all of a sudden, what's this film about? Well, it's about Black Lives Matter. . . . They didn't call it that back then. It's about driving while black. It's about stop-and-frisk. It's about integrated swimming pools. It's about the Confederate flag. It's about black churches that are torched by arsonists. It's about the Southern strategy, beginning in the 1960s more fully, took the party of Lincoln, founded in 1844 with one principle, the abolition of slavery, and turned it into and detailed a pact with the devil that Jackie witnessed firsthand. That they would then, because of the civil rights bill, go after disaffected Southern whites who had normally voted Democratic and employ what we call generously the Southern strategy.[29]

Mike Wise of ESPN.com offers further insights from Burns on the public's need to shortchange a complicated legacy for reasons of simplicity and convenience. As Burns argues, "Why did we preserve these stories over the years and embellish them? . . . The only real reason I can think of is because it gave white people skin in the game. They historically could feel singularly responsible for this, rather than deal with the truth: If the black press hadn't strongly advocated over the years, if political pressure outside baseball hadn't coalesced at this time, it never happens." As Wise suggests, "'Cultural appropriation' can be thrown around loosely. But what greater cultural appropriation is there than convincing a group of people that their resilience was needed, but their liberation was inextricably linked to the goodness of well-intentioned white people? It's another of those historically inconvenient truths that Burns makes you confront."[30]

Wise offered an insight as to how we can view Robinson's life and legacy in a fashion to which we are not typically accustomed. As Wise argued, "But this newly unearthed Jackie Robinson is worth the time because it demythologizes a complex, interesting man and why we feel the way we do about him. This documentary strips away the heroic veneer and liberates Robinson from his legend, which makes him feel more raw and human and that much more admirable."[31]

As Ken Burns himself argued in a *Sports Illustrated* article, the American public is quick to see Jackie Robinson as a "mythological figure encrusted with the barnacles of sentimentality and nostalgia." As Burns continued, "We have turned Jackie Robinson into shorthand for our own wishes and desires when the real person is so interesting and so contemporary. . . . Do you want to know him in his full dimension, or would you rather it just be the superficial, syrupy, sugarcoated, Madison Avenue version of the past?"[32] Burns's approach to the documentary, one that offers a view of Jackie Robinson to which we are not typically exposed, is one on which this book attempts to build. In order to do so, it is important to explore the typical Robinson "version of the past" to which Burns refers.

Since 1947 Jackie Robinson's legacy has been depicted in a similar fashion, one that places Robinson in a definitive space of what it "truly" means to be a sports trailblazer in a racial context. However, as Burns recognizes, this offers a shortsighted view of Robinson's complex and nuanced experiences as Major League Baseball's first African American player during and beyond his playing career. This section reveals the typical Jackie Robinson public narrative that has been offered through myriad media depictions since Robinson's playing career.

The first published depiction is from Robinson's own hand in his book *Jackie Robinson: My Own Story*, which was published in 1948. With the assistance of renowned *Pittsburgh Courier* writer Wendell Smith, Robinson walks the reader through his personal experiences leading up to his arrival with the Brooklyn Dodgers in 1947. Throughout the book, Robinson explains in detail numerous experiences that helped pave the way for baseball's integration, his turbulent experiences as a black player, and his impressions of Dodgers general manager Branch Rickey. Robinson provides one particular passage that describes the day he was informed about his pending contract with the Brooklyn Dodgers: "Some writers have called me the fastest man in baseball. That, of course, is a matter of conjecture. But on that morning of April 10, there was no doubt about it. I set some kind of world record for getting dressed. In less time than it takes to tell, I was on my way to the office of the Brooklyn Dodgers. One hour later, surrounded by Mr. Rickey and his immediate staff, I signed my contract and became the first Negro in modern times to enter the 'sacred portals' of the Major Leagues."[33] Robinson goes on to describe his 1947 season in the latter chapters. As one might imagine, the book includes the trials and challenges that Robinson endured as a black man breaking through to national prominence in white America. This depiction would prove to be typical in subsequent illustrations of Robinson's arrival into Major League Baseball.

Two years later Jackie Robinson shifted from author to actor in the 1950 film *The Jackie Robinson Story*. Robinson plays himself in the lead role of the film, which, much like the aforementioned 1948 book, offers an overview of Robinson's journey to Major League Baseball and a focus on his inaugural 1947 season.[34] The end of the film shows Robinson, after helping the Dodgers clinch the National League pennant, speaking with General Manager Branch Rickey. After a reciprocal congratulatory handshake, the conversation centers on Robinson's invitation to speak to Congress in Washington DC. Robinson asks, "By the way, Mr. Rickey, there's something bothering me. About that invitation to Washington. Do you really think I should go?" As Robinson expresses his trepidation to address Congress publicly, Rickey reassures him with words of encouragement. As Rickey proclaims, "Yes, Jackie, I do. To Washington, to the Senate, to the House of Representatives, to the American people. You've earned the right to speak. They want you to speak about things on your mind, about a threat to peace that's on everybody's mind, Jackie. Now you can fight back." While compressed into a short line of dialogue, this scene is telling. In 1950 America this is the essentially the first public portrayal of Robinson's voyage into the political landscape. Here Robinson is depicted as hesitant to speak his mind, as cautious about making a trip to Congress, as reluctant to speak out without a white authority granting a black man permission to express himself politically. As I will show throughout this book, this is the "typical" Robinson that is portrayed in mainstream public depictions of his legacy. I argue that this film is the starting point for that typical narrative. As I will show in a later chapter, both the black and the white press depicted Robinson in numerous ways throughout his playing career. But those conflicting depictions are not typically part of the representation in contemporary commemorative discourse related to Jackie Robinson.

In 1964, eight years after Robinson retired from his Hall of Fame Major League career with the Brooklyn Dodgers, Robinson authored another book, *Baseball Has Done It*. However, published eight years after his playing days were over, the book did not likely have the same public and media fanfare as his 1948 book or his 1950 film. In it Robinson organized the book into three sections: "The Past," "The Present," "The Future." The first two sections constitute the heavy majority of the 220-page book, leaving only 4 pages for the final section. And of those pages, 3 and a half of them are made up of the words of Branch Rickey. Rickey's excerpt ends with the following passage: "The big challenge to the Negro today is to fight for the right to be equal and then to qualify as an equal. And no less important is the challenge not to compromise for less than equality." Following Rickey's excerpt, Robinson immediately brings an end to the book with seven words: "That's the way I feel about it!"[35] I argue that it's reasonable to see how Robinson's own words can be viewed as following the direction of Rickey, not unlike what viewers see at the end of *The Jackie Robinson Story* fourteen years earlier.

Memory and Sports Mythology

Major League Baseball's construction of Robinson's legacy is less about Jackie Robinson and more about how a hegemonic institution, like Major League Baseball, controls the narrative and the numerous power dynamics involved. By looking at the commemorative discourse and other elements that Major League Baseball includes in its celebration of Robinson's legacy, it is equally as important to examine the elements that Major League Baseball excludes from its celebration, leaving us as critical consumers with a better opportunity to investigate which controversial components are silenced and why they are left out. I begin by analyzing Robinson's public clashes with equally important civil rights figures Paul Robeson and Malcolm X during and after his playing career, then critique the limitations of that portrayal by comparing the presentation of Robinson in the MLB and Negro Leagues museums, and finally examining Robinson's legacy as it is presented by Major League Baseball in the present day. Doing this requires us all to take a hard look at the ways in which we memorialize African American players like Robinson and how Major League Baseball is memorializing him in ways that are intended to create polite chatter about race instead of having the hard conversations about baseball's legacy of racism as well as the truth that African American kids don't feel a part of baseball's history. How do we know that? Because the numbers tell us that more and more African American youth have chosen not to play baseball anymore. In the end, this book provides a more nuanced understanding of how a mainstream, white authority like Major League Baseball has used its game as a way to manage that authority.

The overarching theme of this book utilizes the concept of memory from the perspective that memory should be rooted in social critique rather than understood as merely a static, fixed object of study. That is, memory as a fixed object merely confines memory as something that exists in a vacuum and thus does not allow for analysis that takes into consideration context, history, or cultural change. Conversely, memory rooted in social critique takes memory out of a vacuum and indeed takes into consideration the ways in which memories change over time. One primary goal of studies interested in understanding the relationship between rituals of commemoration and cultural meaning is "to understand how public memorializing functions as a site of cultural expression of values, myths, and cultural knowledge."[36] Such a goal allows us to see memory as an object of social critique and as a further way to understand how public commemoration, for example, functions as a text that offers ever-changing expression of values, myths, and knowledge of a given culture.

It is important, then, to examine what sort of things are looked at specifically in terms of public memory. To fabricate, rearrange, or omit aspects of memory is social, cultural, and political action at its broadest level. The appearance of memory in public involves a fragmentary and always fleeting phenomenon.[37] This fleeting element reminds us of the instability and mutability of memory that publics must endure. Such an unstable nature of memory is predicated upon the publicness of memory itself. As Edward Casey argues, being public in no way guarantees constancy over time: to be public means "to be subject to continual reassessment and revision." A lack of constancy illuminates the uncertainty found in public memory. According to Casey, "Often we cannot count on invoking anything like a constant public memory, despite its rhetorical appeal and despite the often urgent needs of citizens (and even more so, politicians) to refer to something like the same heritage or tradition and to be able to transmit this to oneself and others in a consistent and repeatable way."[38] This lack of constancy and uncertainty in memory is predicated upon the conflicting choices made by publics as to what should be included or excluded. Memory involves the fabrication, rearrangement, and omission of details about the past, often pushing accuracy and authenticity to the margins in order to satisfy broader issues of identity formation, power, and authority.[39] As Ana Lucia Araujo argues, "Memory is not related to individual recollection of personal experiences and events but is about the way the past of a group is lived again in the present—the way a group associates its common remembrances with historical events or with a set of historical events."[40] Sculptural monuments commemorating emancipation from slavery, which emerged in the 1870s, were intended to cultivate unity, resolution, and consensus. In order to do so, these sculptures had to stabilize the myth of a unified people, meaning that such things as physical distinctions between whites and blacks had to literally take shape in commemorative sculptures. The body of the "Negro" was depicted as the antithesis of classical whiteness. One such monument was used for the Freedman's

Memorial to Lincoln in Washington DC, in 1876. Thomas Bell erected an image of President Lincoln standing above a freed slave kneeling before the politician, all with the lone phrase of "emancipation" placed below the two figures. One of the first public monuments to include a black body, Bell's sculpture utilized the black man to reestablish the racial hierarchy constructed in prominent "scientific" depictions at the time.[41] The black body emerged in public sculptures in the 1870s, changing the construction of commemoration itself while ultimately changing the identity of the nation. A social critique of these monuments allows critics to see commemoration of emancipation as a form of invention, an introduction of a new "people" (slave and slave owner alike) into national memory. As Francine Saillant and Pedro Simonard proclaim, "There is a wish to use the power of memory to support the community by projecting an image that allows it to regain its power to act."[42] With this in mind, in this book I will be looking at public commemorations, newspaper editorials, museum exhibits, congressional testimony, and public speeches, among others.

Any discussion of public memory must include, somewhat paradoxically, an acknowledgment of public forgetting. As Sturken argues, "A desire for coherence and continuity produces forgetting. . . . The desire for narrative closure thus forces upon historical events the limits of narrative form and enables forgetting." Without forgetting there is no public remembrance. This is predicated on the fact that specific choices must be made in order to construct and articulate a particular memory. Adds Sturken, "All cultural memory and all history are forged in a context in which details, voices, and impressions of the past are forgotten. The writing of a historical narrative necessarily involves the elimination of certain elements." As Dickinson, Blair, and Ott offer, "Perhaps the most common assertion among public memory scholars is that memory is operationalized by forgetting." As we will see later in the book in the examination of two baseball museums, institutions, just like individuals, formalize the process of remembering and forgetting and in so doing "showcase individual preferences, interpretations, and sentiments. . . . Much in the same way that museums shape public memory by 'including' and 'excluding' in their collecting and exhibition practices, individuals also demonstrate a counter-agency in their control over forgetting." As Paula Hamilton and Linda Shopes suggest, "The 'publicness' of memory, on the other hand, opens up questions about why some memories are known and others are forgotten, or emerge in particular ways and are subject to endless repetition in attempts to fix their meaning."[43] Generally, this is useful to my book because my analysis of commemorative texts includes themes, narratives, and artifacts that are both included and excluded in the commemorative discourse. Specifically, Jackie Robinson's contemporary legacy leaves out, or forgets, the controversial Robinson.

Memories do not stand in isolation waiting for their meaning to be discovered. Rather, they are parts of an ongoing conversation about our present, past, and future. Importantly, "memory studies and memory are complex and multi-layered, resisting easy narratives."[44] There are choices made that result in the critic or consumer translating the chosen information into meaning; to the audience, memory is meaningful only through the way or ways it is depicted. While there are choices made both by the creator of the memory and by those who critique it, both must decide what is significant about that particular depiction. Both the producer and the consumer of public memory, then, are involved in a process of interpretation, and, as Perelman and Olbrechts-Tyteca remind us, "Interpretation cannot be merely a simple choice but also a creation, an invention of significance." Public memory, then, is an inventive process, one that calls for creator and critic alike to provide meaning for a particular memory within a social context. As Jane Goodall and Christopher Lee contend, "Public memory emerges when individuals, families and social groups encounter each other in time and space and negotiate a common view of shared events."[45] This perspective is useful as we examine the controversial aspects of Robinson's life, both during and after his playing career, and will help us to understand how certain memories can impact Robinson's legacy itself.

Examining public memory as a cultural construction will allow me to show that the contestation and struggle over how memories get articulated are germane to understanding the past's impact on the present. As Mandziuk states, "By their very nature as interpretive, symbolic acts, public commemorations are significant sites of struggle over the nature of the past and its meaning for the present." One of the things I will be examining specifically in this book is commemorative discourse. As Sturken writes, "What memories tell us, more than anything, is the stakes held by individuals and institutions in attributing meaning to the past." She goes on to explain that the process of memory "is bound up in complex political stakes and meanings. It both defines a culture and is the means by which its divisions and conflicting agendas are revealed. To define a memory," Sturken explains, is "to enter into a debate about what that memory means." As Seth Bruggeman argues, "Public historians have known for some time that we trust museums and historic sites more than almost any other institutional source of historic knowledge. What we cannot forget, however, . . . is that the process by which memory is made at public monuments is always political."[46] Based on this perspective, we must consider why one group's version of a public memory gets privileged over others. This perspective is useful to this book because it will allow us to consider how Robinson's legacy is portrayed in various forms. For instance, we will be able to see how different museums seem to invite different sorts of memories and how Robinson's entire political career has been pretty much erased from his popular legacy, as well as how Major League Baseball reframes potential challenges to the integration narrative in a contemporary setting.

The Negro Leagues, a prosperous and profitable institution on its own terms, has often taken a backseat to Jackie Robinson within the context of Major League Baseball's integration narrative. The legacy of Jackie Robinson that gets privileged more than others is one that erases, or excludes, the devastating consequences that Robinson's integration had on the Negro Leagues.[47] This tension creates a commemoration that is a site of contestation. As Jane Greer and Laurie Grobman contend, "Public memory is an especially fruitful space for democratic and social justice activities as diverse constituents negotiate the meanings of the past and how that past informs the present moment and guides future actions." Major League Baseball's attempt to define Jackie Robinson's memory is significant because it exemplifies "how the processes of public memorializing function as sites for engaging—or eliding—difficult ideological battles over race."[48] That is, Major League Baseball recognizes its role in erasing the existence of the Negro Leagues. Such recognition fuels M L B's need to right a wrong. The predominantly white leadership of Major League Baseball may have been motivated by a need to try to right past wrongs, constructing Robinson's contemporary legacy as an attempt to reconcile its past racial injustices. This begs the question: Is Major League Baseball's construction of Robinson's contemporary legacy perhaps an attempt to reconcile its past racial injustices?

Understanding why one group's version of a public memory gets privileged over others is rather straightforward: the dominant group in charge controls the narrative. That is, Major League Baseball's control of Jackie Robinson's legacy may suggest that M L B is attempting to reconcile past injuries. There is no way to know the particular motivation for sure, but it stands to reason that there is indeed a need on Major League Baseball's part to correct a past injustice. For instance, Major League Baseball is an institution controlled by whites; thus, they control the integration narrative, a narrative that paints the white-dominant institution in a more positive light. This narrative is evidenced through the lack of any mention of Robinson's critique of the state of race relations in America, a well-documented critique in front of the House Un-American Activities Committee (H UAC) in 1947. Further evidence of Major League Baseball's control of

Robinson's narrative is seen through the lack of any mention of Robinson's controversial public debate with prominent members of the black community, namely, Malcolm X and Congressman Adam Clayton Powell. Specifically, we see no mention of Robinson's racial critique or his public debates in either the National Baseball Hall of Fame and Museum or any of Major League Baseball's commemorations of Jackie Robinson's legacy. As memory scholar Regina Faden argues, "Museums can help people find the place and the words to talk about slavery and race." Faden offers the words of Lonnie Bunch, founding director of the National Museum of African American History and Culture: "[Bunch] sends out a challenge and raises the bar for museums: 'What is missing is a new synthesis—a *new integration*—that encourages visitors to see that exploring issues of race is essential to their understanding of American culture.'"[49]

This mediated process of remembering Robinson's legacy reduces controversy, celebrates racial equality, and invokes the American public's amnesia about the social implications that Robinson's inclusion meant to both black and white communities. As Philip Lee and Pradip Ninan Thomas contend, "This politics of remembering . . . essentially constitutes a struggle for power, so that wherever justice is compromised, wherever a politics of enforced amnesia reigns, it falls to civil society to be the defender and spokesperson of history and public memory." As Daniel Grano argues, "Forgetting is not just a failure to remember or commemorate. It is often a problem of selective representation, a particular and ideologically directed use of partially recalled history."[50] Once again, this amnesia is evidenced in Major League Baseball's contemporary memory of Robinson's impact on white America.

It should not be overlooked that much of Robinson's impact, as well as that of other African Americans, took place within the context of American sports. Sport, in this specific case, became the initial and most public of venues in which Robinson established a historical move toward racial equality. And because sport is the primary context in which this book is examined, it is useful, then, to see sport as a site of public memory. As Patrick Miller and David Wiggins assert, "To much of the rest of the world, sports have defined race relations in the United States—for better and for worse." According to Miller and Wiggins, "Ultimately, if sport stands as one of the ways to erase the color line during the twenty-first century, it cannot stand outside such traditional notions as racial pride and community solidarity, or conventionally broader paths to social mobility and social justice." As Stephen Wieting explains, "Societies have since regularly employed sport to celebrate and remember cherished cultural values. Sport is not the only vehicle societies use for collective memory, but this activity has proved serviceable by virtue of its common appeal, expansiveness in the stimulation of our senses, and capacity for a decisive resolution." Wieting's point speaks to the importance of viewing sport as a site of public memory and how such a viewpoint offers us myriad ways to examine sport beyond the scope of physical play. As Grano argues, "While attention to memory may characterize other cultural institutions, sport has no equal when it comes to obsessions with legacy. Turn on any network dedicated to sport in the immediate afterglow of an elite performance and you will see flash polls, a cobbled-together top-ten list, and a panel of retired athletes, all adjudicating its historical status. This is just a microcosm of constant efforts to mark, measure, debate, and recall history through commemorative specials, 'all-time greatest' lists, interview shows, and so on."[51] Clearly, then, sport must be understood as something more than merely a physical contest, to which we now turn our attention.

As Michael Butterworth writes, "Various other moments and incidents surely come to mind, a reminder of how widely dispersed are the sources of identity and just how rich a site of inquiry sport can be." That site of inquiry to which Butterworth refers is integral to how we view Jackie Robinson's legacy on public culture. As Butterworth continues, "More specifically, how we communicate about sport, how sport is communicated to us, and what is communicated by sport each represent critical opportunities to evaluate, critique, and improve our public culture." And evaluate, critique, and improve our understandings of Robinson' lasting impact on American public culture we must. We must do these things not just because of Robinson's individual impact but because it provides us an opportunity to explore the role that sport plays in shaping complex issues, particularly issues that relate to constructions of power. As Luke Winslow contends, "Sport in the United States has become arguably the most important modality through which popular ideas about complex social, political, and economic issues are contested, struggled over, and affirmed. Sport is not a totally unique institution in that sense; it does not operate in a vacuum. Rather, sport shapes and reflects larger patterns of social interaction and structural significance." And how we remember, and more specifically how we construct, Robinson's public legacy can provide a significant example of how "sport provides a context for the critical examination of dominant cultural practices and the ideological struggle over the institutions that construct hierarchies of power."[52] Major League Baseball, as we will see later in the book, certainly is one such institution that represents a hierarchy of power through which we construct Robinson's legacy.

As Dave Zirin contends, "Sports as a whole do not represent black and white, good or bad, red state or blue state issues. Sports are neither to be defended nor vilified. Instead we need to look at sports for what they are, so we can take apart the disgusting, the beautiful, the ridiculous, and even the radical." Thomas Oates and Zack Furness further this sentiment, claiming, "Many scholars have challenged the rejection of the relationship between sports and politics, whose books and articles have helped roundly reject the long-standing truism that sports and politics do not mix." As they further argue, "Sport, as one can probably imagine, offers some of the most fertile terrain for engaging in such forms of analysis and critique."[53] Along similar lines, as Winslow argues,

Sport has the potential to be a unique bastion of a post-racial, equal opportunity in a country deeply scarred by a white supremacist history. For many black Americans, when access to more formal institutions of legal, political, and social power are closed off, sport offers an opportunity to assume the breadwinning role that is fundamental to the masculine identity. Even if very few ascend to the professional ranks, sport enables many black athletes to momentarily transgress the racial constraints imposed on their lives, and in so doing, redefine black political claims to freedom, equality, and material success. We must also appreciate the way sport fulfills one of the most important requirements for redressing prejudice, stereotypes, and bigotry in white Americans: direct interaction with people who do not look and act like they do.[54]

While sport in general is a conduit between sport and society, baseball specifically has provided a relationship between sport and culture in myriad ways. Baseball historian Benjamin Rader opened his 2008 treatise on baseball history with an ode to baseball's much-romanticized relationship to America on a broad scale:

"It's our game," exclaimed poet Walt Whitman more than a century ago, "that's the chief fact in connection with it: America's game." He went on to explain that baseball "has the snap, go, fling of the American atmosphere—belongs as much to our institutions, fits into them as significantly, as our constitutions, laws: is just as important in the sum total of our historic life." Perhaps Whitman exaggerated baseball's importance and congruency with American life, but few would contend that the sport has been merely a simple or occasional diversion. Indeed, if forced to make a choice, most would side with Whitman. They would insist that baseball achieved a special prominence and permanence in the United States that in some respects makes its significance equivalent to that of business, politics, religion, ethnicity, or race. Until recently, those attempting to tell the story of how baseball became so "important in the sum total of our historic life" focused almost exclusively on the history of the game between the foul lines.[55]

And it has been the attempts "to tell the story" of baseball that have provided such fertile ground for cultivating baseball's mythology. In need of a mythology to sell the game, "The entrepreneurs in charge of the representative nines in the larger cities established an entity that became known as organized baseball. . . . They concocted an elaborate myth of the game's origins, erected great civic monuments in the form of ballparks made of steel and concrete, and instituted an annual fall rite known as the World Series."[56] That mythology is one that is centered on what are deemed uniquely American values, and baseball "has worked hard to maintain that status. To do so, baseball—and major league baseball (MLB) in particular—has tried to associate itself with the values of the American dream."[57]

Baseball historian Robert Elias explains baseball's role in America's efforts to elevate imperialistic and nationalistic endeavors, offering, "When the United States began projecting itself as a global power in the late nineteenth century, baseball was enlisted in America's imperial quests. . . . Baseball was used to sell and export the American dream. . . . And at home, baseball was employed to help manage immigration and the nation's own internal colonies, as well as to promote American identity and nationalism." Richard Crepeau offers a similar contention, arguing, "As the National Pastime, baseball also became a means of expressing American nationalism. . . . The 1930s were marked by the national crisis of the Great Depression. Clearly there was no dearth of opportunity for the expression of nationalist and patriotic spirit, and baseball took full advantage of these opportunities." Historian John Dreifort reinforces this claim, contending, "Not only did the game provide a welcome respite from the grimness and dislocations of the Depression era, but it also generated a revolution of its own in the way in which the game was played. It produced a galaxy of epic heroes whose accomplishments and fame immortalized them among the century's greatest athletic legends."[58]

While commemoration and sport are integral components of Robinson's legacy, an examination of Robinson's legacy would not be as productive if the issue of race was not addressed. Race plays a significant role within the discourse that surrounds sport in the United States. Quite often American sports fans view the racial sports landscape within America as post–Jackie Robinson. That is, with Robinson's inclusion in baseball in the mid-twentieth century, the role of race in sport is often viewed as an afterthought, particularly when we feel it necessary to view American sports as a space of racial equality. The famous meeting between the Brooklyn Dodgers executive and Jackie Robinson in 1945 has become a catalyst for intersecting race and sport. As Rader contends,

> This fateful meeting not only heralded the reversal of organized baseball's long-term ban against black players but also signified the beginning of a new era of white-black relations in the United States. Because baseball enjoyed the distinction of being the national game, racial integration within it was of vast symbolic importance. If it was proper and possible for blacks and whites to play baseball together, then why should they continue to be separated in the armed forces, the schoolrooms, the courtrooms, the workplaces, and the neighborhoods of America? Once the racial wall in the national game had been breached, it seemed indisputable that all other barriers to blacks should be removed as well. . . .
>
> Throughout most of its history, baseball mirrored the nation's racial, ethnic, and religious practices. During the same era that the South (and to a somewhat lesser degree the North) fastened on the nation a rigid system of racial segregation, organized baseball unofficially excluded blacks from its game. For a shining, sterling moment in its history, however, the sport embarked on a "great experiment" in race relations. Well before any other major institution in the nation had acted to end Jim Crow and a full seven years before the famous 1954 Brown Supreme Court decision ending school segregation, baseball terminated its color ban. And unlike the primetime television sitcoms and dramas of the day, in which blacks appeared sparingly if at all, African American ballplayers were a highly visible presence on the nation's television screens.[59]

Chapter Outline

You will notice a relative chronological ordering to the texts, events, and institutions addressed in the following chapters. That is, I address these topics in the order that I do because I want the chapters to construct an overarching narrative that illuminates how a contemporary reading of Jackie Robinson's legacy has been invented through past discourses. The book is laid out in four substantive chapters.

Chapter 1: Robinson's Postplaying Career

Jackie Robinson, the renowned remover of baseball's color line turned political figure, has long been represented as a revered cultural icon for racial equality. Robinson's inclusion in organized baseball in 1947 perpetuates the notion that sport is a meritocracy—that is, one gets judged on his or her merit rather than color, character, or class. Thus, baseball's contemporary integration narrative frames the memory of Robinson's legacy as one that constitutes a more just America, placing racial inequality behind us. Robinson's political involvement during and beyond his baseball career has made him accessible in a plethora of forms, including his autobiography, Jules Tygiel's scholarly endeavor *Baseball's Great Experiment*, and Robinson's own syndicated column in the *New York Post* and *New York Amsterdam News* during the 1950s, just to name a few. The rhetorical construction of Jackie Robinson's memory is the result of various attempts to commemorate his legacy as a convenient symbol for racial equality.

While this chapter will not be exploring a specific memorial per se, there is an interest in the contestation that takes place in constructing public memories. Particularly, examining how a univocal history of Robinson's cultural legacy gets constructed will enable us to see that while Robinson's status as a pioneering baseball player has often been commented on, his status as a political activist has received less attention.

During the 1950s and '60s, Jackie Robinson pursued political aspirations for life after baseball. It was in the *New York Post* and *New York Amsterdam News* that Robinson published a nationally syndicated column to speak out about racial politics and the state of black Americans. In 1963 this column became the site for a heated exchange between Robinson and Malcolm X, at a time when Robinson's conservative political philosophy and Malcolm's radical perspectives were at their respective peaks. Agitated by Malcolm's denigration of moderate blacks and specifically his attack on Dr. Ralph Bunche, the undersecretary to the United Nations, Robinson expressed his respect for Bunche and voiced his outrage toward Malcolm X's attacks. Malcolm X responded to Robinson's column via public letter. By analyzing specific excerpts from both men's letters, we will see how Robinson was perceived as serving merely as an instrument for perpetuating the dominant authority's desire to sustain a superior position in the context of race relations. This schism between Robinson and Malcolm X culminated in further columns and personal letter writing between the two men.

This chapter will examine the publicized debate between Jackie Robinson and Malcolm X, as articulated in the two separate issues of the *New York Amsterdam News*. Doing so will allow us to locate Robinson in a larger political context, particularly regarding the ways he aligned himself with the Republican Party in a post–World War II era. Consequently, Robinson's public confrontation with Malcolm X brings to the fore various ways in which the black community was split in terms of political ideology. Similar to the exchange between Robinson and Robeson described in chapter 2, the public clash between Robinson and Malcolm X often gets "forgotten" in terms of Robinson's public legacy. The rhetorical discourse surrounding this clash highlights the ways in which a contemporary mainstream memory of Robinson "forgets" his controversial political involvement and "remembers" only the positive aspects of his iconic legacy. The stakes in remembering only part of this story, then, are high. First, only remembering part of the story negates the political voice that athletes have had throughout contemporary

American history. Second, it perpetuates the myth that Robinson was deemed a hero and celebrated by all of America. As we will see, this was not entirely the case. There are four primary themes in this chapter that help illuminate the importance of understanding the political aspects of Jackie Robinson's life: the battle over legitimacy, the battle over agency, the battle over the mainstream, and the battle over coalition building.

Chapter 2: The Robinson-Robeson Clash

On April 19, 1949, renowned African American entertainer and sports hero Paul Robeson addressed the House Un-American Activities Committee; several months later, Robinson was asked to respond. This chapter focuses on this public clash between two of the highest-profile African American men of their day, to recover the ways in which Robinson was perceived by the American public and how this may have contributed to shutting down the necessary discursive exchange found in democratic practice. Ultimately, I argue that Jackie Robinson's testimony in front of the House Un-American Activities Committee is an act of dissent on his own terms but was read as an act of assent on white political terms. Viewing Robinson's testimony as an act of dissent offers a newfound perspective of Robinson's legacy. Rather than viewing Robinson as an obedient minority, we can begin to see how an act of political and social dissent is swept under the rug in order to fit the neat, uncomplicated narrative of Major League Baseball's racial integration. Specifically, the objects of study in this chapter include several primary texts. These include significant aspects of Robinson's speech in front of HUAC, the black press's coverage of that testimony, and the mainstream press's coverage of that same testimony. Robinson's perceived assent and dissent, and the tension between the two, becomes the theme of this chapter.

First, by examining Robinson's speech, specifically his emphasis on his identity as a "colored person" in America, we will see how Robinson's emphasis on his racial identity eloquently sets up his argument that there is great difficulty in balancing his role as an anticommunist, patriotic American as well as a man of color fighting for racial equality, even if that means supporting a fellow black American who supports communist views.

After examining Robinson's HUAC speech, there is the important issue of examining the black press's account of Robinson's testimony. Specifically, by analyzing specific excerpts from prominent black newspapers at the time, we will be able to see how the black newspapers framed the testimony, intentionally or unintentionally, as one that, for lack of a better phrase, threw Paul Robeson under the bus. The black press's exclusions of certain parts of Robinson's speech created a tension within the black community, resulting in many individuals of color, both prominent and common, picking sides as to who truly represented the black community.

Finally, by examining specific excerpts from mainstream newspapers' coverage of Robinson's speech, we will be able to see how the mainstream press coverage of Robinson's speech excluded significant excerpts of his testimony, excerpts that clearly articulate Robinson's support of Paul Robeson. These exclusions, coupled with the mainstream press's inclusions of excerpts that paint Robinson as a patriotic American first and a citizen of color second, contextualize a rather neat, uncomplicated representation of Robinson.

Consequently, by analyzing Robinson's speech, and the coverage given to the event by the black press and by the mainstream press, we will see that Robinson's testimony, or at least the coverage of it, led to Paul Robeson's erasure from the public landscape. Furthermore, with Robeson's erasure from the public landscape, Robinson's critique of racism in America gets erased along with it. This erasure plays a significant role in terms of how the contemporary public memory of Robinson's legacy is framed in a solely positive way, ignoring the controversial aspects of his political life. Consequently, as we will see in chapter 4, the examination of "Jackie Robinson Day" points out that Major League Baseball makes no mention of and pays no homage to this aspect of Robinson's life. The rhetorical discourse surrounding Robinson's controversial exchange with Robeson culminates in a public amnesia of Robinson's controversial political persona. By "forgetting" that Robinson was indeed politically contentious, we never learn the entire legacy that Robinson has left behind, thus depriving us of some significant aspects of this chapter in racial and political history.

Chapter 3: Cooperstown and Kansas City

My purpose in this chapter is to view the ways in which African Americans have been included and excluded in sport, specifically baseball, and thus how this inclusion and exclusion can offer an understanding of American culture more broadly. I compare two museums—the National Baseball Hall of Fame and Museum and the Negro Leagues Baseball Museum (NLBM)—that present two competing narratives about the role of race in baseball. These two museums function metonymically, as what Kenneth Burke referred to as "representative anecdotes."[60] Specifically, I argue that the National Baseball Hall of Fame and Museum *individualizes* the role of race by using Jackie Robinson to represent the entire legacy of black baseball. In contrast, the Negro Leagues Baseball Museum presents a *collectivistic* narrative that does not focus so closely on any single player. Furthermore, each of these differing narratives stands in a somewhat different relationship to the myth of meritocracy, complicating the way merit informs the role of baseball in American culture. That is, Major League Baseball focuses on particular individual players, in this case Jackie Robinson, which in turn makes it easier to control the racially inclusive narrative that Major League Baseball puts forth.

The Negro Leagues Baseball Museum, on the other hand, does not focus so closely on any single player. Rather, the museum illustrates the ways in which black baseball was a collectivistic and communal endeavor within the black community. Thus, the focus on individual players is not the point, but rather the ways in which the black community had to work together to make black baseball a successful institution. Each of these disparate narratives complicates the way merit informs the role of baseball in American culture.

The chapter further examines the inclusion and exclusion of African Americans in sport, and thus how this inclusion and exclusion can offer an understanding of American culture on a larger scale. That is, the two museums have come to represent the ways in which race is discussed in sport, particularly how race is discussed in baseball circles.

The National Baseball Hall of Fame and Museum represents the mainstream perspective of Jackie Robinson's legacy. The numerous artifacts and exhibits throughout the entire museum construct a narrative that indeed includes the African American legacy within the game. The narrative is one that portrays Major League Baseball as an inclusive institution. The choices made in order to reconstruct a past are done so in the present to legitimize contemporary personal, political, and public circumstances.[61] Such choices can be found in the memory of black baseball through the Negro Leagues Baseball Museum.

To give a memory expressive form, basically, means that a specific memory is performed for other witnesses, witnesses who constitute an audience. The form in which these memories usually occur is through an act of commemoration, via memorial, ritual, or monument. According to Paul Connerton, knowledge of the past is "conveyed and sustained by . . . performances."[62] Such performances sustain the rhetorical nature of memory, particularly ritual performances. A commemoration such as the Negro Leagues Baseball Museum, for instance, might serve as a means of transmitting public memory via the participants involved. I argue that the commemorative rhetoric of the Negro Leagues Baseball Museum offers a more expansive, comprehensive memory than the mainstream contemporary memory of African Americans in sports.

The Negro Leagues Baseball Museum tells us something beyond African American history, the Negro Leagues, or Jackie

Robinson. The museum illustrates a racially segregated institution in a way that calls to attention both the discriminatory roots of black baseball's cultivation as well as black baseball's prosperous and profitable elements. Visitors get a sobering view of the Negro Leagues from the perspective of those who participated in them rather than just the contemporary mainstream depiction of black baseball's legacy. The point is one of contrast, allowing us an opportunity to best discern the thinness of the dominant narrative by looking at such a museum.

The National Baseball Hall of Fame and Museum is a space that represents the national perspective of the game. Thus, it covers the game in more breadth than depth, resulting in a lack of focus on any one particular era or faction of the game's history. A focus on more specificity of one particular faction of the game, in this case black baseball, will provide an additional perspective on racial inclusion and exclusion within baseball. Thus, the Negro Leagues Baseball Museum is a space that offers a more specific focus, as well as a nonmainstream perspective, of racial inclusion. The theme of the individualistic versus collectivistic approaches taken by the National Baseball Hall of Fame and Museum and the Negro Leagues Baseball Museum, respectively, is the primary focal point in this chapter. This theme will allow us to see how the contemporary memory of Robinson's legacy is appropriated by Major League Baseball and how that appropriation individualizes the mythos of baseball as a meritocracy.

Chapter 4: Jackie Robinson Day

On April 15, 2004, thirty thousand baseball fans stood in a cold Shea Stadium in Flushing, New York, to watch the commemoration of one of the twentieth century's most memorable landmark pioneers. The celebration of Jackie Robinson Day was taking place, an attempt by Major League Baseball to construct the legacy of the incomparable remover of baseball's color barrier. Just one week prior to this ceremony, Major League Baseball announced that April 15 would now be an annual tribute to Jackie Robinson's integration into organized baseball in 1947.

The inaugural celebration included the retirement of Robinson's number 42 across all MLB organizations. Never again would a player wear this sacred uniform number, preserving the legacy of a man who fifty-seven years earlier made sports history. Major League Baseball commissioner Bud Selig led the ceremony with a speech that illuminated not only Robinson's impact on the game but his impact on society more broadly. Selig's presentation was supplemented by video images of Robinson from his playing days, as his widow and daughter stood nearby. The memory of Jackie Robinson was now "official." The public memory of his impact on the game, society, and history was secure.

At the outset we may believe that baseball's creation of Jackie Robinson Day served nothing more than an epideictic function, celebrating the desire to remember an incomparable social icon. But if we examine the discourse more closely, we begin to see that there is much more at stake here than the ways in which we preserve a figure from the past. As Marouf Hasian Jr. and Cheree Carlson argue, "Collective memories are selectively chosen and highlighted to fit the needs of a particular social group." In the case of Jackie Robinson Day, then, the question might be: Is it clear whose needs are being addressed? For example, Selig's presentation did not address the significant impact that Robinson's integration had on the Negro Leagues, which was by many standards considered a prosperous and profitable institution known at the time. In fact, Robinson's legacy is one that tends to privilege the benefits his integration had on the larger American landscape and neglects the dire consequences his integration had on the black community. Selig's similar neglect attempts to secure a rather limited and uncomplicated legacy for Jackie Robinson. Additionally, what was the impetus for this commemoration? There has never been a public declaration of the motivation behind Jackie Robinson Day at the particular time it was constructed. That is, the commemoration fell on the fifty-seventh anniversary, a seemingly arbitrary number, whereas most significant commemorations take place on a "round-number" anniversary. However, it did coincide with a moment of crisis for Major League Baseball's public image. For instance, baseball's now infamous steroid scandal was looming behind the scenes, and grumblings of a potential player lockout were on the horizon. As Filip Bondy wrote the following day in the *New York Daily News*: "It was Jackie Robinson Day last night at Shea, an anniversary of the Dodger's debut game that will be recognized now by baseball every season on April 15. His elegant widow, Rachel, spoke about the family's scholastic foundation. Bud Selig called the occasion in 1947 'the most powerful moment in baseball history.'" As seen in this passage, the emphasis on baseball's triumph over past racial injustices can be seen as a way to deflect the growing criticism of baseball's contemporary state of affairs. This chapter explores the ways in which Jackie Robinson Day becomes a site that "controls our interpretation of the past and subsequent behavior in the future."[63]

As we will see, Major League Baseball's construction of Jackie Robinson's legacy is a site wherein we might study a contest over the ownership of a bit of history. Ultimately, Jackie Robinson Day opens a rhetorical space that invites us to question how a particular social group comes to own a specific public memory. In Major League Baseball's case, it creates such a space by constructing "Jackie Robinson" as a tokenist rhetoric. I argue that once Jackie Robinson struggled through the obstacles of discrimination to achieve social prominence, his persona is appropriated by the dominant ideology of liberalism. Jackie Robinson Day serves as a "rhetorical justification of liberal meritocracy."[64] That is, Jackie Robinson Day functions as a tokenist rhetoric in order for Major League Baseball to sustain the belief that baseball, as a significant rhetorical space, will always be remembered as a meritocracy. The overarching theme that runs throughout this chapter is one that focuses on what Robinson's contemporary legacy contains. Then, we will see how the contemporary legacy excludes numerous controversial aspects of Robinson's life outside the playing field.

Conclusion: Taking Inventory of a Legacy

The concluding chapter is included in order to answer the following questions—questions that arise after the analysis in the four primary chapters: What do we learn from such a configuration of these texts? Why study two disparate museums? What does the relationship between Paul Robeson and Jackie Robinson bring to the relationship of Malcolm X and Jackie Robinson? And what can a contemporary commemorative ceremony every April 15 tell us about how these other texts impact our modern view of an iconic baseball player? Part of the answer to these questions is illumination. An analysis of the National Baseball Hall of Fame and Museum and the Negro Leagues Baseball Museum illuminates the ways in which black baseball represented yet another view of black athletes, particularly Robinson's legacy, in America at the mid-twentieth century as well as today. The relationship of Robinson and Robeson illuminates how Robinson was viewed by both white and black America. Robinson's controversial political views, particularly those publicized in a debate with an even more controversial figure in Malcolm X, illuminate a new chapter in Robinson's legacy. Finally, an analysis of a present-day construction of Robinson's legacy illuminates how the legacy has gone through various changes over the past seven decades. The configuration of texts outlined in the chapters above will offer a sequential progression of how Robinson's commemorative legacy has endured, and will continue to endure, a plethora of interpretations of an otherwise seemingly convenient, uncomplicated legacy.

1

Robinson's Postplaying Career

A Political Impact

I think I've been much more aggressive since I left baseball.
—JACKIE ROBINSON

The contemporary mainstream legacy of Jackie Robinson is often remembered as one that portrays a patriotic pioneer. American mainstream memories of Jackie Robinson do not typically include a Robinson voicing a sharp critique of fellow black political figures, despite evidence to the contrary. In this chapter we see a Robinson who portrays just that: an outspoken member of the black community calling out fellow prominent figures for exercising what Robinson deems inappropriate and dangerous views.

During the 1950s and '60s, Jackie Robinson pursued political aspirations for life after baseball. It was in the *New York Post* and *New York Amsterdam News* that Robinson published a nationally syndicated column to speak out about racial politics and the state of black Americans. Throughout the late 1940s until his death in 1972, Robinson was quite a prolific letter writer, particularly including correspondence with many prominent politicians and public leaders. His correspondents included the likes of Richard Nixon; Barry Goldwater; Nelson Rockefeller; John F. Kennedy; Martin Luther King; Lyndon Johnson; Ralph

Bunche; Roy Wilkins; New York mayor John Lindsay; Hubert Humphrey; Clifford Alexander Jr., White House deputy special counsel; George Fowler, chairman of the New York State Commission for Human Rights; Everett Hutchinson, chair of the Interstate Commerce Commission; A. Philip Randolph, international president of the Brotherhood of Sleeping Car Porters; Emil Rieve, vice president of the AFL-CIO; and Clarence Townes, director of minorities for the Republican National Committee, among many others.[1] Robinson wrote myriad public letters as well as his newspaper column. Sometimes Robinson conflated the two, writing public letters in his newspaper column. The two letters of Robinson's examined in this chapter, those to Adam Clayton Powell and Malcolm X, are a continuation, even a hybrid of sorts, of Robinson's writing outlets. One of the most significant correspondences was that between Jackie Robinson and Malcolm X, coming at a time when Robinson's conservative political philosophy and Malcolm's radical perspectives were considered to be at their respective peaks.

Robinson expressed his respect for Ralph Bunche and voiced his outrage toward Malcolm X's attacks of Bunche. Malcolm X responded to Robinson's column via public letter in the same newspapers. Additionally, on March 30, 1963, Robinson's public letter to Congressman Adam Clayton Powell caused a stir that became the impetus for Malcolm's public rejoinder to Robinson.[2] Robinson's initial letter criticized Powell, a representative from Harlem, for his alleged congressional corruption as well as his association with Malcolm X. Later that year on November 30, 1963, Malcolm returned the favor with a public letter to Robinson.

Jackie Robinson's political involvement continued to grow outside his playing career, becoming even more overt and public after retirement from baseball. After he hangs up his Dodgers uniform for good, Robinson's political voice really begins to take shape, becomes more purposeful, and transforms the ways in which we may remember the more passive and undisruptive Jackie Robinson with which many of his supporters and admirers have grown accustomed to remembering. We start to see an aggressive Robinson, a man who makes clear distinctions between whom he supports politically and publicly. These distinctions pull no punches and contrast sharply with the popular version of Robinson to which we are typically exposed. The postbaseball Jackie Robinson persona is examined in this chapter, as we will start to see the transformation from Jackie Robinson, the baseball icon, to Jackie Robinson, the political advocate.

As we will see throughout the letters examined in this chapter, there are four themes that illustrate Robinson's rhetorical efforts to lay claim as a leader in the black community. Those four themes include the battle over legitimacy, the battle over agency, the battle over the mainstream, and the battle over coalition building. These themes are important to this book for three important reasons. First, they illustrate the rhetorical struggles Jackie Robinson had to endure in order to sustain his visibility within the civil rights movement. Second, they provide a new lens through which to view Robinson's otherwise uncomplicated memory. Finally, they offer a glimpse of Robinson's political identity. This chapter not only will tell us some things about how Jackie Robinson's memory doesn't fit into neat categories, but will also use this case study to tell us something about race in America, and more specifically about race in American sports.

The section that follows offers a thematic analysis rather than a strict sequential examination of the letters exchanged by all three men. That is, rather than merely employ the method of looking at each individual letter paragraph by paragraph, we will focus on the themes that are present in the letters and how various excerpts illustrate each theme. To get a clearer understanding of the impetus for each letter, we turn to a brief background of Robinson and Powell's exchange. This exchange sets the foundation for the exchange between Robinson and Malcolm, which came several months later.

Robinson and Powell: A Background

In his open letter to Adam Clayton Powell Jr., Robinson criticizes the congressman for allegedly, during a mid-March rally in

Harlem, urging African Americans to "boycott major civil rights organizations that they did not control." Despite a public denial that he had urged such a boycott, Powell repeatedly insisted that African Americans take leadership roles in civil rights organizations. As Powell stated in March 1963, "We must seize control of these organizations. We must put into policy control those persons who represent the black masses." The initial letter addressing Congressman Powell provoked a plethora of letters to the editor the following week in the April 6 edition of the *Amsterdam News*. As for Powell's response to Robinson, the *Amsterdam News* did not publish a reply.[3] It is unknown, or at least undocumented, if Powell did in fact respond to Robinson and it simply was not published or if Powell simply did not respond at all.

The Battle over Legitimacy

Throughout his letter to Congressman Powell as well as his letter to Malcolm X, we see the first of four themes: Robinson's engagement in a battle over legitimacy. More specifically, both men claim to speak for African Americans. For instance, Robinson's letter to Congressman Powell, written in the *New York Amsterdam News* on March 30, 1963, was forthright and commanding. The letter opened with the following statement: "Most columnists who write open letters to public personalities don't really want an answer. Let me state, at the beginning, that I would appreciate an answer from the person to whom I am directing this open letter and, if it is forthcoming, I will carry every line in this space, regardless of what it says." Robinson's opening statements frame himself as someone who is proactively pursuing a dialogue with his adversary, in this case a congressional representative. This is the first step to staking claim to who truly speaks for the black community. Rather than present himself as someone who is merely grandstanding, Robinson attempts to illustrate his desire to publicly and openly engage in contentious conversation with those who present a problem to the image of the black community. Interestingly, this differs from the initial image of Jackie Robinson that mainstream America was introduced to sixteen years earlier. The image of Jackie Robinson of 1947 was one that was contained, more or less, by management in order to temper the anticipated backlash of baseball's racial integration. A famous exchange from 1945 reveals this expectation regarding Jackie Robinson's role: "[Robinson:] 'Mr. Rickey, do you want a ballplayer who's afraid to fight back?' [Rickey:] 'I want a player with guts enough not to fight back.'"[4]

As documented through endless accounts of Robinson's career, Robinson portrayed the image as illustrated in Rickey's above plea. This image is often the image that mainstream America remembers of Jackie Robinson—the docile, obedient figure who did not engage in public confrontation. However, as we saw from previous discussions, even the most controversial of engagements, particularly in front of the House Un-American Activities Committee, have been "forgotten" in Robinson's historical legacy.

Robinson's battle for legitimacy continues in the opening comments of his letter to Powell, as he attempts to illustrate what Powell's responsibility is during times of social crisis. As Robinson writes, "Most people who use the word 'friend' use it loosely. I don't. But when I believe a friend is in the wrong, I feel I have the right to tell him so and if the wrong I think he committed was a public act or utterance, then I feel I have the right to tell him so publicly. This letter is for you—Congressman Adam Clayton Powell, Jr." When calling Powell out by name, Robinson uses not only Powell's full name but his title as well, an indication of Robinson's focus on Powell's role as a public servant. The focus on Powell's role as a public servant is meaningful because it further reinforces the idea that Robinson is not afraid to go after a public official who has a responsibility to his constituents. This can be seen as an attempt by Robinson to garner public support rather than merely disparaging an individual with whom he disagrees.

In the final three paragraphs of the letter, Robinson continues his explanation of his criticism. The first of the final three paragraphs begins to soften a little yet sustains its critical edge. As Robinson writes, "Whatever you may believe, Adam, I write this letter more in sadness than in anger. I, like many others, have been troubled by what has seemed to be your growing insensitivity to the cause of our people and your seemingly increasing disregard for your responsibilities to the job you have been sent to Washington to do." The first line makes an explicit effort to signal a tone shift. To suggest that he writes this letter "more in sadness than in anger" appears to be an effort to maintain the personal tone consistent throughout the letter. That personal tone suggests that Robinson sees Powell as someone who has lost his grasp on what his responsibility is to the black community. Thus, Powell no longer should be seen as someone who represents the black community. As Robinson continues in the conclusion of his letter, he addresses the enemy issue. Specifically, he aligns himself with the sentiments of other members of the black community, though in this case the sentiment comes from an individual rather than an entire people. As Robinson writes, "Recently, on the campus of Howard University, I received a tongue-lashing from a student who demanded to know how I could balance my belief and personal principles with my consistent defense of a 'demagogue like Adam Powell.' I replied that I too felt you had been derelict in your duties on many occasions, but that I did not wish to help our common enemies." By claiming to be on the receiving end of criticism from other members of the black community, Robinson positions himself as someone who must also answer to the shortcomings of Adam Clayton Powell. That is, Robinson claims that his relationship with Powell has resulted in public criticism of that relationship, and thus he felt the need to separate himself from Powell on some level. However, Robinson uses the words of another person in order to identify Powell as a "demagogue." Through this strategy, Robinson is able to not only condemn Powell but also use specific derogatory terms without claiming to have said them himself. This further aligns Robinson with the public sentiment of an entire community. This is key because part of what is going on here is that this letter, as well as the letter to Malcolm X discussed later in this section, represents an argument about just what the "public sentiment" of the African American community really is. That is, Robinson claims to know what the pulse of the African American community really is, something that can be identified only by someone who speaks for African Americans.

As Robinson continues in his letter to Powell,

> I can only conclude, Adam, that this latest tantrum of yours stems from the fact that you are infuriated because Roy Wilkins and the Board of the NAACP did not rush to your defense in your recent battle with your fellow Congressmen.
>
> You set up the usual crybaby yell that you were being persecuted because you are a black man when it was pretty obvious that you had placed yourself in a vulnerable position to be condemned by many people with many different motives. The Negro people are growing up, Adam. I do not believe they are sympathetic any longer to the business of supporting anything anyone does—wrong or right—simply because he belongs to the race. . . . It was pretty obvious that you had placed yourself in a vulnerable position to be condemned by many people with many different motives.

Robinson is voicing a perspective that he himself actually spoke out against in front of the HUAC hearings fourteen years earlier. As we recall from previous discussions, Robinson intimated that Robeson did not speak for the entire black community. As Robinson stated then, "Paul Robeson's statement in Paris to the effect that American Negroes would refuse to fight in any way against Russia . . . sounds very silly to me. . . . I've got too much invested for my wife and child and myself in the future of this country . . . to throw it away." As a result, we are witnessing a progression of Robinson's thought process; Jackie Robinson is progressing from thinking that no single individual's voice can represent the sentiments of an entire community to believing that one individual's voice, while not speaking for every member of a community, can articulate the sentiments that are significantly visible within a community as a whole. This progression is obscured when we are not given a more complete picture. Having only a snapshot of Robinson's political thought process is problematic because it reduces the ways we remember the political tone of the black community during this time.

Essentially, Robinson's suggestion that he knows the pulse of all black Americans is certainly not without its merit, but it parallels Paul Robeson's similar suggestion, that one man's view represents the view of an entire people. Ironically, Robinson's critiques of both Robeson and now Powell suggest that these two men do not represent the black community. Essentially, Robinson's suggestion in the letter to Powell parallels his similar suggestion that one man's view represents the view of an entire people. However, Robinson's critique suggests that he can do something that Powell cannot do—represent the voice of the black community.

As we have seen thus far, Robinson has shown a willingness to openly dispute the proclamations by those with whom he disagrees, even if, or perhaps especially if, that includes an African American congressman. Specifically, we have seen Robinson's sharp critical edge take shape in his public claim that Congressman Powell has lost touch with his responsibility as a public servant, particularly as one who serves the black community. Such a critical edge compelled Robinson to somewhat separate himself from Powell, which further shows a progression of Robinson's political thinking. In terms of this book overall, these insights provide further evidence that the Jackie Robinson we have come to learn as a soft-spoken, compliant, and submissive figure is anything but that. Moreover, as we will continue to see in the next section, Jackie Robinson as an outspoken political voice continues to take shape in ways that legitimize his claim as a voice representative of the black community, something we have rarely been exposed to in contemporary versions of Robinson's legacy.

From Powell to Malcolm X: Continuing the Battle over Legitimacy

As we turn to Robinson's letters to Malcolm, we see Robinson continuing to engage in a battle over who represents the black community. That is, Robinson positions himself as a voice of the larger black community. Robinson employs a consistent strategy and almost identical phrasing to illustrate his disdain of both Malcolm and Powell. We are witnessing both a progression and a consistency in Robinson's rhetoric, as his attitude moves from claiming no individual speaks for an entire people to asserting that an entire people can be unified by an individual voice. Robinson, much like in his letter to Powell, immediately goes on the offensive. In the following paragraph, Robinson sharpens his criticism of Malcolm as he invokes the name of Elijah Muhammad as well as painting Malcolm as an individual who is divisive and possesses a hateful disposition, a disposition that could not represent the entire black community. As Robinson writes, "Those of us who are so committed have no intention of supporting the idea of a separate black state where the Honorable Muhammad can be the ruler and you, his immediate successor—and all because you, Malcolm, hate white people. Too many of our young people have gone to jail and too many millions of dollars have been invested in our fight for equality for us to pay serious heed to your advice. Whether you like this country or not is of little concern to me." Robinson first positions himself as a representative of the black sentiment shared by many in the black community. The notion that Robinson and others of his ilk don't have any intentions of advocating the idea of a separate black state draws a clear line in the sand as to where the black community is divided. Second, Robinson further reinforces his sharp critical edge by explicitly portraying Malcolm as hateful, specifically evidenced with the phrase "you, Malcolm, hate white people." By calling Malcolm out in no uncertain terms, Robinson positions himself as a member of the black community who, at least in the eyes of white America, should never be conflated with Malcolm X or with the sentiments of Islam. Finally, Robinson uses a strategy that parallels a similar strategy he used when testifying in front of the House Un-American Activities Committee against the anti-U.S. sentiments of Paul Robeson fourteen years earlier. During that particular testimony in 1949, Robinson used the term "investment," which he utilizes in his letter to Malcolm, as evidenced in the section that suggests that too many members of the black community have gone to jail and invested too much money to follow Malcolm's advice. Additionally, the "investment" to which Robinson refers is something that he argues cannot be discarded because of one individual black man's opinion.

Jackie responds in explicit terms to Malcolm, offering the following: "You say I have never shown my appreciation to the Negro masses. I assume that is why NAACP branches all over the country constantly invite me to address them. I guess this is the reason the NAACP gave me its highest award, the Spingarn Medal and why Dr. Martin King has consistently invited me to participate in the Southern Freedom Fight and invited me to co-chair with him the drive to raise funds to re-build the burned churches in Georgia. By the way, Malcolm, I don't remember our receiving your contribution." In this response, Robinson positions himself as an individual who is a supported member of the black community, while Malcolm has run the risk of being separated from the black community. More specifically, Robinson is calling Malcolm a hypocrite, primarily because his actions don't match his words. Once again, what we are witnessing here is, at least in part, a battle over who speaks for the "true" sentiments of African Americans. From Robinson's perspective, Malcolm's unwillingness to contribute to such things like Robinson's charitable efforts, such as the drive to raise funds for burned churches, doesn't match Malcolm's discourse that attempts to liberate black folks. Perhaps this is an unfair charge on Robinson's part, but a significant charge that once again positions Malcolm even further outside the voices of the black community, subsequently placing Robinson as a representative voice of the black community once again. Furthermore, such a sharply critical perspective of Robinson is something that contrasts the more passive, obedient Robinson that is portrayed in contemporary memories.

As Robinson's letter continues, we see an ever more critical Robinson, refusing to shy away from his notion of patriotic obligations. This critical edge continues as the letter progresses:

"Negroes are not fooled by your vicious theories that they are dying for freedom to please the white man. Negroes are fighting for freedom and rejecting your racism because we feel our stake in America is worth fighting for. Whom do you think you are kidding, Malcolm, when you say that Negro leaders ought to be 'thankful' that you were not personally present in Birmingham or Mississippi after racial atrocities had been committed there? The inference seems to be that you would have played some dramatic, avenging role. I don't think you would have." First, the primary charge here is boasting. From Robinson's viewpoint, Malcolm claims he will oversee numerous dramatic endeavors, but never follows through. Second, just as the previous paragraph depicted, Robinson's use of the "investment" metaphor is employed once again, only this time he uses the phrase "our stake in America," conflating himself with members of the black community who are distinct from the members of the black Muslim community. Additionally, the second half of the above paragraph indicates that Robinson is calling Malcolm's bluff. For instance, Robinson is clearly suggesting that Malcolm would in reality do nothing he claims he would. If the reader acknowledges the consistent themes in Robinson's discourse between the letters to both Powell and Malcolm, this interpretation appears to be highly likely. Furthermore, Robinson's use of word choice in those last few sentences of the paragraph suggests that Robinson is critiquing Malcolm for not following up his words with action. This once again offers a portrayal of Robinson that is distinct from his uncomplicated, obedient status found in his public legacy. It also suggests that Robinson is willing to publicly call out any leaders within the black community he believes are moving in the wrong direction.

Following the defense of his associations with the "white boss," Robinson moves into a brief discussion regarding his testimony in front of HUAC: "I will not dignify your attempted slur against my appearance before the House Un-American Activities Committee some years back. All I can say is that if I were called upon to defend my country today, I would gladly do so. Nor do I hide behind any coat-tails as you do when caught in one of your numerous outlandish statements. Your usual 'out' is to duck responsibility by stating, 'The Honorable Elijah Muhammad says . . .'" In this passage Robinson is employing two notable strategies. First, Robinson uses the phrase "some years back," indicating that the HUAC situation is a thing of the past, an issue that has little bearing on the present state of affairs. Subsequently, Robinson portrays himself as someone who does not dwell on the past and would in fact not change course if presented with the same circumstances today. Second, the passage attempts to paint Malcolm X as something of a puppet figure, an image that is quite distinct from Robinson himself, an image that suggests he is his own man. Essentially, Robinson suggests that Malcolm is not free to speak his own mind, while Robinson is. This strategy is similar to the one Robinson used to paint Congressman Powell as a child, calling him a "crybaby" who throws "tantrums," while referring to himself as a grownup. In the above passage, Robinson does essentially the same thing, arguing that Malcolm displays numerous outbursts and does so while hiding behind his elders. Robinson's tone in this particular passage contains the same sharp critical edge as illustrated in the original letter to Congressman Powell. Again, this portrays Robinson as someone who is a voice of the black community, as any individual who "cries" or "throws tantrums" could not and should not be viewed as a voice for the black masses. Specifically, it strikes the reader that Robinson is treating both Adam Clayton Powell and Malcolm as children, addressing them as children, consequently infantilizing them. This infantilizing allows Robinson to essentially declare that he is an authority on these matters, someone to whom his adversaries should answer. This infantilizing is further addressed later in the chapter. This portrayal of Robinson is significantly distinct from the public memory of Robinson that remains today.

A Battle over Agency

The second theme present in Robinson's letters is a battle over agency, as each rhetor attempts to diminish the agency of the other. For instance, Robinson's public criticism of Powell didn't come from just anywhere. His criticism stems from Powell's public suggestion that members of the black community begin rejecting the stance of controversial black figures. As Robinson writes, "I refer to your vicious attacks upon the National Association for the Advancement of Colored People, your intemperate and ill-advised suggestion that the Negro people boycott the NAACP because of the participations in its affairs of white people and your rallying call to the Negro people to support Malcolm X and the Black Muslims." By making such a characterization of Powell's strategy, Robinson puts himself in the position of giving Powell advice on how to execute public sentiment, something that we saw Brooklyn Dodgers president Branch Rickey do during his pursuit of Robinson as a ballplayer. Additionally, Robinson characterizes Powell's suggestion as "intemperate" and "ill-advised." While Rickey did not characterize Robinson in negative terms by any means, Rickey did advise Robinson on how to fight back against public infuriation by "not fighting back." This is significant because Robinson's willingness to "not fight back" during his playing days—arguably the most important thing he did that garnered mainstream public support—is precisely what he is *not* doing in his opening sentiments to Congressman Powell. Here Robinson makes his first mention of two specific groups, the NAACP and black Muslims, as well as a specific individual in Malcolm X.

The letter's opening comments also include the personalizing of the intended recipient. As Robinson writes, "You know, Adam, that the NAACP, whatever shortcomings it may have, has been and still is the greatest organization working in behalf of all those principles of freedom and human dignity for the black man in America which was ever put together in this nation." The use of his first name rather than the formal "Congressman" could be interpreted as an attempt to illustrate how he, Robinson, does in fact consider Powell "a friend," as indicated in the letter's opening remarks. But there is an apparent tension between this form of address and the more formal form that Robinson uses to open his letter. For instance, the use of the congressman's first name depicts a blatant disrespect of Powell. We see a strategic move by Robinson to not only sharpen his critique but also publicly communicate that a chasm exists between two men who are at odds, particularly two black men. Within the scope of the racial landscape in America at that time, Robinson's strategy illustrates at least some semblance of discord among the black community, further taking Powell's agency away from him.

Furthermore, the opening statement in the letter to Congressman Powell shows us a much different image of Robinson, one that is anything but docile and obedient. Rather, it pulls no punches in terms of indicating for whom this letter, and overall message, is intended. Typically, any public letter would indicate to whom the letter is directed, but Robinson does so in a way that shows he is taking control of his own voice. Specifically, he states that most people writing such a public letter don't want an answer from the recipient. However, such a statement indicates not only that he, unlike most people, wants a response to his letter but also that he, Robinson, is in control of how he wants this letter to be viewed: as a demand for a response.

Back to Malcolm: The Struggle for Agency Continues

As we turn to the letter from Malcolm X, published in the *New York Amsterdam News* on November 30, 1963, exactly eight months after Robinson's letter to Powell, we continue to see the battle over each rhetor's agency.

First, Malcolm's letter to Jackie was a response to the denigration of Congressman Powell. Malcolm's letter opened with an explicit salutation, indicating either a hint of sarcasm or a sincere sentiment. Malcolm's letter opens, "Dear Good Friend, Jackie Roosevelt Robinson." The ambiguity that Malcolm employs while initially addressing Robinson points to Malcolm's attempt to illustrate the nature of their relationship, that of adversaries. That is, Malcolm is portraying a sense of respect to Robinson and a sense of tension. While they both have something in common as black Americans striving for racial equality, they also are positioned as enemies regarding the ways they both see fit to achieve that same goal, thus minimizing Robinson's agency. The role as adversary is made more apparent in his next point. For instance, Malcolm refers to Dodgers general manager Branch Rickey's role in Robinson's playing career. This perhaps suggests that Robinson was not considered, at least not by some, a standout player until "after" Branch Rickey "lifted you to the Major Leagues." It is certain that Malcolm did not think Robinson became a great player until after Rickey promoted him to the Major Leagues. Consequently, the status of Robinson's pre–Major League Baseball greatness is called into question here, offering a viewpoint that when reviewing Robinson's national legacy, perhaps it was the national stage that took precedence rather than his own individual achievements. More specifically, Malcolm is criticizing Robinson in a way that attempts to reduce his ethos and strip him of his agency. By calling into question Robinson's ethos, Malcolm attempts to reduce the extent to which people, specifically white people, would be willing to hear Robinson's voice as the voice of the black community more generally.

Essentially, Malcolm is critiquing Robinson's personal agency, attempting to minimize the degree to which Robinson himself is responsible for his success. Second, Malcolm's use of the phrase "the 'right' negro" when referring to Branch Rickey's choice of Robinson for baseball's racial integration echoes much of white America's sentiments when Robinson broke baseball's color barrier. That is, Rickey had to pick "the right" player to represent a palatable approach to including minority players in America's favorite pastime. The third theme that Malcolm incorporated into the opening paragraph was that of the capitalist motivations behind Rickey's historic endeavor. The implication is evident that Malcolm accuses Rickey of having an insincere penchant for civil rights and that Rickey's true motivation was finding a palatable representative for racial integration. Thus, Robinson's agency is once again stripped, suggesting that Rickey, not Robinson, was the impetus behind baseball's racial integration.

As we continue with Malcolm's letter, we see more than a sug-

gestion that Jackie Robinson contributed to the capitalist motivations of Major League Baseball. Specifically, in the second
paragraph Malcolm addresses Robinson's appearance in front
of the House Un-American Activities Committee in 1949 and
the conflict with Paul Robeson. Similar to Robinson's strategy
of framing Congressman Powell as an enemy, Malcolm utilizes
the strategy of invoking an enemy. By doing so, Malcolm is once
again attempting to minimize Robinson's agency and does so
in three ways. First, the repeated use of Paul Robeson's name
immediately puts Robinson at odds, once again, with yet another
prominent black figure. Second, we see Malcolm's continued
use of the "white boss" terminology, once again reinforcing the
racial relationship between a white authority and black servant.
Third, we also see the reinforcement of the notion that Robinson's greatness should be called into question, as Malcolm explicitly states that Rickey "lifted you from poverty and obscurity to
the Major Leagues." In this instance, Malcolm is claiming that
a black man may be more willing to be the "obedient" servant
when a white authority has something prominent to offer him.
Also, the Negro Leagues are equated with poverty and obscurity. Essentially, these three tactics parallel Robinson's strategy
noted earlier with Powell.

As Malcolm's letter progresses, we next see the inclusion of
yet another controversial figure's name, that of President Richard
Nixon. Additionally, Malcolm provides several themes throughout
portions of the letter. First, Malcolm makes explicit reference to
Robinson the baseball player in the context of politics. More specifically, Malcolm refers to Robinson as an "ex–baseball player,"
indicating that his prowess on the playing field has long since
passed. We see publicly for the first time Robinson's agency as
a baseball icon being deemed as no longer carrying the same
weight it once did. Also, Malcolm is diminishing Robinson's cre-
dentials as a political player. That is, Robinson is *merely* a baseball player, and a long-retired one at that, and thus he has no
authority as a political commentator. This critique parallels the
earlier discussion about the traditional imagined split between

sports and politics. Malcolm is calling upon this tradition to diminish Robinson's political ethos. Second, the emphasis on the term "MISLEAD" in all capitals is of course meant to stand out, while at the same time reinforcing the negative association with Richard Nixon. The strong use of the derogatory language, particularly the term "dumb" when referring to others following Robinson's lead, illustrates Malcolm's sharp critical edge, an edge that is reciprocated in Robinson's letter as well.

Malcolm then continues to mention the status of black Muslims and their involvement in the ongoing racial tension within the black community. The primary theme worthy of note here is the defense of Malcolm's denigration of Ralph Bunche. Similar to much of Malcolm's rhetoric, this paragraph reinforces his philosophy that generally endorsed an attack only in self-defense. More specifically, Malcolm calls into question Robinson's motives for his initial attack of Congressman Powell. That is, Malcolm is suggesting not only that his "attack" on Bunche is done in self-defense but that his "attack" on Robinson is done out of self-defense as well. This portion of Malcolm's letter positions Robinson as the aggressor. Again, this is an image that stands in sharp contrast to Robinson's public memory. In addition, Malcolm is actually *giving* Robinson some forms of agency, particularly as the aggressor against a member of his own race. Malcolm does this while at the same time *taking away* other forms of Robinson's agency, particularly as a hero of his race and as a baseball star. Robinson's agency as an aggressor against a member of his own race gives Malcolm a justification for indeed attacking Robinson out of necessity.

A Battle over the Mainstream

The third theme of the letters is that of the battle over the mainstream. More specifically, Robinson engages in a battle over a multiracial mainstream. We will see how Robinson associates himself with a black-white mainstream, as evidenced in his letters to Powell and Malcolm. Malcolm, in his response, critiques Robinson for this very association.

In his letter to Powell, Robinson justifies his public denounce-ment of the congressman. As Robinson writes, "I write it because it is my sincere belief that you have grievously set back the cause of the Negro, let your race down and failed miserably in the role which our people justly expect you to play as an important national leader of the Negro in this nation." Robinson uses the phrase "our people." By doing so, Robinson is suggesting that Powell, while a prominent leader in the black community, does not effectively represent the black community. More specifically, Robinson imagines Powell's role as different from his own. The use of such phrases signifies a sharp contrast from Robinson's portrayal of Paul Robeson in front of the House Un-American Activities Committee. Furthermore, if we compare the black press's portrayal of Robinson after his HUAC testimony regarding Paul Robeson and communism, we see the black press offering a similar critique of Robinson. The parallel of the two critiques, that of Powell by Robinson and that of Robinson by the black press, illustrates the transformation of Jackie Robinson's pub-lic image from subservient black man to dissenting political voice. Consequently, Robinson has, for the second time at this point in his career, made a sharp public denouncement of two other prominent black figures, as both critiques similarly sug-gest that the targeted black figures do not represent the black community as a whole.

When Robinson condemns Powell for his suggestion that "Negro people boycott the NAACP because of the participations in its affairs of white people," Robinson is clearly emphasizing an integrationist perspective. This is indeed the image of Jackie Robinson that has been publicly remembered in contemporary mainstream America—an image that condemns the denigra-tion of white America.

Perhaps most significant in the above passage is Robinson's first mention of Malcolm X and the black Muslims. More spe-cifically, Robinson has shifted, momentarily, the attention away from Powell and toward the controversial Malcolm X. As Rob-inson implies in the above passage, Powell is not one who typically fell in the category of Malcolm X supporter, but Powell's "rallying call to the Negro people to support Malcolm X and the Black Muslims" suggests that Powell has moved in a direction he had previously rejected.

The letter then moves from its introduction to a further dissection of Powell's "ill-advised" alignment with Malcolm X. Robinson refers to the work of Arthur Spingarn, NAACP president from 1940 to 1966, as well as Kivie Kaplan, a philanthropist who would serve as Spingarn's successor as NAACP president from 1966 to 1975. As Robinson writes, "You also know that people like the Spingarns and Kivie Kaplan have done a dedicated job and organized more moral and financial support for this cause than any ten Negroes, including yourself. You know also, in spite of the fact that you and I share deep respect for Minister Malcolm X as an individual, that the way pointed by the Black Muslims is not the true way to the solution of the Negro problem." Though Robinson expresses admiration for Malcolm X as an individual, he condemns the solutions put forth by the black Muslims. This condemnation of black Muslims puts in no uncertain terms the disdain for and desire to remain separate from this particular segment of black America. Such a critique also reinforces the integrationist notions from the previous excerpts noted above. This desire to remain separate from a segment of the black population may garner favor with white America, but it contrasts sharply from Robinson's remarks in that same passage. As Robinson writes, "For you are aware—and you have preached for many years—that the answer for the Negro is to be found, not in segregation or in separation, but by his insistence upon moving into his rightful place—the same place as that of any other American—within in our society." Granted, the "separation" to which Robinson is referring is that of separating black America from white America. However, Robinson's disdain for any kind of racial separation is emphasized in the latter passage, while the separation from black Muslims is ironically suggested in the beginning of the passage. This speaks to the complicated divide and difficult choice that many black

Americans had to make at that time: pick a side within the black community. Robinson's suggestion to move to a "rightful place" embodies the complexity of his perspective. Unfortunately, as Robinson's complexity has been forgotten, his political participation and activism get forgotten along with it.

As we return to the portion of his letter to Powell that calls him out for being a "crybaby" and throwing a "tantrum," as well as suggesting that the black community is "growing up," Robinson sharpens his critique even more. Robinson is executing three strategies here. First, we notice a second use of Congressman Powell's first name, continuing the personalizing—and infantilizing—of his target. The choice of terms such as Powell's first name, "crybaby," "tantrum," and "growing up," strengthens the bite even further, almost as though Robinson is in a position of power and exercising his authority over a child. The excerpt is essentially chastising Powell, almost as if to say, "We're growing up, Adam, and leaving your childish temper tantrums behind us." Second, he alludes to what mainstream America might view as "usual" when racial strife is discussed in the cultural landscape. Robinson's choice of phrase, "the usual crybaby yell," coupled with a complaint that Powell was claiming to be persecuted because of his racial status, could certainly be viewed as Robinson attempting to garner favor with white America. Here we see one black man publicly infantilizing another, calling him out for crying foul in the context of racial strife. This could be viewed as Robinson embodying the "obedient" black man. In other words, Jackie Robinson is assuming for the moment the perspective of a white person who might view someone like Adam Clayton Powell as a stereotypical black person who sees racial slights at every turn, even when they're not really there. For instance, the Reverend Jesse Jackson, or at least the public perception of him, might be a useful contemporary example to illustrate this perspective.

As we move to Malcolm's letter to Robinson, we also see the battle over the mainstream. For instance, Malcolm insists that Robinson is but a servant to the white man. We see Malcolm's insistence that Robinson operates on a level that only serves to satisfy the white man, a reiteration of his earlier comments about Jackie serving his "white bosses." As Malcolm's letter continues, we see Robinson depicted in such a manner. For instance, Malcolm suggests that Robinson illustrates a level of naïveté, particularly regarding any relationships with members of the white community. What's more, there is a slight hint that Malcolm is referring to Robinson as perhaps a "hidden" enemy. Through the use of the phrase "open enemies of truth and justice," Malcolm may be suggesting that he at least knows who his enemies are, while Robinson can't tell the difference between his friends and his enemies. By ending the letter in this fashion, Malcolm does not offer a clear indication as to what he exactly means in the very last line.

The Last Word: Robinson's Response to Malcolm

While it took eight months for Malcolm to publicly respond to Robinson's initial letter, it only took two weeks for Robinson to provide a public rejoinder. On December 14, 1963, Robinson offered sentiments in the *New York Amsterdam News* in defense of his initial letter to Powell as well as responses to Malcolm's remarks. Throughout his letter to Malcolm, Jackie incorporates the same tone he used in the initial letter to Powell. As we see in the letter's opening comments, the reader must distinguish between either a hint of sarcasm or a genuine proclamation regarding Malcolm's response: "Dear Malcolm: Frankly, your front-page letter to me in THE NEW YORK AMSTERDAM NEWS is one of the things I shall cherish. Coming from you, an attack is a tribute. I am also honored to have been placed in the distinguished company of Dr. Ralph Bunche whom you have also attacked." Through this opening paragraph we see Robinson's immediate attempt to be seen as part of the mainstream. He does this through the strategy of framing Malcolm X as someone outside the mainstream. Robinson's logic suggests that Malcolm X is such a radical that if he critiques you, then that must mean you are actually in the mainstream. By employing this logic, Robinson sees himself not only as a member of the main-stream but as a member of the mainstream who holds a prominent role. The deflection of any possible victim status allows Robinson to frame the rest of his letter as a statement written by someone who understands and recognizes his own prominent role in the black community, while simultaneously portraying Malcolm as someone whose public denigrations are so prolific, and therefore anticipated, that they have lost some of their impact. Thus, there is a parallel between Robinson's criticism of Powell and Malcolm. For instance, Robinson suggests that Powell is at times a "typical" crybaby and that Malcolm "typically" slings unfounded criticisms. Thus, Robinson is in some way depicting both Powell and Malcolm as behaving in predictable ways, which is in contrast to Robinson's own ways of acting and thinking. This then establishes Robinson as someone who is an independent thinker and not locked into a routine way of thinking, unlike his adversaries. Perhaps, then, this adds a new layer to the way that Robinson sees Powell. Rather than merely casting Powell as a "typical" sort of overly sensitive race man, perhaps he is calling out both Powell and Malcolm as engaging in predictable, typical, and nonindependent thinking, which stands in contrast to his own way of thinking. Furthermore, by invoking the name of Dr. Ralph Bunche as a fellow recipient of Malcolm's attack, Robinson is now conflated with someone else who is respected and revered in the black community. Thus, the opening paragraph illustrates Robinson's adeptness at constructing a response that, similar to his initial letter, pulls no punches and invokes a sharpness to his critical edge. This opening paragraph, like many of Robinson's public portrayals, is a depiction of Robinson that does not fit neatly into the mainstream public memory of an obedient, soft-spoken Jackie Robinson.

In the next section of Robinson's letter, he addresses the themes of the "white boss" almost immediately, noting in the second paragraph the following defense of his associations with prominent white figures: "I am proud of my associations with the men you choose to call my 'white bosses'—Mr. Branch Rickey, my boss at Chock Full O' Nuts, Mr. William Black, and Governor Nelson Rockefeller. I am also proud that so many others whom you would undoubtedly label as 'white bosses,' marched with us to Washington and have been and are now working with our leaders to help achieve equality here in America." By invoking the names of not only Brooklyn Dodgers general manager Branch Rickey but also William Black and Nelson Rockefeller, Robinson reinforces his prominent status with not just "white bosses" but with white iconic figures. At the same time, Robinson is also criticizing Malcolm's stance (at least as of 1963) that all white people are evil. By doing so, Robinson is pointing out that many white people, and most specifically the white people he mentions, are not evil. This further positions Robinson as a black man with whom white America can further identify and be more willing to support, thus further placing him in the mainstream.

Robinson, as noted earlier, calls Malcolm's bluff when claiming that members of the black community should be "thankful" that he was not present in Birmingham or Mississippi after racially motivated crimes were committed, as he, Malcolm, infers that he would have taken an avenging role. While calling such a bluff addresses the battle over legitimacy, it also addresses the battle over the mainstream. For instance, Robinson indicates that Malcolm sees him as a naive figure, as a black man who fails to see the hypocrisy in the white man's discourse. Furthermore, as we return to Robinson's letter, we see Robinson once again addressing any indication that he is naive when it comes to his relationships with members of the white community. As Robinson writes, "You mouth a big and bitter battle, Malcolm, but it is noticeable that your militancy is mainly expressed in Harlem where it is safe. I have always contended for your right—as for that of every American—to say and think and believe what you choose. I just happen to believe you are supporting and advocating policies which could not possibly interest the masses. Thank God for our Dr. Bunche, our Roy Wilkins, our Dr. King and Mr. Randolph. I am also grateful for those people you consider 'white bosses.'" First, Robinson contends that every American has the right "to say and think and believe what you choose." Here we see Robinson reinforcing what is considered by many as a popular, mainstream view when it comes to freedom of expression—that despite any differences of opinion, all Americans, black or white, still have the right to be heard. This reinforcement carries over to the following sentence, particularly in terms of unifying the black community through such expression. Robinson uses the specific pronoun "our" when referring to the black community as a whole. By referring to Dr. Bunche, Roy Wilkins, and Dr. King as "ours," Robinson suggests that they are members of a specific dynamic of the black community, an inclusive use of the pronoun. Robinson's word choice of "our" suggests a unity within the black community for which Robinson had previously argued in his letter.

At another section of his letter, Robinson employs a similar statement he made fourteen years earlier during his HUAC testimony. As we will see in chapter 2 regarding the ways in which portions of Robinson's HUAC testimony were taken out of context by both the white and the black press, much of Robinson's critique of America's racial landscape at that time was excluded from his public memory. As Robinson states in the next section of his letter to Malcolm, "America is not perfect, by a long shot, but I happen to like it here and will do all I can to help make it the kind of place where my children and theirs can live in dignity." Here, Robinson incorporates a critique of America's racial landscape, quite similar to the critique he made in front of HUAC. Robinson's critique is eloquent in its brevity. What's more, Robinson's statement that he hopes one day America is "the kind of place where my children and theirs can live in dignity" is similar to a sentiment articulated by Martin Luther King less than four months earlier, when Dr. King proclaimed: "I have a dream that one day my four little children will live in a country where they will be judged not by the color of their skin but by the content of their character."[5] Robinson's paraphrase of King is yet another tactic that he can use to try to position himself in the mainstream and consequently marginalize Malcolm

X. While King himself was hardly within the mainstream, Robinson's tactic places himself in the mainstream by echoing the sentiments that many Americans saw leading the racial landscape, slowly but surely, in a new direction.

Finally, as Robinson continues his letter, we see an inclusive sentiment toward equality as well as an explicit rejection of Malcolm's leadership strategies. As Robinson writes, "I shall always be happy to associate myself with decent Americans of either race who believe in justice for all. I hate to think of where we would be if we followed your leadership. Strictly in my personal opinion, it is a sick leadership which should be rightfully rejected by the vast majority of Americans." Robinson employs a sharp critical edge similar to that of Malcolm's. Robinson truly has the last word, as this is the final letter of the public exchange of letters and illustrates his willingness to stand firm on not only his public stances but also his denouncement of Malcolm's discourse. One recurrent theme we see throughout these letters is that as rhetors, both Jackie Robinson and Malcolm X are trying to line up an assemblage of supporters behind them rhetorically. That is, they are both suggesting that they have more supporters than the other. As a result, we are witnessing, in some sense, a battle for mainstream support.

The Battle over Coalition Building

The fourth theme present in the letters is the battle over coalition building. More specifically, Robinson attempts to build up a rhetorical coalition of sorts, bringing a "common sense" found within the black community to his side. In one instance, an excerpt examined earlier, Robinson states, "Whatever you may believe, Adam, I write this letter more in sadness than in anger. I, like many others, have been troubled by what has seemed to be your growing insensitivity to the cause of our people and your seemingly increasing disregard for your responsibilities to the job you have been sent to Washington to do." First, as we see at the end of the passage, Robinson moves to the notion of personal responsibility. Robinson claims that Powell put himself in a "vulnerable position." This passage suggests that Powell, and only Powell, is to blame for any public criticism against him. Additionally, Robinson is attempting to build up a rhetorical coalition, bringing a notion like "common sense" to his side. Second, Robinson aligns himself with the sentiment of "many others," which may strengthen his criticism, as well as continue to build a rhetorical coalition that attempts to bring common sense to his side, as noted earlier. That is, while Robinson is speaking out as an individual, he again claims to represent the perspective of a community. Once again, Robinson continues to emphasize the role of personal responsibility. Robinson argues that Adam Clayton Powell is derelict in his duties and that he has "been troubled by . . . your seemingly increasing disregard for your responsibilities to the job you have been sent to Washington to do." This statement illustrates Robinson's plea for Powell to take personal responsibility when it comes to fulfilling the black community's expectations of their representative's role in Washington.

The next passage of the letter reiterates Robinson's specific strategies: "As I close this letter, Adam, I must confess with a deep sense of sadness, that I no longer know who your enemies really are. Like many others, I have hesitated to say this because you have done a magnificent job in years gone by and because I did not want to give ammunition to those enemies of yours who have been the enemies of the Negro people." We see in this passage five strategies that reinforce Robinson's approach throughout the letter. First, Robinson invokes the presence of an enemy, perhaps to compensate for his lack of credibility as a relative newcomer to public debate. By no means does he not have experience in the world of political and racial strife at this point in his life, but his role as a staunch, outspoken, and public advocate is still a relatively new endeavor. While there is no one better known than he in both the sports and the political worlds in the early 1960s, Robinson demonstrates a lack of personal and public ethos when it comes to critiquing his adversaries, specifically Congressman Powell. This is complementary to the "common sense" theme of African Americans to which Robinson alludes throughout the letter. Just as Robinson aligns himself with the African American and white American mainstream, so too does he establish enemies against which to define the mainstream. In this case, the mention of an enemy is used to suggest that the line between "friend" and "enemy" has been blurred both within and outside the black community, making future attempts to fight said enemy more difficult. Second, the use of the pronoun "I" is used three times in one sentence, reinforcing the direct ownership that Robinson is taking for his criticism of Powell. More specifically, the use of the pronoun "I" in these passages illustrates how Robinson recognizes his role as a prominent individual whose public declarations would be scrutinized more heavily than many others in the black community. Third, he refers to Congressman Powell by his first name yet again, further bolstering the personal tone and infantilizing nature of the letter's intended recipient. Fourth, the notion of "sadness" reinforces the softening of the critical edge, suggesting more of a disappointment rather than a mere public tongue-lashing. Finally, Robinson uses the phrase "like many others" to forge an alignment with a larger community, suggesting that his sentiments are a reflection of a larger community rather than appearing as a mere personal attack. Robinson also makes it a point to praise the work that Powell has done in the past. Rather than making an indirect or general mention of Powell's work, Robinson makes it explicitly clear that Powell's previous efforts are praiseworthy. Thus, Powell, like Malcolm X, is a man to be admired personally so long as his sentiments are disparate from other controversial black figures.

Beyond the use of specific pronouns, Robinson has now addressed the enemies of the black community. In the next passage, Robinson makes very specific mention of the segregationists: "The people who were your enemies and ours—the segregationists—are probably thinking very highly of you right now although they probably have contempt even for an enemy who would desert his own cause. At any rate, you have played right into their hands. They want nothing better than to hurt the NAACP and you have volunteered to give that aim a tremendous boost." Robinson's word choice here mentions the segregationists as the enemy, though he refers to them as "your enemies and ours." Undoubtedly, Robinson means that the segregationists are Powell's political enemies as well as enemies of the black community in general.

Robinson's Political Persona: Taking Ownership

This analysis has shown a side of Jackie Robinson's political persona that is primarily absent from his contemporary legacy. Specifically, this analysis reveals four key insights about Robinson's rhetoric. First, by analyzing his public letters criticizing Congressman Adam Powell and Malcolm X, we have seen that Jackie Robinson made it an occasional practice to make sharp critiques of his targets, regardless of their community or national standing. Robinson's sharp critique of Congressman Powell and Malcolm X suggests a contentious persona that is absent from many contemporary versions of his memory. Through Robinson's rhetoric, we notice that Robinson was not afraid to explicitly address the presence of numerous enemies within both mainstream American culture and the black community. The letters analyzed in this chapter add another dimension to the public memory of Jackie Robinson. The passages analyzed here tell us something about race in sports in America. For instance, the letters suggest that sports are not just a mere escape from our everyday realities. The racial tensions that clearly emerged between Robinson and other prominent black figures are not an escape; they are quite real and represent a larger narrative regarding our racial realities. Also, the letters tell us that the battle over who represents a community's voice is a constant one, and one for which there is no definitive answer. The letters also equip us with more evidence that this historical figure was more than a mere representation of a particular community agenda. The agenda that Robinson set in these public letters served not only members of both the black and mainstream communities but Robinson's individual and political interests as well—the interests seldom remembered in contemporary versions of Robinson's memory.

As author Michael Long proclaims about Robinson's political persona and prolific letter correspondence, "Here, at last, was a Jackie Robinson far beyond the baseball diamond. An angry black man who grabbed a pen and wrote rage-filled letters about segregation and discrimination. A fiery prophet who rebuked politicians for telling African Americans to exercise patience and forbearance when pursuing their constitutional rights. A fervent patriot committed to using his celebrity status and considerable resources to overcome the racial divide *right now* so that his children would have a brighter, better future." In terms of the impact of the letters, adds Long, it is as though we are "meeting a new—or perhaps another—Jackie Robinson."[6] That "other Jackie Robinson" is depicted effectively in his disparaging letters to Congressman Powell and Malcolm X.

But Long's analysis misses the significance of the recurring themes throughout these letters. Robinson's letters employ recurring themes that are consistent through much of his political discourse. The two letters analyzed in this chapter are not so much about offering hope as they are about condemning controversial and opposing viewpoints that Robinson sees as problematic. Specifically, Robinson's recurring themes, or what Carl Burgchardt deems "rhetorical imprints," include the following: Robinson censures his targets for their stunting of racial progress, for their ill-advised urging of members of the black community to shun the NAACP, for their alignment with other controversial figures, for their suggestions to support separatist philosophies, for their "usual crybaby yell" when condemned publicly, for their presumption that members of the black community will support them solely because of their race, for their growing insensitivity to the cause of the black community, for their ammunition given to opponents of the civil rights movement, for their denigration of white authorities who are sympathetic to the cause of the black community, for their "us versus them" mentality, and for their dereliction of duties as leaders of the black community. According to Burgchardt, a rhetorical imprint is a set of "distinctive verbal characteristics that supports the content of numerous speeches and articles in different contexts."[7] Robinson's rhetorical imprint is useful because it helps distinguish the "real" Robinson (the fiery, combative, controversial, political figure) from the "remembered" Robinson (the obedient, uncontroversial, patriotic figure). Robinson, in his letters as noted above, repeatedly rebuked Powell for his dereliction of duties, for his "usual crybaby yell," and for his "set back of the negro." Furthermore, he rebuked Malcolm X for his "separatist philosophies," his depiction of "white bosses," as well as his "racist views." The recurring employment of such sharp, critical denouncements suggests that Robinson was well aware of the public perception of him as an "Uncle Tom." The rhetorical imprints Robinson uses provide us with a "different" Robinson than that to which we have grown accustomed. The different Robinson to which we are exposed here provides us with a new lens through which to view not only Robinson's memory, but also the political and racial landscape of this chapter of the American civil rights movement. For instance, if the Jackie Robinson with which mainstream America is familiar can also be viewed as an outspoken, controversial, and overtly political voice, then we as critics have more choices for how to explore the historical implications of a changed public memory.

Third, Robinson documents his political beliefs and philosophies through these public letters, thus constructing a narrative about his political identity. By doing so, particularly with two individuals whom he viewed as adversaries, his experiences and actions are organized over the course of his life, particularly his political experiences and actions, and those are documented in the letters to prominent political figures, including Powell and Malcolm over the course of two decades. During that time, Robinson uses these letters, specifically the ones to Powell and Malcolm, to construct a revision of his narrative self. That is, while the Jackie Robinson portrayed in these letters was not a new persona of Robinson in his own eyes, it was a new persona to many readers who were newly exposed to Robinson's political discourse. Robinson's political identity manifests itself in his attempt to publicly articulate his critical insights regarding the contemporary American racial landscape, a version of his identity that runs counter to the neat, obedient version to which most Americans have become accustomed. That typical version is analyzed in the following chapter.

Finally, in Robinson's letters, he offers *his* account of America's racial landscape. Through his denigration and condemnation of these matters, Robinson takes ownership of *his* political persona. He pulls no punches. He states in no uncertain terms what the stakes are in the fight for civil rights. By taking ownership of *his* political persona, Robinson provides a concrete and documented version of his political outlook on the American racial landscape. As noted throughout the analysis of the letters themselves, this version of Robinson is seldom, if ever, portrayed in contemporary commemorations of Robinson's legacy. Subsequently, Robinson executes an authoritative memory, one in which the individual under the microscope is the one who actively and consciously portrays him- or herself in the manner he or she wishes others to see him or her. An authoritative memory allows the subject being remembered some agency, usually in a particular way in which he or she chooses to be remembered. This type of memory is difficult to achieve, mainly because over time the ways in which a culture or community chooses to remember a particular subject changes based on the needs of the day. Unfortunately for Robinson, this portrayal does not typically withstand the modern-day constructions of his legacy, something we have seen in the introduction. Robinson's political persona portrayed in these letters will eventually be appropriated in ways that best suit the commemorator, as evidenced in Major League Baseball's Jackie Robinson Day commemoration. But at the time the letters were written, Robinson seized control and took ownership of his political identity. Major League Baseball, through its construction of Robinson's contemporary legacy, took that control and ownership out of Robinson's hands a half century later. This tells us something about race and sport in America. For instance, Robinson, as analyzed through his letters, represents the difficulties and risks of standing as an individual and making a statement about race in America, as opposed to making a statement by, more quietly, attempting to become a part of a group. In his baseball career, Robinson was hired because he could quietly become a member of a group. After his playing career, however, Robinson became a more vocal individual. This has something to do, in part, with the way that we talk about race in this country because we tend to privilege those who seem to ask for quiet integration, à la Martin Luther King Jr., while rejecting those who seek a voice to make a more individualistic criticism, à la Malcolm X, and similarly perhaps Robinson after baseball.

As we look back to the role Jackie Robinson played in not just Major League Baseball but the Negro Leagues as well, there are numerous things to consider in terms of how Jackie Robinson managed his public image both during and after his playing career. For instance, Jackie Robinson's emerging political persona further obscures the history of the Negro Leagues. That is, the more Robinson's political voice comes to the forefront, the easier it is to forget how he had a hand in both the popularizing and the eventual demise of the Negro Leagues. It also suggests that the Negro League players may have been more politically active, in general, if they had had the opportunity that Robinson did and thus would not be relegated to some of the forgotten annals of black baseball. Furthermore, it suggests that Jackie Robinson can be seen as a proud representative of the Negro Leagues, though he is consistently remembered as a representative of the Major Leagues first and foremost. Because this chapter has been primarily concerned with Robinson's management of his public image, it is important to consider how this narrow concern relates to, and in fact is essential to, the larger arguments that have been made about the Negro Leagues and the politics of race in baseball.

2

The Robinson-Robeson Clash

A Siren Song Sung in Bass

I do have an increased respect for Paul Robeson, who, over the span of
that 20 years—since 1949—sacrificed himself, his career and the wealth
and comfort he once enjoyed because, I believe, he was sincerely trying
to help his people.

—JACKIE ROBINSON

Jackie Robinson has often been examined, understandably, in
a baseball context, a context in which politics, or any political
edge for that matter, has not been constructed for public con-
sumption. This chapter parallels that same argument, but we
turn our attention to how members of both black America and
white America constructed Robinson's status *during* his playing career. Robinson's emphasis on his racial identity eloquently
sets up his argument that there is great difficulty in balancing
his role as an anticommunist, patriotic American with his role
as a man of color fighting for racial equality.

Robinson's political views began to take shape on a national
stage just a few years into his playing career. In the 1940s communism was on America's mind, and often being suspected
of being a communist was sufficient cause for a government
investigation. Prominent singer and actor Paul Robeson was

the target of just such an investigation, and Jackie Robinson was invited to denounce Robeson's public criticism of American foreign policy at the Hearings of the House Un-American Activities Committee Regarding Communist Infiltration of Minority Groups.[1] Robinson accepted the invitation, marking the beginning of a political clash that would emerge as a significant historical moment in the lives and careers of both men.

On July 8, 1949, Jackie Robinson received a public request from John S. Wood, a Democrat from Georgia and chairman of the House Un-American Activities Committee, to appear before the committee to testify on matters of "black Americans and their loyalty to the nation."[2] It was ten days later, on July 18, 1949, that Robinson appeared before the U.S. House of Representatives to testify before the House Un-American Activities Committee Regarding Communist Infiltration of Minority Groups.

When Jackie Robinson was invited to address the HUAC session, he was asked to denounce a prominent member of the black community. That member, Paul Robeson, was already established as a political agitator by the American government. The choice for Robinson to contest Robeson publicly was not an easy one. As explained in Robinson's biography, "Jack had no special desire to join a fight against Robeson."[3] But if Robinson's decision to contest Robeson's statements was ultimately predicated upon spite for those opposed to his HUAC participation, it should be no surprise that his comments may be read as an act of political assent, at least at some level, on white terms.

Too often the examination of a historical text stops at a mere recounting of the past event. For our purposes here, moving beyond a recovery of an event is necessary if we are to obtain a distinction between "mere history" and rhetorical inquiry. So what can studying the historical context of the Robinson-Robeson conflict offer us in terms of valuable purchase for practicing democratic dissent? How does it allow us to theorize democratic dissent in a contemporary context? First, as Stephen Hartnett argues, "We . . . enhance and enliven our understanding of the past when we recognize the conflictual and intertextual nature of democratic dissent." Yet my goal here has been to move beyond mere enhancement of understanding our past. For the purposes of this book, it is necessary to delve into the rhetorical nature of important historical events like Robinson and Robeson's public discourse so that we may learn how mainstream political sentiment can blunt much of the critical edge put forth by performers of democratic dissent. Thus, it is productive to view a historical event such as this one as a series of rhetorical problems. Thinking of the Robinson-Robeson conflict as a rhetorically historic moment does not, and should not, reduce the moment to a mere judgment of right and wrong. Rather, thinking of it as a series of rhetorical problems has the potential to produce multiple viable perspectives of the robust nature of democratic practice. By examining Robinson and Robeson in this way, perhaps we can recover "significant aspects about those events that other perspectives miss."[4]

By analyzing the backgrounds and relationship of Jackie Robinson and Paul Robeson, Robinson's speech, and the coverage given to the event by the black press and by the mainstream white press, we will see that Robinson's testimony, or at least the coverage of it, led to the diminishing of Paul Robeson's status in popular culture. Furthermore, with Paul Robeson's diminished status, Jackie Robinson's critique of racism in America was also diminished. This diminishment plays a significant role in terms of how the contemporary public memory of Robinson's legacy is framed in a solely positive way, ignoring the controversial aspects of his political life. The rhetorical discourse surrounding Robinson's controversial exchange with Robeson culminates in a public amnesia of Robinson's controversial political persona.

This chapter recovers the way(s) in which Robinson was perceived by the American public and how this may have contributed to shutting down the necessary discursive exchange found in democratic practice. Ultimately, I argue that Jackie Robinson's testimony in front of the House Un-American Activities Committee is an act of dissent on his own terms, but was read as an act of assent on white political terms.

I will show how viewing Robinson's discourse in terms of synecdoche allows for the historical narrative regarding Robinson's HUAC testimony to get constructed in ways that bring democratic practice to the fore. Moreover, this analysis shows how sport and politics are significantly interrelated. Sport, in this specific case, became the initial and most public of venues in which Robinson established a historical move toward racial equality. The Robinson-Robeson saga is a prime example of how certain corners of society deem sport as a nonpolitical space yet, at the same time, ironically use that space as a catalyst for political motives.

First, I will examine the background of Paul Robeson and how he played a role in Major League Baseball's racial integration. We will see how Robinson and Robeson's relationship set the stage for Jackie Robinson as an "ideal" agent to publicly denounce Paul Robeson's procommunist sympathies. Second, I examine Robinson's HUAC testimony, specifically his emphasis on his identity as a "colored person" in America.

After examining Robinson's HUAC speech, I will then examine the black press's accounts of Robinson's testimony. Specifically, I will analyze specific excerpts from prominent black newspapers at the time. Many of the black newspapers framed the testimony, intentionally or unintentionally, as one that, for lack of a better phrase, threw Paul Robeson under the bus. In other words, much of the black press framed Robinson's testimony as one that harshly criticized Paul Robeson for his procommunist sentiments and consequently made it appear as if Jackie Robinson was separating himself from Robeson and urging others to do the same. The black press's exclusions of certain parts of Robinson's speech created a tension within the black community, resulting in many individuals of color, both prominent and common, picking sides as to who truly represented the black community.

Finally, I will examine specific excerpts from mainstream newspapers' coverage of Robinson's speech. The mainstream press coverage of Robinson's speech excluded significant excerpts of his testimony, excerpts that clearly articulate Robinson's support of Paul Robeson. These exclusions, coupled with the mainstream press's inclusions of excerpts that paint Robinson as a patriotic American first and a citizen of color second, contextualize a rather neat, uncomplicated representation of Robinson.

Paul Robeson and Jackie Robinson: The Beginning and Crossroads

The Paul Robeson Saga

Athletically speaking, in some sense, Paul Robeson was the Jackie Robinson of his day. The fact that Robinson's and Robeson's lives paralleled one another makes a compelling case for focusing on the exchange between the two men. In the first half of the twentieth century, Paul Robeson was "one of the most famous and admired of living black Americans."[5] As Barbara Beeching explains, "Today he is remembered as an outstanding African American singer, actor, and All-American athlete, but in the 1930s and 1940s he was also among the country's most respected black leaders." Paul Robeson was "one of many intellectuals who espoused liberal and leftist views [and] he became a champion of racial justice, with a campaign for human rights at the center of his agenda." Lisa Brock describes him as "a politically committed anti-racist internationalist, who, because of his sweeping talent and power, became the most dangerous man in the U.S."[6] Growing up in the early 1900s, Robeson was raised with a social and political perspective that paralleled that of W. E. B. DuBois, rejecting the premise of the famous Supreme Court ruling *Plessy v. Ferguson*, attacking racial prejudice where he saw it, and refusing to become accommodated to an unjust system. This perspective allowed Robeson to realize his physical and mental capabilities, capabilities that superseded his peers. Upon earning a scholarship to Rutgers University, Robeson became an All-American football player in 1917 and 1918. In fact, Robeson's athletic achievements allowed much of the American public to take notice of a black man excelling in a white-dominated society. While at Rutgers Paul Robeson earned twelve varsity letters in football, basketball, baseball, and track and field. Such athletic prowess even led to a brief career in what is now known as the National Football League, landing a spot on the first championship team of the league.[7]

Robeson moved on to law school at Columbia in 1920. Upon completing his law degree, Robeson was denied membership by the American Bar Association because of his race, leading to a career in which he eventually flourished—singing and acting. This became the impetus for much of Robeson's acceptance among both black and white communities, receiving favorable reviews and audience reaction. Traveling Europe and England for most of the 1920s and 1930s, Robeson became "more politically aware as areas of the world moved toward fascism during the 1930s . . . [questioning] the imperialistic policies of European nations and America toward colonial Africa, of fascist Italy toward Ethiopia, and of Nazi Germany toward the Spanish Civil War."[8] Received warmly by Europe, it was a trip to the Soviet Union in 1934 where "he was treated with a humanity he had never known [that started] him down the road toward a commitment to radical socialism."[9] Upon arriving in Moscow, Robeson considered there to be a lack of racial prejudice, writing, "I, the son of a slave, walk this earth in complete dignity."[10] From then on, Robeson consistently protested fascist thought while praising the Soviet Union. Much of the fascist thought he criticized came from America. His popularity in America began to wane somewhat after the war, "along with the growing enmity between the United States and the USSR."[11]

It was September 1939 when Robeson returned to America, the same month Jackie Robinson began attending the University of California at Los Angeles as a four-sport athlete. Jackie Robinson's pursuit of baseball on a professional level led to Paul Robeson's involvement in desegregating Major League Baseball. To Robeson, "it seemed hypocritical . . . that America would fight to end the myth of Aryan supremacy in Germany while the nation preserved its own myth of racial supremacy at home."[12] Pressure to desegregate baseball increased as the United States entered World War II. Paul Robeson was one of the more prominent black leaders to apply such pressure.

In 1943 the New York Legislature introduced a resolution that protested the exclusion of African Americans from the Major Leagues. Peter V. Cocchione, Brooklyn's communist councilman, pioneered "a resolution calling for desegregation of baseball." With this new legislation, the Negro Publishers Association requested a visit with Major League Baseball commissioner Kenesaw Mountain Landis, hoping to discuss the issue of black ballplayers in organized white baseball. Landis fulfilled the request, marking the first time the issue of baseball integration was officially explored. As Ronald Smith explains, "Eight black newspapermen and Paul Robeson attended the meeting. Robeson's presence dominated the session."[13]

At the December meeting, Commissioner Landis introduced Paul Robeson, remarking that Robeson was brought in "because you all know him. You all know that he is a great man in public life, a great American." Robeson addressed Major League Baseball team owners, stating, "I come here as an American and former athlete. I come because I feel this problem deeply." As the first African American to play in Shakespeare's *Othello* two months earlier on Broadway, Robeson used this as a springboard for his plea, arguing that "if he could be a black in an otherwise all-white play, then a Negro in a white cast should no longer be incredible to baseball owners."[14] Understanding the fears and anxieties that were perceived to come along with the burden of baseball integration, Robeson reassured the owners that "my football experience showed me such fears are groundless."[15] The owners followed Robeson's remarks with "a rousing ovation," while choosing not to question Robeson further. While his presence and testimony at this meeting did not have an immediate impact on baseball's stringent racial policies, Robeson is considered by many to have had a hand in the eventual breaking of baseball's color line.[16]

The Impetus for Jackie Robinson's Testimony: Paul Robeson's
Remarks to the World Congress

Several years later, on April 19, 1949, when probed about his position regarding Americans' stance on communism at the World Congress of the Partisans of Peace, Robeson addressed the Congress: "It is unthinkable that American Negroes would go to war on behalf of those who have oppressed us for generations against a country [the Soviet Union] which in one generation has raised our people to the full dignity of mankind." In their reaction to Robeson's speech, most black leaders criticized his comments.[17] For example, Max Yergan, a member of the Council of African Affairs, stated, "We American Negroes can be deeply grateful Mr. Paul Robeson did not speak for us in Paris a few days ago."[18] A member of the National Association for the Advancement of Colored People board of directors, Dr. Channing Tobias, proclaimed that Robeson was "an ingrate." Walter White, head of the NAACP, stated publicly: "We will not shirk equal responsibilities. . . . We will meet the responsibilities imposed upon all America." The *Chicago Defender* included one headline that read "Nuts to Mr. Robeson," and the *Pittsburgh Courier* declared Robeson's sentiments a "pathetic statement." President of the National Council of Negro Women Mary McLeod Bethune echoed the recurring sentiment: "I am chagrined at his presumption. . . . I think he has missed his cue and has entered the stage during the wrong scene."[19] Finally, Edgar G. Brown, director of the National Negro Council, "went further by calling Robeson's speech communist propaganda."[20] These reactions become a key component in understanding later how Robinson's HUAC testimony gets reduced to a simple narrative of political assent on white America's terms.

The House Un-American Activities Committee was notorious for singling out Americans who seemingly posed a threat to national security. HUAC was established primarily to explore any and all communist involvement among American citizens.[21] At the very least, targets were sought in order to immobilize them, if nothing else. Walter Goodman claimed that HUAC's "endless harassment of individuals for disagreeable opinions and actions has created anxiety, revulsion, indignation, [and] outrage."[22]

Jackie Robinson as "Ideal" Dissenter

In the annals of sport history, Jackie Robinson is accurately characterized as the embodiment of courage. However, this was not done entirely on his own. Rather, it was considered a collective effort on the part of several individuals.[23] Branch Rickey, general manager of the Brooklyn Dodgers, transgressed the color barrier with the introduction of Robinson, Major League Baseball's first African American player of the twentieth century. This endeavor has often been constructed as a heroic endeavor on the part of both Branch Rickey and Jackie Robinson. However, the heroism often projected upon Branch Rickey is one that has come under scrutiny in recent years. As Bill Mardo argues,

> Let's be perfectly frank. Branch Rickey signed Robinson after a long and bitter campaign of social protest: ten years of struggle by key black sportswriters and their papers, ten years of struggle by progressive trade unionists, ten years of struggle by some politicians of conscience, ten years of struggle by the Communist Party, and ten years of struggle by the *Daily Worker* Sports Page and its sportswriters. And from 1936 to 1946, democratic-minded baseball fans rang doorbells, pounded the pavements, picketed outside ballparks, and collected signatures on petitions urging that America's national pastime become national not in name alone but in fact.[24]

A viable perspective, then, of Robinson's ability to stand center stage on a political platform like the House Un-American Activities Committee is one that brings his ties to a political community to the fore. In previous discussions, we saw how Major League Baseball individualizes black baseball primarily through Robinson alone. Similarly, despite the collective efforts to break baseball's color barrier, here we see Mardo arguing that the media portray Jackie Robinson this way.

On the brink of the Cold War, with American anxieties and

angst regarding communism in full force, Americans looked for patriotic stability and national certainty from their leaders. Of course, a "leader" in this case had to be one of strong moral conviction, one willing to perform his patriotic obligation without hesitation. What better figure than the remover of America's national pastime?

Robinson's HUAC Testimony

It was on July 18, 1949, that Jackie Robinson found himself in a new political space that transcended sport, a space that momentarily removed him from the role of athlete and placed him in the role of political symbol. It was on this date that Robinson appeared before the U.S. House of Representatives to testify before the House Un-American Activities Committee Regarding Communist Infiltration of Minority Groups. Robinson was intended to represent the "model minority" that "neo-conservatives celebrated and presented both to counter the dependence of the underclass and to affirm their commitment to racial equality."[25]

Dissent and Assent: A Synecdochical Tension

In response to Robeson's remarks, the House Un-American Activities Committee strategically assembled a political platform for Jackie Robinson in order to secure patriotic sentiment, while simultaneously "construct[ing] the political gallows for ex-athletic great and premier singer and actor, Paul Robeson."[26] While Robinson's presence before a congressional hearing evoked a sense of responsible moral suasion, it was the motivation lurking behind his testimony that has brought questions of democratic inconsistencies, evidenced here as dissent and assent, to the fore. Robinson's testimony was strategically erected by the House Un-American Activities Committee to denounce the political Robeson's discourse. Not surprisingly, Robeson's declaration was seen by many as a threat to America's opposition to communism, and Robeson was thus widely considered a political agitator. Consequently, in the midst of prevalent anticommunist sentiment throughout the American political and social landscape, a move had to be made to denounce such sympathy for communist Russia. In other words, the House Un-American Activities Committee implicitly expected Jackie Robinson to represent a synecdoche of Americanism, a symbol that represented the political sentiment of the larger American society.

As we will see throughout this chapter, Jackie Robinson's testimony was called into question by many members of the black community. This raises several questions. For instance, how could an advocate of freedom of expression such as Jackie Robinson have his loyalty to the black community questioned? Why was Robinson roundly criticized for critiquing Paul Robeson when prominent black leaders had already critiqued Robeson themselves? Perhaps a useful heuristic for answering these questions is to explore the ways in which Robinson's HUAC testimony was read notably in terms of synecdoche. Synecdoche is most useful for this analysis, as Kenneth Burke claims that a "synecdochical form is present in all theories of political representation, where some part of the social body (either traditionally established, or elected, or coming into authority by revolution) is held to be 'representative' of the society as a whole." It is useful to understand Robinson's appearance before the HUAC as an instance of synecdochical representation, similar or analogous to the "political representation" that Kenneth Burke describes as an exemplar of synecdoche. Just as Burke notes that "some part of the social body" may be elected as "'representative' of the society as a whole," in Jackie Robinson's case the HUAC committee selected him to represent African American sentiment as a whole. This reading of Robinson helps us to understand how his testimony gets reduced to a representation of a larger group. As we will see, Robinson's testimony establishes him, according to the mainstream American public, as a representative of the larger democratic polity. This inaccurate representation of Robinson is a lesson in understanding the importance of taking dissent seriously, for "when dissent occurs . . . it is all too readily reduced by ruling elites to a political irrelevancy."[27] In other words, not only is the representation of Robinson as an individual representing a larger group an inaccurate depiction of him, but his intended dissent is also reduced when he is assumed to be representing the larger black community as a whole. His individual voice, then, fails to stand out.

Thus far we have seen ways in which Jackie Robinson was read synecdochically. Just as there was debate about whether Paul Robeson was seen to be representing the black community as a whole, Robinson's HUAC testimony was debated among members of both the black and the white communities as to whether his political sentiments were held to be representative of the society as a whole.

Mainstream Press Coverage of Robinson's Testimony

Congressman Morgan Moulder, a Democrat from Missouri, began the exchange with this statement: "Mr. Robinson, this hearing regarding communist infiltration of minority groups is being conducted 'to give an opportunity to you and others to combat the idea Paul Robeson has given by his statements.'" Robinson offered this famous response: "Paul Robeson's statement in Paris to the effect that American Negroes would refuse to fight in any way against Russia . . . sounds very silly to me. . . . I've got too much invested for my wife and child and myself in the future of this country . . . to throw it away because of a siren song sung in bass."[28] Extending his comments on the "silliness" of Paul Robeson's statement, Jackie Robinson had proclaimed that Robeson had the right "to sound silly if he wants to, but not to threaten 'an organized boycott by 15 million members of my race.'"[29]

For instance, Robinson declared, "That doesn't mean we're going to stop fighting race discrimination in this country. It means that we're going to fight it all the harder because our stake in the future is so big."[30] Robinson's critique continued:

> Every single Negro who is worth his salt is going to resent any kind of slurs and discrimination. This has got absolutely nothing to do with what Communists may or may not be trying to

do. This includes Jim Crowism in the Army, in jobs, on trains and in buses. Because it is a Communist who denounces injustice in the courts, police brutality and lynching, when it happens, doesn't change the truth of the charges. [Blacks] were stirred up long before there was a Communist Party, and they'll stay stirred up long after the party has disappeared—unless Jim Crow has disappeared by then as well.[31]

David Hinckley points out that Robinson's testimony "was a gamble most historians think ultimately failed—not because Robinson didn't make a strong and even radical point, but because most headline writers seized on something else." That "something else" was the statement regarding the "silliness" of Robeson's statements. Unfortunately for Robinson, as Hinckley states, "that was the next day's headline almost everywhere. This wasn't the message Robinson considered important, as evidenced by the fact that he devoted most of his statement to warning that the big threat to America was its own failure to deliver the rights and opportunities the Constitution promised."[32] In its original form, Robinson's testimony was a synecdoche for dissent from the political status quo. That is, Robinson's testimony was a representative part of some larger discourse of dissent. Robinson's testimony, as it was portrayed in the media, became a synecdoche for anti-Robeson sentiment.

However, as Hinckley suggests, Robinson had "told the House Un-American Activities Committee that Commies, whom the committee saw as the whole problem, were not the problem at all," but this was not the way it was represented in the press. The *New York Daily News*, for example, headlined Robinson's testimony on page 2 the next day, reading "JACKIE HITS A DOUBLE—P. ROBESON, JIM CROW." Despite the newspaper's explicit mention of Jim Crow, indicating Robinson's dissent from racial segregation in America, other newspapers and news reporters, just as HUAC did, "found it more newsworthy that Robinson had criticized Robeson, for many years an ally in pushing to integrate baseball."[33] So now we start to see a shift in how Robinson was portrayed in the media. Robinson had gone from serving as a synecdoche for black dissent from mainstream white American political thought to Robinson serving as a synecdoche for white assent to mainstream anticommunist political thought. In other words, where Jackie Robinson's actual testimony did seem calculated to serve as a synecdochical critique of race relations in the United States, reports in the press made it seem instead that his remarks joined the white critique of Paul Robeson. In fact, Robinson's use of the term "silly" perhaps helped the statement to backfire. While Robinson may have been trying to dismiss the attention to Robeson's comments as being silly, he instead seemed to be saying that Robeson himself was silly. If this was indeed the case, it only reinforced a strategy of whites to emphasize points of disagreement among African Americans, making it more difficult for African Americans to sustain a united front.

Perhaps not surprisingly, given that the white press was framing Robinson's testimony according to the prejudices of their readership, the reaction from the white public regarding Robinson's testimony was a positive one. As Arnold Rampersad explains, "The next morning, and in the ensuing days and weeks, a deluge of congratulations poured over him—especially in the white press. Newspaper editorials and cartoons sang his praises, and the *New York Post* even offered an excerpt from his speech as an editorial entitled 'Credo of an American.'" The *Daily News* echoed a similar sentiment, writing, "Quite a man, this Jackie Robinson. . . . Quite a ball player. And quite a credit . . . to all the American people."[34] Consequently, Robinson's testimony had been reduced to a synecdoche for anticommunist ideology, but more significantly a synecdoche for mainstream Americanism as a whole. Robinson's testimony could be seen as being read as patriotic assent to a mainstream American ideological worldview, primarily because talking about freedom (as a part) was read as talking about America (as a whole). This reading is in contrast to the black community's reception of Robinson's remarks.

Black Press Coverage of Robinson's Testimony

Much of black America read Robinson's testimony in a similar vein as white America did, interpreting it as political assent to a patriotic American ideological worldview, but also on white terms. But at the same time, while other prominent black leaders had critiqued Paul Robeson, many members of the black community did not want it to seem as though Jackie Robinson spoke for them all. This, as to be suspected, created tension. The New York newspaper *Age* reported that citizens of Harlem were "split sharply on the issue." According to Robinson's biography, the same newspaper described Robinson as having "come back from Washington 'in the dual role' of leader of his race and 'handkerchief head.'"[35] Additionally, one writer from Pittsburgh "asserted that Robinson had been a 'stooge' for HUAC and had put Negroes on the defensive, hamstringing the civil rights movements."[36]

Robinson's double gesture, one of black dissent along with affirmation of Americanism, was being insufficiently balanced on the side of assent. In other words, Robinson's testimony as a synecdoche for supporting a sentiment of white Americanism was being emphasized, erasing his dissent from the status quo from the picture. The *Pittsburgh Courier*, a prominent black newspaper at the time, included a story of a woman exclaiming that "the habit of 'bad mouthing' is a slavery trait and should have been outgrown ere this time." The *Philadelphia Afro-American* provided an angry account from a person in Boston who said "Paul Robeson was fighting for his people's rights when Jackie Robinson was in knee pants."[37]

Again, we are able to see how Robinson's testimony was read synecdochically, but this time by much of the black community. As his testimony was represented and reduced, Robinson was seen to have turned his back on a former ally, Robeson, while also turning his back on the black community. To read his HUAC participation in this way can understandably be seen as a division of much of the black community in America. Though this reading was a grossly inaccurate one, it lingered within the black community for years to come, especially after the subsequent downfall and public erasure of Paul Robeson.

Following Robinson's HUAC testimony, Paul Robeson suffered a major decline in his popularity and consequently virtually disappeared from the American public landscape. Smith explains, "Concert managers soon refused to book him, and his recordings were often taken out of record shops." Even alumni of Rutgers University called for the removal of his name from the college records. Furthermore, "The *American Sports Annual* deleted Robeson's name from its list of football All-American selections for the years 1917 and 1918." As if that wasn't enough, Secretary of State John Foster Dulles had Robeson's passport canceled in attempts to deny him economic and personal independence.[38] These efforts were successfully made to put black America back "in its place." Consequently, Robinson was now perceived by many to have had a hand in putting black America in such a place.

Swinging for Democratic Space

I have argued that Jackie Robinson's testimony in front of the House Un-American Activities Committee was a synecdoche for black dissent, but was inaccurately read as a synecdoche for assent on behalf of white interests. This is significant in terms of the implications regarding how Jackie Robinson's contemporary legacy has been presently constructed. For instance, we have witnessed how Robinson's testimony led to Robeson's erasure from the public landscape, causing Robinson's critique of racism in America to be erased along with it. Also, the Robinson-Robeson saga becomes a cautionary tale in understanding how mainstream political sentiment can cause democratic dissent to lose much of its critical edge. Furthermore, we have seen how sport has become a suitable and significant space for theorizing democratic dissent and political practice. Each of these conclusions is explained in greater detail below.

First, on July 18, 1949, Jackie Robinson occupied a space that foregrounded what DuBois called "double-consciousness." He had to juggle the double identity of both a black man speaking out against racial segregation *and* a patriotic American who denounced a procommunist ideology. By emphasizing his dissatisfaction with America's practice of racial segregation *on his own terms*, an exercise not expected by HUAC, Robinson was on the verge of creating a space for robust democratic dissent. However, though Robinson attempted to publicly dissent against racism on his own terms, he was portrayed as affirming the core notions of Americanism, notions such as anticommunism, white dominance, and patriotism.

Second, a significant critique of racism such as Robinson's is essential in understanding the give-and-take of democratic practice. However, when Paul Robeson was erased from the public spotlight, the critical edge of Jackie Robinson's testimony was erased as well, partially damaging the credibility of dissent and how it can be weakened at times in a democratic space. Moreover, erasing Paul Robeson damaged the power of Jackie Robinson's testimony, and thus diminished the usefulness of Robinson's testimony as a model of the sort of give-and-take that is essential for democratic practice. According to Bob Ivie, the sharp edge of criticism is necessary in order for dissent to challenge existing policies, conventions, and attitudes. Sharp criticism, then, is what enables dissent to gain any sense of traction. Without a sharp critical edge, dissent is much less likely to challenge the status quo effectively. With that in mind, blunting Jackie Robinson's critical edge resulted in the failure of executing a prime opportunity to challenge the American racist political system on its own terms. This is extremely dangerous when trying to gain traction for the importance and necessity of democratic practice. The media's oversimplification of the disagreement between Robinson and Robeson (thus making it sound like Robinson was representing a white mainstream voice) is what blunts the edge of criticism. Consequently, the edge of Robinson's dissent from racism in America was underrepresented in the press, constituting a lack of balance between Robinson's dissent and assent. Such an imbalance is dangerous, as "the possibility of credible dissent relies on achieving a certain productive tension between affirming and disconcerting the political order. Optimal credibility, by this account, implies a kind of rough equivalency . . . of the two gestures—that is, a double gesture of non-conforming solidarity."[39] Consequently, because Robinson did not express a credible gesture of nonconformity, because his move to critique racism on seemingly white political terms was not sufficiently balanced on the side of assent, his dissent was therefore eradicated by both black and white communities who needed him to represent a strong symbol, or synecdoche in this case, of Americanism. Robinson's motive of nonconformity is in tension with a motive of assimilation to white political terms. Robinson's motives of nonconformity and assimilation are complementary motives and should be kept separate and distinct so both can be heard.

Third, Jackie Robinson's black identity was disciplined, as he needed to disconfirm Paul Robeson's black edge by trumping the race card. Robinson believed that his testimony in front of the House Un-American Activities Committee would underscore his belief that African Americans are indeed patriotic, with a stake in the direction of the country, while Jim Crow continued to deny them equal rights and opportunities. Robinson intended to affirm Robeson's criticism of racism in America while simultaneously critiquing the direction of Robeson's procommunism sentiment. However, this double gesture lacked the necessary edge for effective critique because Robinson lacked control of the media, and thus his message. That is, Robinson's testimony was framed by the white and black press to erase the matter of racism from the equation, therefore blunting his critique of racism in America. HUAC's motives painted the white community as wanting to read Robinson's political stance as one that portrayed themes of patriotism and anticommunism, while suggesting that the black community wanted Robinson's testimony to be read not as African American but ultimately *American*. To be clear, there is a distinct difference between HUAC's motives and the way in which both the black and the white communities were painted. Certainly, not all whites wanted Robinson to be anticommunist, and not all blacks wanted Robinson's comments to be *American*. Yet as Robinson's dissent from America's racist ideologies got read as assent to a white American political perspective, Robinson was framed as standing for and affirming white dominance. However, this was not actually the case. By analyzing Robinson's speech, and the coverage given to the event by the black press and by the mainstream press, we see that Robinson's testimony, or at least the coverage of it, led to Paul Robeson's diminished status within the public landscape. The rhetorical discourse surrounding Robinson's exchange with Robeson cultivates a "forgetting" of Robinson's controversial political persona.

I agree with Stephen Hartnett's assertion that "American democracy is most fascinating when studied through the voices of citizens engaged in critical dialogue with . . . its most pressing political crises, especially when these voices slowly oscillate between dissent and assent." It is this last part of the passage, the oscillation between dissent and assent, that intrigues me. Here we have two examples of prominent public advocates participating within the constructs of democratic space, engaging in political deliberation that foregrounds two key premises of patriotic participation: dissent and assent. Paul Robeson, on the one hand, can be read as *dissenting from* the proclamation that black Americans could, would, and should defend America against a communist threat. Conversely, Jackie Robinson appears to be read as *assenting to* the popular American paradigm that communist Russia does indeed pose a serious threat to American national security on all fronts. Therefore, according to Robinson's testimony, the situation requires the sacrifice of any and all Americans, black or white, who view such a threat as significant. In American political culture, according to Ivie, the act of dissent is not a privileged endeavor. Assent, however, tends to be considered a privileged move, especially when it expounds on core values such as patriotism, liberty, and democracy. As Hartnett claims, "When in a pickle, invoke freedom or liberty, for few Americans would dare express opposition to such grand concepts."[40] For a rhetor to follow this advice is a move that would, in most cases, be viewed as socially and politically beneficial. In this chapter, we have seen what happens when invoking the notions of freedom and liberty results in the public misreading of the orator's overarching message. In the end, the Robinson-Robeson saga becomes a cautionary tale in understanding how mainstream political sentiment can cause democratic dissent to lose much of its critical edge.

Fourth, while investigating the political discourse between Paul Robeson and Jackie Robinson, we must not overlook the fact that the two men had much more in common with one another politically and socially than is generally acknowledged in the white historical narrative. As Bill Mardo point outs, "To talk about Jackie, for me, means to talk about Paul Robeson. . . . Too many times, the comments about Robinson and Robeson seem wrongly centered on what allegedly separated Jackie and Paul—and I'm here to tell you that rarely are two historic figures so closely *connected*."[41] What Mardo brings to the fore in this assertion is the myth that has been perpetuated over the past half century: that despite Jackie Robinson and Paul Robeson being political enemies, the two men were not socially and politically disconnected.

Consequently, the political discourse between Jackie Robinson and Paul Robeson has been rhetorically constructed in a way that has hindered our ability to view the Robinson-Robeson collision as one that is culturally productive in the context of democratic practice. The notion of what Chantal Mouffe calls agonism is useful here, as framing Robeson and Robinson in an agonistic space becomes germane to the overarching rhetorical narrative of the Robinson-Robeson conflict. According to Mouffe, agonism "is a different mode of manifestation of antagonism because it involves a relation not between enemies but between 'adversaries.'" Adversaries, for Mouffe, are defined "in a paradoxical way as 'friendly enemies,' that is, persons who are friends because they share a common symbolic space but also enemies because they want to organize this common symbolic space in different ways." Giving presence to the similarities between the two men in addition to their differences, rather than solely presenting their differences, makes for better cultural critique. Examining how Robinson and Robeson had more political similarities than differences helps us get a clearer understanding as to how privileging an agonistic space is rhetorically and culturally productive. For instance, if we subscribe to this notion of agonism as suggested by Mouffe, we can read the conflict between Robinson and Robeson as one not concerned with "overcoming . . . this us/ them opposition—which is an impossibility—but the different way in which it is established."[42] Thus, by reading Robinson's testimony this way, we see that Robeson is not a domestic "other" that needs to be controlled; rather, he needs to be embraced for what his adversarial characteristics can bring to the table of democratic dissent. In terms of the overall book, this helps us see how Robinson's legacy is not just one of convenience but a way to complicate our understanding of his political past. This can in turn provide an outlet for examining Robinson's legacy not just beyond Major League Baseball's contemporary version of it but also in terms of how we can further the discussion and continue to peel back the layers of Robinson's controversial and complicated past.

Fifth, this analysis shows how the relationship between sport and politics is significantly interrelated. With an understanding of Robinson's role in the American political landscape beyond the baseball diamond, we start to see not only how sport and politics are interrelated but also how such a relationship can provide a space for learning how to engage sport as a site for democratic practice and dissent. There is no question that breaking the color barrier itself two years earlier was overtly political, but now Robinson's testimony before HUAC transgressed the boundaries of the baseball field and gained presence inside the doors of America's congressional community. The Robinson-Robeson relationship exemplifies how sport is often considered nonpolitical but is simultaneously used for pushing political agendas. For example, HUAC brought Robinson before the committee precisely because HUAC believed that sports were *not* connected to politics. Thus, Robinson was painted as a figure who could be counted on to provide nonpolitical commentary that would neutralize Paul Robeson's political statements. Thus, HUAC's hope to neutralize the political endeavors of Robeson was done through what it believed would be seen as a nonpolitical figure in Robinson.

While the Robinson-Robeson clash can be seen as a significant political and historical moment, the relationship between sport and politics is one that tends to get chided as an undesirable and unlikable move. As Shelly Anderson wrote in the *Pittsburgh Post-Gazette*, "It's difficult to keep politics out of sports and vice versa, but that doesn't mean we have to like it when they overlap." In a culture where sport and politics are supposed to be separate institutions, any intersection of the two may be deemed inappropriate. As Anderson argues, "Often, the crossover seems out of place."[43]

However, Michael Butterworth correctly argues that despite this desire to keep these two institutions disconnected, "baseball performs a political function." He goes on to claim that political discourse allows a sport such as baseball to "be used ideologically to discipline the notion of what is 'American' and, consequently, what is not."[44] We will continue to see Robinson as an example of that political, and American, space in the chapters that follow.

Finally, exploring Robinson and Robeson through rhetorical history offers us a way to link the past to the present. The argument that historical analysis helps us comprehend the present "by placing it in the context of the past" is certainly not a new contention.[45] But Kenneth Burke's notion of humble irony is useful here. According to Burke, "True irony, humble irony, is based upon a sense of fundamental kinship with the enemy, as one needs him, is indebted to him, is not merely outside him as an observer but contains him within." Along similar lines, recounting historical events is fine so long as one is aware of the tendency to privilege the "expectations and norms of the present, hence treating the past as if it were alien, other, the 'enemy.'" As Hartnett points out, "Humble irony, however, recognizes that our present is indeed indebted to the past our forebears created and lived. . . . Burke is asking us, then, to be humble regarding our rush to judge the past." Practicing such humility can allow us to open doors to the connected world of historical analysis and, more important, rhetorical and cultural critique. Yet when examining a rhetorical text like the Robinson-Robeson conflict, how can such an examination of a text more than a half century old be useful to us in the present day? According to David Zarefsky, "Not all issues engaged by the history of rhetoric are 'hot button' issues of the moment. Rather, the point is that even studies of theory are called upon to make a contribution to theory that in some way transcends the particular case under study and participates in a larger scholarly conversation."[46] The growing concern over the state of the democratic public sphere is germane to a rhetorical analysis of the Robinson-Robeson dialogue. Seeing as how Robinson is analyzed in this book as an orator above anything else, rhetorical inquiry becomes an essential part of the process.

3

Cooperstown and Kansas City

The Museum Narratives

We already have a Baseball Hall of Fame. We don't want a separate Hall of Fame. Our best players should go into the Baseball Hall of Fame.

—BUCK O'NEIL, cofounder of the Negro Leagues Baseball Museum

From 1920 to the mid-1960s black ballplayers barred from white baseball had formed numerous leagues in which to play, mainly on the East Coast and in the Midwest. While the Negro Leagues represent only one chapter in American history, that chapter is profound and prodigious in its own right, something on which this chapter focuses. The rhetorical effects of two prominent baseball museums are examined in this chapter—the National Baseball Hall of Fame and Museum and the Negro Leagues Baseball Museum. Through a comparison of the rhetorical effects of these two museums, I show that the National Baseball Hall of Fame and Museum enacts a similar sleight of hand, one that becomes more evident when compared with the Negro Leagues Baseball Museum.

These two museums both include and exclude African Americans in sport in various ways.[1] Both museums construct a narrative, or narratives, for the viewer to engage. However, there is not just one definitive narrative that represents an entire history of a movement, institution, or moment. The two museums analyzed here serve as what Kenneth Burke called "representative anecdotes."[2] That is, the narratives that are constructed by these two museums attempt to represent a particular perspective of baseball's racial history. I argue that an analysis of both museums offers a unique opportunity to explore the various forms of resistance within the racial landscape in American sport.

The purpose of this chapter is to examine the inclusion and exclusion of African Americans in sport, and thus how this inclusion and exclusion can offer an understanding of American culture on a larger scale. I argue that Major League Baseball uses Jackie Robinson in a way that *individualizes* the role of race, thus representing the entire legacy of black baseball. The Negro Leagues Baseball Museum, on the other hand, does not focus so closely on any single player, but rather presents a more *collectivist* narrative. Each of these disparate narratives complicates the way merit informs the role of baseball in American culture.

In the sections that follow, two major yet differing commemorations of baseball's integration are illustrated. The first is the National Baseball Hall of Fame and Museum's account of racial integration of America's pastime. The second is the Negro Leagues Baseball Museum's account of the same integration. Throughout the analysis I provide extended captions that are mounted on the exhibit walls. These captions are the primary channel through which the exhibits are explained throughout the museum. Thus, I supply in some instances long block quotations and then provide commentary on them. I believe this is the most effective method to use, as it ensures that no details will be left out in the ways the museum explains the exhibits. As Carole Blair and Neil Michel explain in their analysis of the Civil Rights Memorial, the captions and inscriptions of any commemorative text offer a useful way to analyze its impact. As they state, "Its design components, e.g., color, shape, size, and inscriptions, combine and recombine with its contexts to create a web of multiple performances, spectacles that both reproduce and transform historically the tactics of the Civil Rights movement."[3] It should be noted that the way the captions mentioned above are presented intact helps preserve as much as possible the way that they are presented to the public. More specifically, my analysis emphasizes the importance of comparing two different museums' explanations of baseball legacies. Thus, it is important to be specific and accurate when describing what each exhibit caption actually states.

More specifically, this chapter will first provide a general overview of the National Baseball Hall of Fame and Museum, then will delve into an analysis of how the museum constructs a specific memory of Jackie Robinson and the racial integration of the game. We then will move to an examination of the Negro Leagues Baseball Museum, looking specifically at how this museum's depiction of baseball's racial integration is quite different from the version provided by its counterpart. The chapter concludes with a discussion of how the distinction of both museums' portrayals of black baseball offers a unique view of competing historical narratives.

There are notable differences between how Major League Baseball and Negro League baseball give Robinson's memory expressive form. The Negro Leagues Baseball Museum, for instance, uses Robinson's memory as merely a chapter in the legacy of black baseball in the twentieth century. By employing this strategy, the Negro Leagues Baseball Museum suggests that black baseball goes beyond one individual's achievements. In other words, Major League Baseball individualizes the legacy of black baseball through Robinson, whereas Negro League baseball collectivizes it. Major League Baseball's individualizing of Robinson's legacy reinforces the idea that meritocracy works if only *individual* merit is considered. The Negro Leagues Baseball Museum, however, does not solely consider individual merit as a necessary component to the legacy of black baseball. What the museum emphasizes is the collective approach to how black baseball survived on the margins of Major League Baseball. Baseball as a meritocracy, then, exists in the eyes of Major League Baseball via the Hall of Fame and Museum. In contrast, in the eyes of the Negro Leagues via the Negro Leagues Baseball Museum, baseball is not as much of a meritocracy but a space in which racial exclusion was prominent. Visitors get a sobering view of the Negro Leagues from the perspective of those who participated in them rather than just the contemporary mainstream depiction of black baseball's legacy. The point is one of contrast, allowing the viewer an opportunity to best discern the thinness of the dominant narrative by looking at such a museum.

The difference between the museums' commemoration of baseball's racial history is quite sharp. An examination of the differences is significant because, first, studying the commemorative narratives of both the Negro Leagues Baseball Museum and the National Baseball Hall of Fame and Museum offers a more expansive, comprehensive history than the mainstream contemporary history of African Americans in sports. Second, it allows us to examine how these competing narratives tell us something beyond African American history, the Negro Leagues, or Jackie Robinson. Finally, it shows us how both the collectivistic and the individualistic approaches to an institution's legacy play a role in how commemorative narratives are constructed. These two museums demonstrate two different ways of negotiating the meritocratic ideologies of baseball and how that idea of meritocracy is understood. Having analyses of two different museums is useful because it demonstrates how the same narrative is constructed from two different viewpoints.

In the next section, we will take a descriptive tour of the museums themselves, as this will help us get a better understanding of how Major League Baseball and Negro League Baseball construct the Robinson legacy as well as the legacy of black baseball.

The National Baseball Hall of Fame and Museum: An Overview

As a representation of the mainstream perspective of Jackie Robinson's legacy, the National Baseball Hall of Fame and Museum portrays Major League Baseball as an inclusive institution. The museum is located in Cooperstown, New York, and opened on

June 12, 1939, three years after the first Hall of Fame class was honored in 1936. As stated on the official Hall of Fame website: "The National Baseball Hall of Fame and Museum is an independent, non-profit educational institution dedicated to fostering an appreciation of the historical development of baseball and its impact on our culture by collecting, preserving, exhibiting and interpreting its collections for a global audience as well as honoring those who have made outstanding contributions to our national pastime." That is how the museum is described in present terms. The story of how the museum was actually created is more complex, and it forecasts the more individualistic portrayals of baseball heroes, including Jackie Robinson, inside the present-day museum. In 1933 the small town of Cooperstown, like many towns across the nation, had been devastated by the Great Depression. Stephen Clark, the owner and operator of the town's largest employer, the Singer Sewing Machine company, understood that the town was on the verge of collapse. Clark, one of Cooperstown's leading pillars, knew that he had to help save it. Baseball historian James Lincoln Ray describes how the origin of the National Baseball Hall of Fame was predicated upon the mythology of the origin of baseball itself:

> According to a legend that still prevailed in the 1930s, a young West Point cadet named Abner Doubleday had created the game of baseball in Cooperstown during the summer of 1839. Although that little bit of history later proved to be untrue, Clark probably couldn't have cared one way or the other. The circumstances required that he embrace and propagate the Doubleday myth in order to save his town. That is precisely what he did. In the hopes of attracting tourists to Cooperstown, Clark decided that he would create and operate a new baseball museum, which would be called the National Baseball Hall of Fame. Seeking official support for his idea, Clark lobbied for and obtained the approval of his new Hall of Fame from the Presidents of the National and American Leagues and from Kenesaw M. Landis, who had been baseball's commissioner since the 1919 Black Sox scandal. All three baseball men supported Clark's

idea, and began sending baseball memorabilia and artifacts to his offices in Cooperstown. By late 1935, Clark and the baseball elite had also enlisted the official support of the Baseball Writers Association of America (bbwaa), and by 1936, it was agreed that members of the bbwaa would elect several of the game's great players for membership in the Hall.[4]

Over the next three years, the bbwaa elected another twenty-one retired players and managers for membership, resulting in such a vast collection of baseball artifacts and memorabilia that Clark was compelled to commission the construction of a new building at 25 Main Street. By 1939 construction was completed, commemorated by a public ceremony that was attended by the members of the 1936 class as well as Commissioner Landis.[5] As Ray explains, "The larger museum was an instant success, attracting some 5,000 tourists to the town in 1940. That was just the beginning, however. Over the next sixty-five years, membership in the Hall of Fame would grow from five players to 280, and visitors to the museum expanded from a few thousand to almost half a million tourists per year. It [has been] reported that the Hall of Fame is responsible for more than half of the town's jobs and annual income."[6] Ray's description of the museum's origin illustrates how the museum was created out of economic necessity and primarily through the efforts of one individual. Thus, the origin of the museum itself is rooted in one individual's efforts to bring economic prosperity to a community. In this case, finances came before preservation and celebration of history. This is not to critique the motivation for the creation of the Hall of Fame or to claim that the preservation and celebration of the game's history have not been a significant factor in the origin of the museum itself. Most museums and public tourism understandably play a major role in a community's economic standing. However, it should be noted that the individual efforts of Stephen Clark show that the National Baseball Hall of Fame was not a grassroots effort tied closely to a particular ethnic group, in contrast to the Negro Leagues Baseball Museum, as discussed later in the chapter. Furthermore, the National Baseball Hall of Fame and Museum is not closely tied to a collective identity or history, which, again, is in contrast to the Negro Leagues Museum. Rather, as we will see in the following sections, the narrative that the National Baseball Hall of Fame and Museum constructs is one that depicts Major League Baseball as an inclusive space, and the museum does so by focusing on the individualistic nature of baseball's legacy rather than a collectivistic approach.

The museum presents a physically inviting exterior, creating an atmosphere of inclusion, a physical and figurative parallel to the ways in which Major League Baseball depicts its own history: as a history of inclusion. The building is a familiar beige brick, with three inviting archways located at the front. The two primary sections of the front of the building jut outward about sixty feet, giving the three archways a somewhat corridor feel. The building is designed to be user-friendly, as there are parking spaces and meters directly in front of the building, including handicapped-accessible spaces along with numerous other parking lots within the vicinity. It is quite a noticeable building, surrounded by numerous gift shops and memorabilia stores. The building is only two stories tall but stands out compared to the surrounding buildings on its street. What the building lacks in height it compensates for in depth and width, expanding beyond the entryway by a noticeable margin, almost giving it the appearance of having a separate building attached to it. There are numerous flower beds that brighten up the building's facade as one makes his or her way to the entry, accompanied by two American flags hanging on each side of the entry walls. There are three floors total, including two above street level.

Once inside, there are more than 2.6 million library items, including 35,000 three-dimensional artifacts, such as newspaper clippings and photos, and 130,000 baseball cards dispersed throughout the building.[7] A detailed tour of the inside of the museum is my attempt to have the reader experience the museum in a way similar to the way that a visitor to the actual museum would. It is important for the reader to experience the museum this way because it puts the focus on the individual details of the museum, thus reinforcing the individualistic and inclusive bend on baseball's legacy that the museum portrays both physically and conceptually.

Upon entrance into the museum, the visitor enters a rotunda and has three immediate viewing options: the ticket gate to the left, the Hall of Fame Gallery in the center, and the museum store to the right. The most visually appealing option is in the center of the rotunda, where a glass wall allows the visitor to see all the way through the end of the Hall of Fame Gallery. Just to the left of the glass wall are three bronze statues, left to right, of Lou Gehrig, Jackie Robinson, and Roberto Clemente, respectively. Each statue has a mounted black-and-white photograph on the wall behind it, with the player posing with a child in a baseball-related activity. The exhibit includes a display titled "Character and Courage" on the wall to the right. The display includes the following message:

> Becoming a Hall of Famer takes more than just a great baseball career.
>
> Off-the-field challenges—and how those challenges are met— reveal an inner character that serves men and women throughout their lives.
>
> The life experiences of Lou Gehrig, Jackie Robinson, and Roberto Clemente stand out above all. Each faced personal and social obstacles with strength and dignity that set an example of character and courage for all others to follow.

This exhibit, and specifically this passage, immediately frames the museum's message as one that prioritizes *individual* effort and the overcoming of challenging social circumstances. From the outset, the visitor is prescribed a narrative that values baseball's individual merit over a communal or collective effort that has helped cultivate baseball's legacy.

Upon leaving the rotunda and passing the ticket gate, the visitor enters the first level of the museum. From that point, the visitor can either turn right and remain on the first floor, where an art gallery and the Hall of Fame Gallery are located, or take the staircase to the upper floors. In terms of the first floor, the visitor has access to an art gallery. This moderately sized room, titled "Art of Baseball," is not in the open space, like many of the other exhibits. Rather, it is a room with artwork hanging on all four walls, including various displays mounted on columns standing approximately four feet in height, which are scattered throughout the room. The artwork has the title and artist mounted below each piece, typical of any art gallery. All works of art portray either specific players or stadiums themselves or various general depictions of the game itself, such as a manager and umpire arguing, fans in the stands cheering on the game, or baseball players in action.

Upon exiting the art gallery, the visitor is now getting closer to the actual Hall of Fame Gallery. But before entering that corridor, a corner display spotlights the "John J. 'Buck' O'Neil Lifetime Achievement Award." Included in this display is a life-size bronze statue of Buck O'Neil, a former Negro Leagues baseball player and longtime advocate of black baseball history. The award is described thusly: "Honors an individual whose extraordinary efforts to enhance baseball's positive impact on society has broadened the game's appeal, and whose character, integrity and dignity reflect the qualities embodied by Buck O'Neil throughout his life and career." Once again, and within the first one hundred feet of the entrance into the museum, visitors are exposed to a dedicated exhibit of a former player's individual efforts to impact the game.

Upon leaving this display, the Hall of Fame Gallery is preceded by the "Inductee Row." This display immediately precedes the gallery of wall-mounted plaques that can be seen in the forthcoming open hall. Inductee Row includes photographs and wall-mounted text describing the most recent inductees into the Hall of Fame. On the ramp down Inductee Row, leading into the Hall of Fame Gallery, museum visitors can see artifacts representing the illustrious careers of all the inductees, as well as portraits of some of the more recent Hall of Famers at their induction ceremonies. It is the Hall of Fame Gallery that is the primary focal point of the entire National Baseball Hall of Fame and Museum. Thus, this section of the chapter gives particular attention to the gallery's detail.

Based on the amount of space dedicated to this exhibit, it is clear that the Hall of Fame Gallery was designed to be the primary focal point of the museum. Any exhibits that are closer in proximity to the gallery don't appear to indicate any more importance than other exhibits in the museum. There is enough open space from the final exhibits leading up to the gallery that there appears to be no relationship between proximity to the gallery and importance. Upon entering the hallway, it is easy to notice how much larger this exhibit is than any others in the museum. The ceiling is approximately twenty feet high, with several marble columns on each side of the room. At first entry, there is a wooden podium with a bronze plaque on top serving as a directory for the gallery. Down the center of the hall are three wooden benches designed for seating. The floor is granite, noticeably different from the carpeting housed throughout the rest of the museum. The marble columns to the left and the right serve as a gateway to the bronze plaques on the oak walls. The plaques are displayed in two rows around the entire gallery, one on top of the other. Each section of the wall mounts about a dozen plaques in each section, making it a much less crowded wall space than the other exhibits, keeping the viewer from feeling a sense of information overload. Thus, the walls are rather empty other than the plaques, leaving about ten feet of empty space above the plaques, making the plaques the focal point on each wall. The expansive use of space and the specific arrangement of the plaques indicate an attempt to encourage the viewer to focus on the individual player, putting an emphasis on the individualistic nature of baseball history. This is because the empty space around the plaques tends to isolate them. The gallery's focus on the individual players is accomplished by allowing the viewer to read about only one player at a time. There are no pictures, no artifacts, no other displays other than the busts with information on them that explain the individual's accomplishments during his career.

At the back of the gallery on the center wall, there is a large archway, almost a cathedral-like structure, with several plaques of players and numerous achievements within the game, including memorable dates and milestone statistics. Today, the Hall of Fame features more than three hundred members, including the most recent inductees. Throughout the gallery there are more than two hundred former Major League players, nearly forty Negro Leaguers, nearly thirty executives or pioneers, more than twenty managers, and ten umpires. The structure of the gallery makes it stand out from all other exhibits in the museum, mainly due to its large size, making it the primary focal point of the visitor's viewing experience.

At the back of the Hall of Fame Gallery, the visitor can proceed to an inclined walkway that leads to several popular culture and media exhibits. The first is titled "Baseball at the Movies." Here, the viewer is shown excerpts of numerous films about baseball, most of which are mainstream Hollywood releases, from black-and-white films as early as the 1940s to films released during the current decade. The next space is titled "Scribes and Mikemen," a display dedicated to the journalists who covered the game and announcers who called the game for their respective teams. This space is relatively small in comparison to the others, with the typical photographs and newspaper clippings seen in the previous exhibits. The inclusion of media members allows the viewer to see that these particular reporters and announcers are the ones who either described or reported on the game itself. The smallness of this exhibit suggests that the visitor should remain focused on the game itself rather than on what is said about it. For instance, baseball's inclusion of players of all backgrounds was depicted through the members of the media and conveyed to a mass audience, making baseball's inclusive nature that much more prevalent in the public landscape.

Additionally, there are two separate rooms for display: the

"Bullpen Theater" and the "Sandlot Kids' Clubhouse." The Bull-pen Theater is first, housed in a separate space that includes various multimedia presentation capabilities, such as televisions and interactive question-and-answer displays. There is a lot of open space in the room in order for groups to listen to various presenters speak about the game's past and present. When there is not a tour-guided group in this room, it is an otherwise open and unoccupied space. The adjacent room is the Sandlot Kids' Clubhouse, a room designed with children in mind. There are several wall-mounted displays, but similar to the Bullpen Theater, there is a lot of open space for children to participate in activities, most of which are spread out throughout the room. This space is inclusive to everyone, even children who may or may not be particularly interested in other aspects of the museum itself.

The visitor is then directed back toward the Hall of Fame Gallery. As we revisit the gallery layout in this next section, I focus on the importance of Robinson's plaque, which is among the very few items in the museum to have been updated substantially since originally installed. Specifically, I argue that the updating of Robinson's plaque was done as an attempt to make him appear more robust and Hall of Fame worthy, not just based on playing merits alone but also based on his cultural impact on the game.

The Jackie Robinson plaque itself tells a story of his note-worthy achievements as a player and ambassador of baseball as a social institution. Thus, the plaque becomes worthy of analysis, as it represents a significant symbol of how Major League Baseball has commemorated Robinson's legacy as both a player and a social leader.

Since his induction in July 1962, Robinson's plaque has been on permanent display in the Hall of Fame Gallery, leaving its location just once, to travel to the Civil Rights Game in Memphis on March 29, 2008.[8] This was the text of the original plaque, which was cast for Jackie Robinson in 1962:

JACK ROOSEVELT ROBINSON BROOKLYN N.L. 1947 TO 1956 LEAD-ING N.L. BATTER IN 1949. HOLDS FIELDING MARK FOR SECOND

BASEMAN PLAYING IN 150 OR MORE GAMES WITH .992. LED N.L. IN STOLEN BASES IN 1947 AND 1949. MOST VALUABLE PLAYER IN 1949. LIFETIME BATTING AVERAGE .311. JOINT RECORD HOLDER FOR MOST DOUBLE PLAYS BY SECOND BASEMAN, 137 IN 1951. LED SECOND BASEMEN IN DOUBLE PLAYS 1949–50–51–52.

This original plaque implies that Robinson's most notable achievements were those based on statistics, with no mention of his status as the first black Major League Baseball player of the twentieth century. That, however, was eventually reconsidered.

Forty-six years later, the original plaque was changed. A new plaque has been cast—with the new language revealed for the first time at a special ceremony at the Hall of Fame on June 25, 2008—further documenting Robinson's lasting legacy. The following announcement was posted on the National Baseball Hall of Fame website on April 29, 2008: "The National Baseball Hall of Fame and Museum will unveil a new plaque of Hall of Famer Jackie Robinson, featuring updated language to further honor his legacy, in the summer of 2008. The ceremony will feature Rachel Robinson, Jackie's widow, as she shares her thoughts on her late husband's legacy." Jeff Idelson, president of the National Baseball Hall of Fame and Museum, said of Robinson in the same website article, "Now, 46 years later, his impact is not fully defined without mention of his extreme courage in breaking baseball's color barrier. The time is right to recognize his contribution to history, not only as a Hall of Fame player, but also as a civil rights pioneer."[9] Similar to the museum's exhibits discussed earlier, the president of the Hall of Fame and Museum's own words explicitly state that Robinson's courage, not just his physical talent, is germane to Robinson's legacy, thus further expanding the way merit is defined within the context of baseball.

When the press release was distributed to announce the updating of the original Robinson plaque, Hall of Fame chairman Jane Forbes Clark stated, "We have adjusted plaques over the years that were found to have factual errors, but very rarely do we change the plaque for subjective reasons. We feel very strongly that rewriting Jackie Robinson's plaque is extremely important." The use of the term "subjective" in this statement may actually imply that choosing to display Robinson's plaque without any mention of his breaking of the color barrier was objective rather than subjective. As Clark continued, "Now the totality of Jackie's impact will be encapsulated on his plaque. The plaque is a career snapshot, and Jackie's snapshot was not complete without noting his cultural impact on our game. This is the right moment," Clark explained, "to place on Jackie's plaque his contribution to history not only as a Hall of Fame player but also as a civil rights pioneer."[10]

The National Baseball Hall of Fame and Museum officially unveiled the new Jackie Robinson plaque on June 25, 2008. Included in the official ceremony was Rachel Robinson, Jackie's widow. At the ceremony Rachel stated that her husband "wanted to be judged by the same standards that all the other Hall of Famers had been. He would understand now that we need to go beyond that toward social change, and he would want to be a part of that and be recognized. I don't think he would object to that. He would understand this is an evolution." Rachel Robinson's inclusion at the ceremony is significant because she speaks of Jackie's character and his role in social change. As Robinson continued,

> I vividly remember that joyful weekend. Jack was thrilled to be recognized by the Hall of Fame. . . . A very important part of Jack's life has been acknowledged here today [at the rededication]. As he said 46 years ago, those of us who are fortunate enough to receive such an honor must use it to help others. That was a great theme in his life. . . . When young people now look at Jack's plaque, they will look beyond the statistics and embrace all Jack has meant and all that they can be. We want it to be an inspiration, not just something to take pictures of. We want to give them a sense of direction.[11]

Rachel Robinson's comments reinforce the idea that Jackie's ultimate contribution to the game of baseball was, as she stated, "beyond the statistics." Once again, similar to the black baseball exhibit in the museum, Jackie Robinson's merit is expressed in this ceremony not so much through his on-field accomplishments but rather through his character.

Furthermore, the official unveiling featured remarks by Chairman Clark:

> When he earned election to the Hall of Fame in 1962, Jackie Robinson totaled a career worthy of inclusion, based on performance alone. He told baseball writers that when considering his candidacy, they should only consider his playing ability—what his impact was on the playing field. At his induction in 1962, his plaque reflected his wishes—it only recounted his magnificent playing career. But as we all know, there's no person more central and more important to the history of baseball, for his pioneering ways, than Jackie Robinson. Today, his impact is not fully defined without mention of his extreme courage in crossing baseball's color line. We are proud of the changes we have made.[12]

Indeed, Robinson's significant contributions to changing the racial landscape within baseball put him at the fore of baseball's racial history. Clark's comments provide an interesting context for the inscription of Robinson's plaque. The remarks, in a similar fashion to those provided by Rachel Robinson and Jeff Idelson, reiterate and illustrate the significance of Robinson's social contributions, thus reinforcing the move to update the original plaque nearly a half century later. The social contributions in this case center around Robinson's courage more so than his physical talent, once again expanding the way merit is defined within a baseball context.

As of June 25, 2008, the new plaque reads as follows:

JACK ROOSEVELT ROBINSON
"JACKIE"
BROOKLYN, N.L., 1947–1956
A player of extraordinary ability renowned for his electrifying style of play. Over 10 seasons hit .311, scored more than 100 runs six times, named to six All-Star teams and led Brooklyn to six pen-

nants and its only World Series title, in 1955. The 1947 Rookie of the Year, and the 1949 N.L. MVP when he hit a league-best .342 with 37 steals. Led second basemen in double plays four times and stole home 19 times. Displayed tremendous courage and poise in 1947 when he integrated the modern major leagues in the face of intense adversity.[13]

As seen on the new plaque, the word "courage" is used. Within the context of the new plaque, Jackie Robinson's widow, the Hall of Fame and Museum president, the Hall of Fame chairwoman, and the plaque itself all explicitly use the word "courage" in describing Robinson's contributions to and inclusion within baseball.[14] By explicitly addressing Robinson's character in addition to his statistics, Major League Baseball is employing a shift in its representation of not only Jackie Robinson's legacy but also baseball's redefining of itself as a meritocracy.

This is not to say that this legacy, as constructed through the museum, is not accurate. However, it should be noted that this particular narrative is constructed through a mainstream perspective. This museum is a space that represents the national perspective of the game. Thus, it covers the game in more breadth than depth, resulting in a lack of focus on any one particular era or faction of the game's history. The museum's depictions of Jackie Robinson as an "American hero," Branch Rickey's role in baseball's racial landscape, and Robinson's status as a member of the military all create a multilayered way of considering how the notion of merit can be applied to baseball's integration narrative. Also, the way that the museum portrays Robinson as acted upon as an object of racial inclusion rather than as an agent for social change provides a narrow view of Robinson's own willingness and ability to engender a significant transformation within America's racial landscape. Additionally, the inclusion of women's and Latinos' roles in baseball offers another layer to baseball's integration narrative. And even the way that the Hall of Fame Gallery itself portrays its inductees, including a change to Jackie Robinson's original Hall of Fame plaque, shows that

Major League Baseball consistently individualizes the game in order to preserve the assertion that individual merit is the driving force behind inclusion. A focus on more specificity of one particular faction of the game, in this case black baseball, provides an additional perspective on racial inclusion and exclusion within baseball. Thus, the Negro Leagues Baseball Museum is a space that offers a nonmainstream perspective of racial inclusion.

The museum is designed to perhaps give the visitor a quick glimpse of baseball's inclusive nature rather than providing too much depth that might otherwise explain baseball's shortcomings prior to the eras described in this section. For instance, the exhibits described here include "The Babe Ruth Room," "Diamond Dreams: Women in Baseball," "Pride and Passion: The African American Baseball Experience," "Viva Baseball," and "Today's Game." The exhibits construct a historical review of numerous topics that stand out in baseball history, such as the impact of Babe Ruth, baseball's first superstar; women's inclusion in professional baseball; African Americans' role in baseball history; the Latin influence on the game; and how the game is viewed today.

The location and proximity of each of these displays illustrate once again the recurring motif of baseball's inclusive history. Women, African Americans, and Latinos are placed at the forefront of the museum itself, exposing the viewer to the inclusive narrative at the outset of the museum experience. The placement of these exhibits that emphasize the inclusion of minorities speaks to the museum's attempt to show that once again merit, not just gender or race, is a significant factor in baseball's inclusive narrative. This frames the remainder of the visitor's experience in a way that will reinforce the theme of inclusion throughout the rest of the museum.

Next, the visitor is introduced to "The Babe Ruth Room." This exhibit begins with an old-fashioned turnstile one would find in the earliest stadiums, through which the visitor must pass in order to see the exhibit. Photographs, newspaper clippings, jerseys, and equipment are enclosed in glass, illustrating the life and career of Babe Ruth. This is one of two exhibits in the entire museum dedicated to one player. This encourages the viewer to focus on an individual player rather than a collectivistic legacy of the game. If a considerable amount of attention is given to one player in the forefront of the museum, and that same amount of attention is given to a group that is otherwise considered to be on the margins of baseball's history, it paints Major League Baseball as an institution that includes not just the prominent individuals but also those players otherwise excluded throughout history. That is, women's inclusion in baseball is an important part of the constructed mainstream baseball narrative, as illustrated by the museum. Furthermore, the museum "includes" groups such as women and Latinos but in a way that emphasizes individual exemplars of the groups.

Once the visitor is finished with this exhibit, he or she must again pass through the turnstile in order to exit, then making his or her way to the adjoining exhibit, "Diamond Dreams: Women in Baseball." This display is similar in size to "The Babe Ruth Room," with photographs, newspaper clippings, jerseys, and equipment either enclosed in glass or printed on the walls themselves. The visitor sees a compilation of texts and images that describe the role women had in baseball as either players in their separate professional league—the All-American Girls Professional Baseball League—or as contributors to the men's game. Ultimately, the exhibit portrays the idea that even women had a significant role in baseball's existence, with allusions to the meritocratic ideal that when given the opportunity, professional baseball not only celebrated but exercised the value of inclusion based on merit rather than exclusion based on gender. The similar size and scope of this exhibit compared to the Babe Ruth exhibit is notable because it illustrates the weight and attention put on the legacy of a particular chapter of baseball history. In other words, the similar size of the exhibits dedicated to women as well as a legendary player indicates similar importance of the two. This attempt to use physical size to portray similar importance of two eras of baseball perhaps suggests that Major League

Baseball views women's inclusion as important as one of its most revered icons. This provides the viewer further evidence that baseball is indeed an inclusive space that puts all eras on an equal playing field.

Around the next corner the visitor walks into the exhibit titled "Pride and Passion: The African American Baseball Experience." This exhibit is similar in size to both "The Babe Ruth Room" and the "Women in Baseball" exhibits. Because this exhibit is the primary focus of the analysis of this particular museum, its description will be discussed in greater detail. Thus, in this next section, I argue that the National Baseball Hall of Fame and Museum portrays Jackie Robinson through a specific narrative that reads like the following: (1) Jackie Robinson was brought into the Major Leagues based on merit, but (2) "merit" is more complex than merely physical talent, and in fact (3) Jackie Robinson seems often to be portrayed as an object being acted upon rather than an agent acting on his own motivations.

The African American Baseball Experience Exhibit

When the visitor first walks into the area dedicated to black baseball, he or she sees that it is located in the middle of the five exhibits on this floor. Visually speaking, the visitor is introduced to the exhibit dedicated to Babe Ruth first, then makes his or her way to the exhibit dedicated to women in baseball, then the exhibit dedicated to black baseball comes next, with the remaining two exhibits, the art gallery and the actual Hall of Fame filled with player busts, placed afterward. Thus, the black baseball exhibit is sandwiched, so to speak, between exhibits dedicated to women and Latinos. This conveys the notion that among the different chapters that stand in the margins of baseball history—Latinos, African Americans, and women—the black baseball chapter is the centerpiece of all peripheral spaces. Baseball has included players from these groups at some point in its history, and by strategically locating the black baseball exhibit in the middle between the women's and Latino exhibits, the National Baseball Hall of Fame and Museum frames black baseball as a primary focal point among all marginal groups, a move that is illustrated through the physical location of the black baseball exhibit.

Racial Inclusion: Jackie Robinson and Merit

The adjacent display presents Robinson's heroic status, not just as a player, but also as a symbol of social progress. The text on the wall reads:

"American Hero"

Jackie Robinson became a hero to millions of Americans. He embodied the hope that one day the color of a person's skin would no longer determine the limits of opportunity. Nearly everybody agreed that *Robinson's ability to tolerate prejudice* [emphasis added], and his ability to play, helped many accept that African Americans belonged in the majors and in mainstream American life.

This text moves the narrative further toward the notion that Robinson's physical merits aided in the social acceptance of him as an African American. The excerpt "his ability to play, helped many accept that African Americans belonged . . . in mainstream American life" perpetuates the notion that social acceptance is contingent on merit. Thus, while Robinson's "ability to tolerate prejudice" played a role in his social acceptance, his physical merit had to be considered as well.

The next display includes several images and short captions. The first is a caption titled "Many a skill." It includes a picture on the left of Robinson turning a double play. The explicit use of the word "skill" illustrates the emphasis on the physical traits that not only allowed Robinson to succeed on the field but also allowed for his acceptance by fans. The second image is a bigger picture of Robinson stealing home in the 1955 World Series. This picture, quite famous in baseball circles, is a reminder that not only did Robinson have the physical traits to succeed, but those skills also allowed him to succeed on the biggest stage, the World Series. Consequently, this display could be interpreted as meaning that if Robinson can prove that he can hold up to scrutiny on such a large platform, then why couldn't all African Americans?

In terms of a visual perspective of this exhibit section, the adjacent wall displays Robinson's Brooklyn Dodgers uniform. However, unlike the imprinted images of his jersey elsewhere in the exhibit, the actual jersey is enclosed in glass. Because it is a mere article of clothing with no face, skin color, nor even a player's name, rather just a team name and number, this possibly suggests that baseball is a meritocracy—an institution that pays no mind to skin color. Moreover, it is a team jersey, a part of a uniform worn by a group of individuals, all of whom are included in this particular space regardless of each individual's background. Robinson's jersey visually reminds the viewer of the idea that only those elite players, the players with incredible skill and physical talent, could wear a jersey in the Major Leagues. If Robinson did not have such skill or talent, he never wears that particular uniform.

Beyond Merit: Racial Inclusion and Character

There are many more displays in this particular exhibit that demonstrate an emphasis on Robinson's physical merit. However, in the displays that I describe below, the idea of baseball as an inclusive space is demonstrated in ways that reconfigure baseball's idea of merit by emphasizing the role that the individual's character plays in baseball's mainstream legacy. This more complex understanding of "merit" is a symptom, perhaps, of the rhetorical work that MLB must do in order to present Robinson as an emblem of MLB's inclusiveness. It is as if MLB must show that it recognizes a wide variety of positive attributes and contributions and thus is truly and broadly inclusive.

Following the display of Robinson's jersey mentioned above, the viewer sees a wall-mounted text, one that describes a powerful white man's role in making that desegregation happen— Brooklyn Dodgers general manager Branch Rickey:

Branch Rickey assigned Dodgers scout Clyde Sukeforth to find an African American player with major league talent and the courage to withstand harsh prejudicial treatment. Sukeforth found his man in Kansas City Monarchs shortstop Jackie Robinson. Despite opposition from major league owners, Rickey signed Robinson for the 1946 season with Brooklyn's farm team in Montreal.

Jackie Robinson played the 1946 season with the Montreal Royals, Brooklyn's International League farm team. Rickey hoped that Canada, a country with less racial prejudice, would provide Robinson with a gentler introduction to the minors. Robinson's strong season with the Royals laid the groundwork for his promotion to the Dodgers in 1947.

This text illustrates the inclusive nature of a prominent baseball authority figure and while doing so conveys the notion of baseball as a meritocracy in a very particular way. This wall-mounted text frames Robinson's breaking of the color barrier as one that was made possible only by the intervention of a white authority. Without Rickey, Robinson's legacy never comes to fruition. There are several excerpts from this text that create the impression that it is Robinson's merit as both a gifted player and an individual with strong character that earned him that opportunity. For instance, evidently it was Robinson's "talent" as well as his "courage" that made him a qualified candidate. However, it is never mentioned that Robinson was not necessarily the Dodgers' first choice. It was, by historical accounts, Robinson's teammate Monarchs catcher and eventual Hall of Fame inductee Josh Gibson who was considered the better player. However, there was considerable concern over Gibson's temperament and thus whether he could withstand the public scrutiny on and off the field.[15] So while Robinson's merit as a player was good enough to eventually land him the opportunity with the Dodgers organization, it should be noted that physical merit was not the sole factor in Robinson's inclusion in Major League Baseball. Courage and character were factors as well. However, Gibson's consideration is never mentioned in this wall-mounted text in this specific section or the entire exhibit. It is reasonable to read this narrative as one that paints Gibson as a player who lacked the requisite courage to withstand the anticipated social scrutiny as the first black player in a white man's game. Thus, baseball's exclusion of one black player in Gibson is outweighed by baseball's inclusion of another black player in Robinson because of the way that baseball views individual merit.

The final passage in the above text, that which reads, "Robinson's strong season with the Royals laid the groundwork for his promotion to the Dodgers in 1947," reminds the viewer that while Robinson's physical merit was *not* the sole factor, it was indeed significant. The text indicates that "Robinson's strong season" was one of successful on-field performance. However, interestingly, this excerpt also gives the viewer the impression that the 1946 season in the Minor Leagues was an audition, so to speak, for how he might handle the "harsh prejudicial treatment." Consequently, the notion that baseball is a purely meritocratic institution above all else may be the case only as long as the character of an individual passes an initial test run. That is, an individual may be given the opportunity to display his physical merit on the biggest stage only if he can pass a character test on a smaller stage first. More important, this exhibit puts a twist on the way "merit" is defined within the context of baseball as a meritocratic space. Physical accomplishments do not stand alone in a meritocracy. Baseball as a meritocracy, then, should be understood to include both physical *and* personal traits. In other words, merit does not consist of physical talent alone.

Furthermore, similar to the previous excerpt analyzed above, this passage reinforces the idea that in order for baseball's integration experiment to work, there needed to be an emphasis on the individual's character, more so than his on-field merits. This is significant because, once again, the notion of baseball as a meritocracy, and thus an inclusive space, works only if there is an assurance that character takes precedence over physical ability.

The exhibit displays one particular image of a hate-mail example placed at the bottom, titled "Encountering Hatred." It is an image of a handwritten note that is actually somewhat hard to read. The image is accompanied by a short paragraph, which reads: "Some Americans hated Robinson for crossing the color line and wrote vicious letters to him. Branch Rickey asked Robinson to turn the other cheek during his early years with the Dodgers. Following his major league career, Robinson discussed how difficult it had been to rise above the racial hatred he encountered." The combination of images illustrating Robinson's skill on the field and the plight he experienced off it provides an interesting juxtaposition of Robinson's encounters inside and outside the playing lines. The admiration of his physical play is indicated first, followed by the scorn of what he stood for socially. Thus, there is a distinction made between his physical ability and his social capability. For instance, the above caption includes the excerpt, "Branch Rickey asked Robinson to turn the other cheek during his early years with the Dodgers." In this section of the exhibit, turning the other cheek to racial hatred on and off the field becomes the impetus for Robinson's merit and consequently his inclusion on the field. Robinson's acceptance on the field because of his physical merit, coupled with his lack of acceptance off it, reinforces the notion that baseball is a meritocratic space. In the eyes of the National Baseball Hall of Fame and Museum, one's physical ability coupled with his character get him on the field. As we've seen throughout the above passages, merit is more complicated than physical capability, going beyond merely physical talent. Again, Robinson's courage, shown through his willingness to "turn the other cheek during his early years with the Dodgers," represents a shift in how baseball's meritocracy is defined. In terms of the overall theme of this book, this example allows us to see yet another way in which Major League Baseball's emphasis on portraying itself as a meritocratic space is once again brought to the forefront as it attempts to construct an inclusive legacy.

Jackie Robinson: An Object Rather than Agent

Jackie Robinson can be viewed as not so much a source of empowerment but as someone who is empowered by others. As we have seen to this point, the African Americans in Baseball exhibit places an emphasis on merit, both physical and character merit, as a prerequisite for inclusion. However, this section explores the ways in which the exhibit frames Jackie Robinson as an object being acted upon by others rather than as an agent working on his own motivations.

One particular caption is printed flatly on the wall at eye level, making it visually accessible to the viewer. The visitor, standing toward the front of the exhibit, first sees the following opening paragraph printed on the very first wall to the right:

> As the number of black baseball leagues changed and grew, this form of segregated ball was embraced by local towns and neighborhoods, with teams and players earning both legendary status as well as income for their communities. Following World War II and the loyal service of more than one million segregated African-American soldiers, the game itself finally became a testing ground for integrating American life. Jackie Robinson's "breaking of the color barrier" in 1947 eventually led to desegregation of the sport at every level. Given new opportunity, many talented black players took the majors by storm, dominating the most important awards and making their mark in the record books.
>
> By 1959, every major league team's roster was integrated, but questions concerning true equality at every level of the sport, from the executive office to the locker room, remained. Despite progress on many fronts, such issues continue in baseball today. African-American participation in the sport is at its lowest level in almost 50 years and limited opportunities for management and front office positions are still critical topics for discussion.

This opening caption is important because it frames the exhibit as a space dedicated to the impact desegregated baseball had on the country, while using Robinson's inclusion in Major League Baseball as the representative example of how that desegregation took shape. Furthermore, this passage frames Major League Baseball as "a testing ground for integrating American life," and thus as an inclusive space, a characteristic that the game and its national museum are not shy about emphasizing. In other words, baseball, as indicated in the above text, positions itself as a space that not only mirrors American life but also serves as a precursor, or "testing ground," for the ways in which American life changes and or sustains itself.

After the visitor reads this text, there is the next wall-mounted caption that follows a mere twelve inches away. The close proximity of the two captions keeps the viewer's attention on the integration theme as well as suggests that these two captions are closely related in their purpose. This text is one that illustrates how the original groundwork for a discussion on racial integration in baseball was laid in the early twentieth century. It is an excerpt from Sol White, which reads:

> It is said on good authority that one of the leading players and a manager of the National League is advocating the entrance of colored players in the National League with a view of signing Matthews, the colored man, late of Harvard. It is not expected that he will succeed in his advocacy of such a move, but when such actions come to notice, there are grounds for hoping that some day the bar will drop and some good man will be chosen from out of the colored profession that will be a credit to all, and pave the way for others to follow.

Below the excerpt is a caption that reads:

—Sol White, *History of Colored Base Ball,* 1907
    In Jack Roosevelt Robinson, Branch Rickey found Sol White's "good man" to "pave the way."

Again, the inclusion of Rickey's involvement sets up the idea that racial integration was an active move by a white authority. In this particular instance Rickey is mentioned as the subject of the sentence, which indicates that he is doing the acting, meaning Robinson is being acted upon. Rickey is carrying out an action that is purposeful and has a particular motivation behind it. There is more than mere inclusion at stake in this instance. Rickey's role as the actor establishes a clear hierarchy between Rickey and Robinson. Robinson is being acted upon, which forfeits his ability to be seen as the primary initiator of social change. Rather, Rickey is viewed as the primary initiator.

Without Rickey's action, Robinson, as we view him today, does not exist. Rickey's action, as illustrated in the above text, also affords him a certain level of humanity that is denied Robinson. As a result, Major League Baseball, in this case represented by Branch Rickey, is represented as an inclusive space that puts social justice into action.

Following the focus on Robinson is a more general illustration of African Americans in professional baseball. For instance, the next exhibit the visitor encounters, located closely to the exhibits mentioned above and thus indicating a similar theme, addresses the concerns of racial inclusion. The exhibit displays a wall-mounted flyer that was distributed at Yankee Stadium prior to opening day in 1953. The flyer was distributed by groups affiliated with the American Communist Party.[16] The flyer, and its inclusion in the museum exhibit, creates a picture of baseball as an unjust place, but now with the possibility to see baseball as a site where America can realize its true greatness via racial inclusion. It also shows that the question of racial inclusion in Major League Baseball, across every organization, continued to make its way into the social conscience. As the flyer reads:

"The $64 Question"

Why Does the N.Y. Yankee Management Refuse to Place Negro Players on its Major Team?

What excuse will Mr. George Weiss, General Manager of the N.Y. Yankees give this year?

The urging of the inclusion of "Negro players" is associated here with the notion of "a real all-American team," further reinforcing the idea of America as a potential space of fairness and inclusion. The National Baseball Hall of Fame and Museum recognizes that baseball was once a racially exclusive space. In other words, because Major League Baseball paints itself as an inclusive institution in today's era, they are implicitly recognizing that MLB used to be exclusive.

Robinson's military status is also highlighted within the exhibit. By highlighting this aspect of Robinson's life, it illustrates how

Robinson's legacy is one that expands beyond the baseball field. Even more, it is a way to put emphasis on his patriotic background; he not only played the all-American game of baseball but served his country as well. Just a few feet straight ahead, the viewer sees the following display, depicting Robinson's time in the army:

> "Jack the Soldier"
> Jackie Robinson served in the Army during World War II. Like many African Americans, he felt it was a war to end prejudice as well as a war for democracy. Black soldiers served in segregated units until after the war. Many were highly decorated for their service, and their example helped highlight their right to full participation as citizens when peace came in 1945. Having been in the service made Robinson somewhat older than the usual baseball recruit, but it was an important part of his past for Branch Rickey and baseball fans. (caption reads: "Jackie Robinson in military uniform")

Framing Robinson as a patriotic individual who serves a larger cause makes it easier to include Robinson in such a mainstream space as baseball. That is, a visibly patriotic Robinson made him more attractive to Rickey as the man to integrate baseball. If an individual does not illustrate their support for their country, it makes it more difficult to include them in a mainstream—and patriotic—space such as baseball, a game dubbed as "America's *national* pastime." Patriotism, in this instance, is framed as Robinson serving for a larger American cause—the war effort—rather than as an individual resisting prejudice throughout the country. Moreover, this display illuminates a paradox, as it helps Jackie Robinson appear to be not as individualistic, even within the context of the MLB narrative that frames him specifically as an individual. This paradox is significant because it attempts to show that even an individual like Robinson knows the importance of a larger, more collective effort such as the war effort, which in turn reduces his ability to stand out individually on some level. Furthermore, the term "prejudice" is used in the same sentence early on in the paragraph. The fact that the term "prejudice" is used when illustrating Robinson's military standing indicates a significant strategic move. It offers the reader a way to see how America's favorite game is a space where prejudice can be eliminated.

Directly below his Dodgers jersey is yet another wall-mounted text in paragraph form, then a large imprinted, wall-mounted image of Robinson's military uniform, followed by a picture of Branch Rickey. This display sandwiches two different visual representations of the Brooklyn Dodgers organization. In between the images are a paragraph-length caption and an image introducing us to and reminding us of Robinson's patriotic service to his country, that of his military uniform. This aesthetic strategy literally lines up the ways in which the integration narrative can be read. The first and last images are of a Dodgers uniform and the Dodgers general manager, respectively. Thus, Robinson's legacy is contingent on the help of a white authority figure and his patriotism.

After this excerpt, the viewer moves on to the next wall-mounted text, highlighting Jackie Robinson as the representative symbol for such integration possibilities. There are numerous imprinted pictures of his number 42 Brooklyn Dodgers jersey on the wall, a visual indication that Robinson's next big move was to the Major Leagues. The wall-mounted text reads in paragraph form as follows: "As World War II ended, many African Americans believed that 'separate but equal' could no longer be tolerated because while much was separate, little was equal. Highly decorated black regiments helped foster the pride and impetus that demanded change in all parts of American life. Following the death of commissioner Kenesaw Mountain Landis, Brooklyn Dodgers president Branch Rickey and Jackie Robinson took the lead in testing America's tolerance for integrated baseball. Under pressure, the major and minor leagues began to desegregate, but slowly and on their own terms." The reference to the death of baseball commissioner Kenesaw Mountain Landis does three things. First, it implies that Landis was opposed to the idea of racially integrated baseball, and thus nothing could be done until after his passing. Consequently, baseball as a meritocracy is at the mercy of a timetable. Second, it suggests yet another individualist narrative. In this case the integration of baseball was delayed by a racist individual. The way to remedy that problem was with not only a white authority but a nonracist white authority. Finally, it suggests that active protest to racially segregated baseball could not be sustained as long as a racist white authority was in charge. Thus, baseball as a meritocracy was at the mercy of an authority's prejudice. These three observations about the Landis plaque provide us with the ability to see how resistance within the racial landscape of sport is sometimes feasible only when an authority no longer maintains his ultimate power.

Beyond the African American Experience:
The Remaining Exhibits

After the visitor makes his or her way from the African American exhibit, he or she walks into the adjoining space, titled "Viva Baseball," an exhibit similar to those described above, with enclosed glass displaying newspaper clippings, photographs, jerseys, and equipment. This display describes baseball's role in the Caribbean countries. On the floor, there is a large map of the Caribbean countries in which baseball is most prominent. The size of the map on the floor is hard to miss, leaving, once again, the viewer encouraged to pay special attention to the inclusive nature of baseball's history. Baseball's influence is literally seen all over the map in this instance, illustrating not only baseball's expansive presence around the world but also its willingness to include players from all locations and backgrounds.

The next stop is in the "Cooperstown Room," which examines the history of the Hall of Fame and the "home of baseball," Cooperstown, New York. This is not a particularly large space, as it is structured in a way that allows the visitor to see the rest of the exhibits ahead of him or her. This creates an inclusive exhibit space, as numerous exhibits are visually included when standing at the front of the room. This arrangement, again, offers a physical and figurative analogy to the inclusive history constructed by Major League Baseball. That is, the exhibit space is open and inviting, the precise way in which Major League Baseball wants fans and visitors to see the institution.

After the Cooperstown Room the visitor walks into the next space, "The Baseball Experience." Here the visitor finds a digitally enhanced thirteen-minute multimedia presentation in the 191-seat Grandstand Theater, preparing visitors for the story of the game's widely chronicled history. If the visitor chooses to enter the theater, he or she sees that there is a combination of individual seats and bleachers, providing the viewer with the feeling of being at the ballpark, which once again reinforces the individual nature of the museum while making him or her feel included in the action. The visitor can choose to engage this presentation or move to the next space, which is a wall-mounted display titled "Taking the Field: The 19th Century." This display describes in general terms baseball's early beginnings, conveying a relatively shorter description of the game's formative years. There is not much specific detail, and there are few images, which conveys a lack of emphasis on baseball's origins, origins that were racially exclusive. However, the timeline of baseball's foundation is included in an adjoining space, a display aptly titled "20th Century Baseball Timeline." Unlike the preceding timeline display, this display is categorized and separated into various smaller spaces, focusing on five distinct chapters in baseball history, with each chapter represented through its exhibit. This display focuses more on breadth than depth, so the numerous chapters of baseball history in the exhibit force the visitor to divide his or her attention among the details.

This leads the visitor to the final exhibit on the second floor of the museum, which is titled "Today's Game." This is also similar to the previous displays in both artifacts and size, but this exhibit focuses on recent years, featuring a locker enclosed in glass that displays recent artifacts from each of the thirty Major League teams, including equipment, jerseys, and various game memorabilia. At this point the visitor has been introduced to similar exhibits, all with similar artifacts and structural designs, telling the story of baseball's application of a meritocratic ideology: that the National Baseball Hall of Fame and Museum emphasizes meritocracy, resulting in baseball being viewed as an inclusive space. However, these exhibits are, after all, labeled by ethnicity, which could suggest that they are included for some sort of politically correct purpose. For instance, the label "Today's Game" perhaps suggests that race is not an issue any longer. It was an issue in the past, in Jackie Robinson's time, but it is not now. At the very least, a more critical view might see the National Baseball Hall of Fame's meritocratic narrative as problematic.

As the visitor has concluded the tour of the initial (officially the second) floor, he or she has the option of going upstairs to the third floor or downstairs to the first. The viewer's option parallels the narrative that baseball is attempting to convey throughout the museum experience. In this case, baseball is illustrating its willingness to open a physical space that offers the visitor a choice. Regardless of the choice that is made, the fact remains that a choice is available, painting baseball as an inclusive space that offers an option to enter the space or not, similar to its post-1947 history.

On the third floor of the museum, the visitor is introduced to six exhibits, most of which are similar in structure to those on the previous floor. The placement of these exhibits on the third floor could be simply a result of not having enough space on the other floors. However, it could be an indication that the aforementioned exhibits are considered more significant than others. Certainly, visitors need to work harder to see them, investing more in the experience. Consequently, it could indicate that the visitor's investment in such exhibits sends the message that the value of an exhibit lies in the visitor's willingness to devote a bit more effort to it. Upon making his or her way to the entry of the third floor, he or she sees the following exhibits: "Sacred Ground," "Hank Aaron: Chasing the Dream," "The Records Room," "Autumn Glory: Postseason Celebration," "Education Gallery," and "Baseball Cards."

First, in "Sacred Ground," the visitor is faced with a relatively open space that displays images and numerous artifacts of the game's different baseball stadiums from past and present. The ballparks represent the physical space that was and is open to players of all backgrounds, and the expansive view of the ballparks in this exhibit further enhances the notion that baseball is a space of few literal and figurative obstacles, making its inclusiveness even more noticeable. The artifacts and pieces of memorabilia from the different parks are displayed comparatively, allowing the viewer to see the similarities and differences in parks of past and present. While the space is not particularly big in size, it is more open than the other spaces on the previous floor. In this case there are fewer walls throughout the middle of the space, allowing the viewer to get a sense of the different aesthetic characteristics of each ballpark. The open space affords the viewer an inclusive view of the numerous ballpark artifacts. Much of the space in this museum is inclusive and open, again indicating the effort made to paint Major League Baseball as just that: inclusive and open to all.

About twenty feet after this space the viewer makes his or her way to the next exhibit, titled "Hank Aaron: Chasing the Dream." The initial wall in this display is quite large, reaching the ceiling and spreading about twenty feet wide. The size of the display indicates that the museum puts a great emphasis on the role that a prominent African American player such as Aaron plays in baseball's legacy. Aaron, another player whose career began in the Negro Leagues just like Robinson, is one of the individuals who has an entire exhibit dedicated solely to him. This is yet another way for the National Baseball Hall of Fame and Museum to illustrate its notable inclusion of African Americans in baseball. The number 715 is mounted in big silver numbers to the left of the initial wall, emphasizing the significance of Aaron's 715th career home run, the milestone that broke Babe Ruth's long-standing 714 career home run total, which was once considered unbreakable. Artifacts in this room include Aaron's game-worn jersey of the record-breaking game in which he hit the 715th home run of his career, as well as various artifacts from his childhood and postplaying career. The artifacts are enclosed in glass, much like the other displays in the museum. There is some mention of his days as a Negro Leagues player, but it pales in comparison to his prominence in the Major Leagues. This is certainly understandable, as Aaron's career spanned nearly a quarter century in the Major Leagues, but the limited mention of his start as a Negro Leagues player allows Major League Baseball to be viewed yet again as a space that is racially inclusive rather than as a space that led to the Negro Leagues' demise due to the recruitment of Negro League players. The feature that stands out the most is Aaron's locker from his playing days in Atlanta's Fulton County Stadium, centered in the middle of the room, making it quite noticeable to the viewer. The exhibit includes his famous "44" jersey, as well as a game-used bat, cleats, hat, and glove. These particular artifacts emphasize one player rather than a team, stadium, or era. The viewer will no doubt know who is the focal point here. The spatial location of the locker encourages the viewer to focus on the individual, a move that contrasts the locker displays in the Negro Leagues Museum, discussed later in the chapter.

The remaining four displays are housed in close proximity, almost giving the impression that they are all part of the same display. To the left is "The Records Room," a space that includes virtually every record holder for every category throughout the game's history. The historical records are mounted on the left, while the updated statistics of every category leader during the present season are mounted on the right. While this is called "The Records Room," it is not closed off from the other displays but adjacent to the remaining three exhibits, which do connect without much spatial interruption. The records are focused on individual accomplishments, putting the focus on the role that individual performance plays in baseball's legacy.

The first of the three remaining displays is titled "Autumn Glory: Postseason Celebration." This exhibit includes photographs, news clippings, equipment, jerseys from past postseasons, and numerous World Series trophies. The adjacent exhibit, "Education Gallery," is visible to the viewer, but a primarily empty space unless being utilized at the present time. This space is used by the Hall of Fame Education Department for various programs. When not in use, it is an otherwise lonely and visually empty space, making it almost unnoticeable. The final exhibit, "Baseball Cards," samples some of the 130,000 baseball cards in the museum's collection, some as old as one hundred years to the more recent cards from the current decade. Similar to "The Records Room," this display includes baseball cards that are focused on individual accomplishments, putting the focus on the role that individual performance plays in baseball's legacy. Furthermore, there are very few baseball cards of African American players, and there are no cards of Negro Leagues players. This again illustrates the focus on individual players and excludes any representation of the Negro Leagues. After the visitor has made the somewhat circular trek around the third-floor exhibits, he or she returns to the stairway leading to the other two floors below.

Negro Leagues Baseball Museum

We can see the expansive detail that the National Baseball Hall of Fame and Museum entails. The Negro Leagues Baseball Museum, however, contrasts in size, scope, and depth. However, as we have seen, the National Baseball Hall of Fame and Museum is specifically designed to be just that: a hall of fame. It is widely regarded by many, if not most, sports fans as the quintessential hall of fame among all sports. The Negro Leagues Baseball Museum, by contrast, was never intended to serve the same role as the National Baseball Hall of Fame. Perhaps the most significant contrast to the Negro Leagues Baseball Museum is found on the museum's website:

> *Important things to know when visiting the Negro Leagues Baseball Museum:*
> **The Negro Leagues Baseball Museum is NOT a Hall of Fame.** Often the museum is referred to as the "Negro Leagues Hall of Fame" or "Black Baseball Hall of Fame" and various names. It is

important to the museum that we not be referred to as such. The NLBM was conceived as a museum to tell the complete story of Negro Leagues Baseball, from the average players to the superstars. We feel VERY strongly that the National Baseball Hall of Fame, in Cooperstown, NY, is the proper place for recognition [of] baseball's greatest players. The Negro Leagues existed in the face of segregation. Baseball's shrines should not be segregated today. Therefore, the NLBM does not hold any special induction ceremonies for honorees. As space allows, we include information on every player, executive, and important figure. However, we do give special recognition in our exhibit to those Negro Leaguers who have been honored in Cooperstown.[17]

It is important to preface this section with that sharp distinction between the two museums' missions. The specific claim that "baseball's shrines should not be segregated today" speaks to the mission of the NLBM and its desire to reflect the collective history of the Negro Leagues, more so than calling special attention to one specific player or group of players. As we will see throughout this section, the collective narrative places the Negro Leagues Baseball Museum in both a celebratory and a contrasting space.

Museum Origins

In the early 1990s Horace M. Peterson III (1945–92), founder of the Black Archives of Mid-America, inspired a group of local historians, business leaders, and former baseball players who came together to create the Negro Leagues Baseball Museum. It functioned out of a small one-room office in the Lincoln Building, which is located in the Historic 18th & Vine Jazz District of Kansas City, Missouri. It quickly incorporated, built a board of directors and staffing, and created a licensing program to support operations.[18]

The museum expanded to a two-thousand-square-foot space in the Lincoln Building in 1994 and included a number of photographs and interactive displays. Designed by ESA Design of

Abilene, Kansas, this exhibit became the flagship for redevelopment in the historic district. From its inception in 1994 until the late 1990s, hundreds of visitors, including school groups and dignitaries, marveled at this once-untold American history. Highlights in the Lincoln Building included the seventy-fifth anniversary reunion of the Negro Leagues and a visit from Vice President Al Gore.[19]

From the late 1800s to the 1960s, the 18th & Vine historic district was the center for black culture and life in Kansas City. It was the hub of activity for home owners, business, jazz music, and baseball enthusiasts. Just outside of the district stands the Paseo YMCA building, which was built as a black YMCA in 1914. It served as a temporary home for baseball players, railroad workers, and others making the transition to big-city life in the Midwest. It was in this district that the Negro National League was founded in 1920. Although the district and the YMCA building were becoming blighted by the 1980s, they were recognized on the National Register of Historic Places.[20]

Plans were under way by city officials during the late 1990s to create a new home to showcase Kansas City's jazz heritage and to revitalize the historic district. City officials and the mayor worked to raise more than $20 million in bonds to build a new facility to host the new American Jazz Museum and a new, permanent, and expanded home for the Negro Leagues Baseball Museum. The new fifty-thousand-square-foot building opened in September 1997, and the Baseball Museum opened in November of that year.[21]

The museum's permanent home uses ten thousand square feet of the new building. Also designed by ESA Design, the new exhibit features multimedia computer stations, several film exhibits, hundreds of photographs, and a growing collection of baseball artifacts. The museum raised more than $2 million to complete design and construction of this space. As was the case with the old museum, this new one has welcomed thousands of visitors and dignitaries since opening, including Presidents Bill Clinton and George W. Bush, General (Ret.) Colin Powell, Jesse Jackson,

Maya Angelou, Judith Jamison, Mike Dukakis, Walter Cronkite, Kareem Abdul-Jabbar, Barry Bonds, Tony LaRussa, Isaac Hayes, Ossie Davis, Sinbad, and many others.[22]

The Negro Leagues Baseball Museum is designed for educational purposes. Visitors experience an immersive environment of information, sound, and nostalgia. Since it is set primarily as a self-guided tour experience, the viewer chooses how much information he or she wants to absorb. Based on the way that the museum is set up physically, the viewer must learn the history of black baseball in order to "take the field" with its legends. The main entrance to the museum looks like an old movie theater, similar to the openings of many old baseball parks, with gray-and-white-tiled flooring and a ticket window located on the exterior wall. Above the ticket window are four large letters in gold, "NLBM," including the museum name below the letters, "Negro Leagues Baseball Museum." The ticket window is located on a blue-green wall, with framed images placed about three feet apart from each other. These images are abstract depictions of black baseball players with no individual player's likeness. This is a subtle, although consistent, indication that the Negro Leagues Baseball Museum constructs a collective story about baseball's role in its respective community, contrasted with the individualistic narrative constructed by the National Baseball Hall of Fame and Museum. The entry way is constructed as a hallway, restricting the visitor's view until he or she is inside. Once the visitor enters the exhibit, he or she must follow the directed path. The path features a design that harks back to the days of old brick baseball stadiums, like old Comiskey Park in Chicago, complete with antique-style turnstiles. The turnstiles, for example, are features of both the National Baseball Hall of Fame and Museum and the Negro Leagues Baseball Museum. Both museums, to varying degrees, attempt to simulate the experience of attending a game in an old ballpark. This can be read as an effort to place the visitor in a previous era, almost like the good old days of baseball's simpler time.

The viewer is purposely "segregated" from other parts of the exhibit by a "chicken-wire" backstop that is connected to a baseball field that includes statues of Negro League players. The chicken-wire backstop is placed in front of the visitor as he or she first enters the museum space. Next to the backstop is a statue of Negro Leagues Baseball Museum cofounder Buck O'Neil, who is positioned as looking on at the baseball game taking place on the other side of the backstop.[23] The museum is an open space, with no separated rooms or walls. This is in contrast to the Hall of Fame Gallery in the National Baseball Museum. The lack of separate rooms here reinforces the collectivistic nature of the Negro Leagues Baseball Museum, as opposed to the National Baseball Hall of Fame and Museum, which constructs the numerous exhibits in specific rooms and clearly defined individual spaces. Thus, the spacing within the museums alone shows the distinction of their constructed narrative: the National Baseball Hall of Fame and Museum views the game as one rooted in individual contributions, whereas the Negro Leagues Baseball Museum views the game as one rooted in a collective effort.

On the other side of the backstop is a small-scale version of a baseball field that is difficult to see in its entirety. It is designed as the final encounter for the visitor as he or she exits the museum, which will be described in greater detail at the end of this section. The visitor, after the initial backstop, is introduced to a relatively small space with artifacts, wall-mounted text, and photographs. Despite these artifacts, there is more wall space in this area than other areas of the museum. As a result, there is much more information and many more artifacts to examine as the visitor makes his or her way to the next small corridor. This visual strategy suggests that any visitor interested in learning more about the black baseball experience must literally move forward to learn more information. After walking the corridor the visitor has access to the museum's small theater, in which a video on the legacy of the Negro Leagues plays every half hour. Narrated by James Earl Jones, the fourteen-minute video provides a brief explanation of the origins of the Negro Leagues as well as still photographs of players and teams. Also included are video highlights of contemporary African American Major League Baseball players in order to illustrate the lasting legacy that black baseball has had on the professional game. As the visitor exits the theater he or she sees the first wall exhibit to the left, with the title "The Early Years" at the top of a half-wall about five feet in height. The photographs, texts, and artifacts in this exhibit shed light on black baseball and its origins after the Civil War, including a large framed passage with the following statement: "1863: The New 'National Pastime' is embraced by free blacks. Talented individual players and all-black teams carve out their place in American sports history."

As the viewer finishes viewing this wall, a simple turn to the right reveals a large wall with a plethora of artifacts, mostly photographs and their accompanying captions. The images are of hundreds of fans in the stands, representing a typical crowd at a Negro Leagues baseball game. The fans are African American, dressed in 1950s style clothing, hovering above the exhibit, almost as though they are looking down upon the artifacts and the museum visitors.

The visitor makes his or her way from this section to the next section, which is directly around the right corner. The next exhibit is titled with two depictions, including "Pioneers" and "Drawing the Line," which discuss the so-called gentlemen's agreement that unofficially banned black players from major professional leagues at the turn of the century. This section of the museum includes various photographs and wall-mounted captions explaining the different ways in which African Americans were excluded from the game, including another prominently framed passage that states, "1887: Opportunities for black players in professional baseball diminish as the country turns its back on Reconstruction." The focal point of this display is in the corner, which is a large black-and-white photograph blown up to approximately five feet tall and three feet wide. The photograph is of the 1884 Toledo Blue Stockings of the American Association, which at that time was considered a Major League. The photograph contains every player on the team, including

Moses Fleetwood Walker, the first black player to play in a Major League until Jackie Robinson's inclusion in 1947. The caption describes Walker's inclusion as a *temporary* endeavor, as sixty-three years passed before Robinson's inclusion in 1947. This exhibit conveys a similar sentiment to the National Baseball Hall of Fame and Museum's exhibits when it comes to baseball as an inclusive space, but the difference is on the temporary status of Walker's inclusion. For instance, the National Baseball Hall of Fame exhibits, as noted above, emphasize baseball's willingness to include African Americans in the game by focusing on an *individual* player. The Negro Leagues Baseball Museum suggests this willingness as well, but the emphasis is on the *temporary* status of baseball's inclusion of blacks as indicated in the Walker exhibit. The following exhibits described below put the focus on black players and black teams and their efforts to survive on the periphery of Major League Baseball, whereas the National Baseball Hall of Fame and Museum puts the emphasis on baseball's existence without African Americans.

As the visitor makes his or her way from the Walker exhibit, he or she then comes to the next exhibit located on the right. This is a relatively small space of the exhibit, perhaps an indication of the lack of attention paid to the Latin influence in black baseball. The exhibit, titled "Beisbol," brings to light the great legacy and connections of black baseball to Latin America. Immediately following the "Beisbol" exhibit, the next exhibit is located on the same wall just a few feet farther away. Here, Robinson is portrayed as an important chapter in black baseball's history, but he is not the focal point. It is titled "Changing Times" and offers a glimpse at the first attempts to integrate in the modern-day game of baseball and its ultimate success with Jackie Robinson in 1945. There is surprisingly not as much space dedicated to this chapter in black baseball's history. There are various photographs, press clippings, and game artifacts like jerseys, gloves, and baseballs in this space. Perhaps this is an indication that the Negro Leagues Baseball Museum, unlike the National Baseball Hall of Fame and Museum, has chosen to focus more on black baseball as a whole rather than focusing on the mainstream emphasis on Jackie Robinson. This provides a sharp distinction in how the two museums portray Robinson's legacy.

The next exhibit, which is located on the same wall just another few feet farther, is titled "The End." The exhibit portrays the closing of the Negro Leagues after Robinson's integration. This exhibit contains more text in the form of wall-mounted summaries, with fewer photographs than the previous exhibits. This too is a relatively small space. The summaries that are mounted on the wall explain how many black communities suffered with the demise of the Negro Leagues. The presence of this exhibit itself also creates a sharp distinction from the National Baseball Hall of Fame and Museum. The fact that the Negro Leagues Baseball Museum draws attention to the negative components of baseball's racial integration adds an intriguing component to the black baseball narrative. The National Baseball Hall of Fame and Museum does not put an emphasis on the downfall of the Negro Leagues once integration became a growing trend. If the National Baseball Hall of Fame and Museum did draw attention to the Negro Leagues' downfall because of racial integration, it would complicate the idea of baseball's inclusive element. That is, the idea that Major League Baseball welcomes any player would have to be expanded to include the idea that such inclusion of players, in this case black players, would inevitably mean that the prosperous Negro Leagues would lose players to the Major Leagues. Baseball's inclusive narrative, then, would not be as neat or uncomplicated. Baseball would need to admit that inclusion of just any player may come with consequences. In this case the consequences would be the downfall of the black communities Major League Baseball was trying to include. One way in which Major League Baseball's mainstream narrative would perhaps need to change would be to include the statistics, anecdotes, and critiques that illustrate how the Negro Leagues suffered as a result of racial integration.

As the visitor turns from the display depicting "The End," the role of the black press is presented in its own dedicated space. The exhibit includes entire Negro League baseball articles from prominent members of the black press, as well as descriptions of the role the black press and specific writers had on the integration of Major League Baseball. This display illustrates the ways in which countless individual efforts, specifically by the black press, were made in order for Negro League baseball to not only gain mainstream exposure but survive, once again reinforcing the collectivistic nature of the museum's narrative. Examples of the black press's collective efforts to bring attention not only to Negro Leagues baseball but also to racial equality through baseball itself include the following captions:

Black sportswriters informed the American people of the existence and injustice of segregated athletics as well as the news of the games.

In the mid-1940s the black press played a pivotal role in shaping modern African-American identity. The black newsweeklies also gave voice for a distinctly black perspective on central events in the African-American community, events that spanned antebellum America to the integration of baseball to the civil rights movement.

After WW II, black sportswriters pushed the race issue, forcing tryouts and placing white team owners and managers in awkward and uncomfortable positions. Historians have given a great deal of credit for Jackie Robinson's big break to sportswriters Wendell Smith, Joe Bostic, and Frank Young.

Black press coverage of baseball shows more specifically how the black newspapers covered American social issues and concerns, from immigration to economic development to race relations. As such, they often provided different perspectives on news for readers.

The black press and the Negro leagues were brothers in the fight for equal opportunity in baseball for more than a quarter-century. The partnership dated back to the League of Colored Base Ball Players, a precursor to the Negro leagues, which was organized in 1886 by Walter S. Brown.

For years, black ballplayers had suffered the oppression of white booking agents and owners. When black sportswriters called for "the

Moses to lead the baseball children out of the wilderness," Andrew "Rube" Foster, a successful player and team owner, answered the call.

When Foster called the meeting for the formation of the Negro Leagues, Elwood C. Knox of the Indianapolis Freeman, Dave Wyatt and A. D. Williams of The Indianapolis Ledger; C.A. Franklin of The Kansas City Call, and Gary B. Lewis of The Chicago Defender were invited to attend.

Wendell Smith was considered by many as the best black sportswriter of his generation. . . . His specialty was addressing the owners of both black and major league teams.

Joe Bostic, like his newspaper, The People's Voice of Harlem, was known for his outspoken condemnation of the injustices of Jim Crow America in the 1940s.

Dr. W. Rollo Wilson was a moderate, and has been credited by some with being the purest baseball writer of his generation. He reserved his criticism for internal matters involving league players, officials and promoters.

Frank A. "Fay" Young, sports editor of The Chicago Defender, was the first full-time black sportswriter. . . . Young, like many other black sportswriters, conveyed social messages along with his coverage of baseball.

After leaving the black press exhibit, the next display, titled "Major Leagues," is placed as the last exhibit on the same wall as the previous two exhibits. This display includes photographs, equipment, and press clippings that highlight the great black players who moved from the Negro Leagues and became stars in the Major Leagues. This display is a precursor to the second-to-last display of the entire museum, titled "Heroes of the Game." This display is a collection of more than thirty lockers that honor those Negro League players who are inducted into the National Baseball Hall of Fame with the inclusion of their official Hall of Fame busts. Perhaps most compelling is the exclusion of Jackie Robinson's locker and consequently his Hall of Fame bust. This further demonstrates the museum's emphasis on those players and individuals who are otherwise placed on the periphery of baseball history and not otherwise easily identified as having a lasting impact on the legacy of black baseball. In other words, there is a very strategic move to show that, despite mainstream narratives on black baseball history, Jackie Robinson is not the lone focal point of that history. The focus, then, is on the collective, not the individual.

When the visitor gets past the lockers he or she encounters the very last exhibit of the museum, a baseball diamond on which he or she is welcomed to walk. Once on the field, the visitor encounters eleven life-size bronze sculptures of Negro League players. Ten of these statues are positioned on the Field of Legends, a mock baseball diamond, where this mythical all-star team looks to be engaged in an epic battle. The field itself is a primary space in the museum, both physically and conceptually. The construction of ten players, plus one onlooker, marks a collectivized expressive form of black baseball's memory. The statues include Josh Gibson at catcher, Martin Dihigo at bat, Satchel Paige pitching, Buck Leonard playing first base, John Henry Lloyd playing second base, Judy Johnson at shortstop, Ray Dandridge playing third base, Cool Papa Bell in left field, Oscar Charleston in center field, and Leon Day in right field. The eleventh statue is that of Buck O'Neil, who is not playing on the field but rather standing behind the fenced backstop, looking on as a coach or manager would. This provides an interesting depiction of O'Neil, who, when hired by the Chicago Cubs, became the first African American coach in Major League Baseball history in 1962. O'Neil emerged as the face of Negro Leagues history, cofounding the Negro Leagues Baseball Museum in the early 1990s. The placement of O'Neil's statue behind the field of players provides a metaphor for many Negro Leagues players, those who could not find a spot on the playing field, in this case literally finding themselves on the outside looking in. Interestingly, the eleven statues do not include Jackie Robinson, who is, in terms of mainstream public memory, the most notable of all Negro League players. The absence of Robinson on the field suggests that the legacy of black baseball goes well beyond the achievements of one individual and marks an attempt to show that black baseball should not be synecdochically reduced to one person. In other words, the museum suggests that black baseball's legacy is not just about Jackie Robinson but about numerous others as well, and those others should not be forgotten. The emphasis is on inclusion of individuals who contribute to the prosperity of black baseball. Individual merit is not a consideration, a sharp contrast from the National Baseball Hall of Fame and Museum.

Jackie Robinson: A Disparate Portrayal

The final section draws on these two historical contextualizations, using them to illustrate the significance of the differences in how Jackie Robinson is portrayed. This analysis will help show how Robinson's legacy within the Negro Leagues context is one legacy within a larger legacy of black baseball, whereas the National Baseball Hall of Fame and Museum uses Robinson's legacy to individualize his role as a pioneer. In short, the distinction of these portrayals offers two different legacies of Jackie Robinson.

The exhibits in the Negro Leagues Baseball Museum do much more than just document the racial history of baseball. Rather, they illustrate the role that Robinson's integration played both in the recognition of black baseball and in the ultimate erasure of it. By comparison, the National Baseball Hall of Fame and Museum emphasizes Robinson's individual legacy, as noted on his original and updated plaques. The Negro Leagues Baseball Museum goes beyond Robinson's role in baseball's integration. Ultimately, Robinson's legacy in the National Baseball Hall of Fame and Museum is one that is individualized, whereas his legacy in the Negro Leagues Baseball Museum is more collectivistic. The legacy constructed by the Negro Leagues Baseball Museum emphasizes the idea that Robinson was indeed a significant symbol in the inclusion of black players in Major League

Baseball but simply one individual in the larger scope of black baseball. The National Baseball Hall of Fame focuses on Robinson's legacy with a synecdochical strategy, meaning Robinson, the individual, represents the Negro Leagues, the whole, as an institution that was competing with the Major Leagues for decades.

The museum provides an illustration of a racially segregated institution that highlights both the discriminatory roots of black baseball's cultivation as well as its prosperous and profitable elements. The National Baseball Hall of Fame and Museum examines Robinson's legacy from an individualistic perspective, putting Robinson at the forefront of baseball's racial history. This is contrasted from the collectivistic approach to baseball's racial history that the Negro Leagues Baseball Museum states. Major League Baseball, as we have seen, felt it necessary to update Robinson's Hall of Fame plaque. For instance, at the National Baseball Hall of Fame and Museum, the new Hall of Fame plaque still mentions Robinson's statistical achievements, as is standard, but the noting of his "tremendous courage and poise in 1947" clearly marks a conscious shift in how Major League Baseball wants Robinson's legacy to be constructed, expressed, and remembered.

Jackie Robinson's promotion to the Major Leagues had implications far beyond the realm of sport; it is deeply interconnected to U.S. race relations more generally. Therefore, the difference between these two portrayals of Jackie Robinson is significant because it illustrates how our memories are constructed with a specific purpose in mind. The National Baseball Hall of Fame and Museum, as we have seen, constructs a narrative that places a premium on the values of individualism and color blindness. However, the emphasis on color blindness doesn't allow for the visibility of black baseball's role in the contemporary status of Major League Baseball as America's favorite pastime. This represents the National Baseball Hall of Fame and Museum as a microcosm of U.S. race relations more broadly, as much of what mainstream America conveys when it comes to race relations is color blindness. Conversely, the Negro Leagues Baseball Museum constructs a narrative that resists such themes, placing a premium on collectivity above all else. This tells us that black base-ball, at least as constructed through the Negro Leagues Baseball Museum, represents a narrative that parallels what many outside the mainstream emphasize when not included: an emphasis on collectivity, calling on a sense of unity within the community in order to portray strength and accord.

4

Jackie Robinson Day
The Contemporary Legacy

There is no question in my mind, Jackie Robinson coming to Major
League Baseball, was the most powerful moment in baseball history. It
transcended baseball.
—BUD SELIG, former Major League Baseball commissioner

Jackie Robinson has been heralded in baseball circles as an iconic
symbol of Major League Baseball's racial integration. With that
iconic status comes both convenience and controversy as to how
that status has been constructed and maintained over the course
of the past half century. There is convenience in how easy it is
to point to Robinson's integration as a focal point in baseball's
willingness to change its racist practices. There is controversy in
how Robinson's legacy gets commemorated, particularly by Major
League Baseball. This chapter looks at how Major League Baseball has commemorated Robinson's legacy in both convenient
and controversial ways. Major League Baseball's commemoration of Jackie Robinson excludes various aspects of Robinson's
life, such as his political activity, his debates with other prominent members of the black community, and his criticism of
Major League Baseball. Conversely, Major League Baseball's
commemoration of Jackie Robinson contains primarily aspects

that reflect a Major League Baseball that is inclusive, racially and culturally tolerant, and willing to correct its past injustices. In other words, Major League Baseball's commemoration of Jackie Robinson is one that stays away from the controversial Robinson and embraces the popular one. The commemoration ceremony analyzed in this chapter is representative of Jackie Robinson's popular, commemorative legacy.

At Shea Stadium, home of the New York Mets in Flushing, New York, thirty thousand fans attended the first "Jackie Robinson Day" on April 15, 2004. I argue that this commemoration was an attempt by Major League Baseball to define the legacy of the man who broke baseball's color barrier more than a half century earlier. In the week prior to this commemoration, Major League Baseball announced that April 15 would now serve as the annual tribute to Jackie Robinson's inclusion to professional baseball. This inaugural ceremony meant that every Major League Baseball organization would retire Robinson's number 42. No player will don this number on his jersey again, save those who were already wearing that number. This gesture was intended to preserve the legacy of an individual who made not only baseball history in 1947 but American history as well. Bud Selig, Major League Baseball commissioner, headed the ceremony with a presentation that illustrated Robinson's impact on the game and society as a whole. Included in the ceremony was a video montage that depicted Robinson from his days as a baseball player, with Robinson's widow and daughter watching the video while standing next to the commissioner. Jackie Robinson's memory and legacy, as well as his impact on the game, society, and history, were now "official."

As discussed in the introduction, public memories help us understand our expression of values, myths, and cultural knowledge. Commemoration, as a specific form of public memory, allows us to see how such expressions seldom remain fixed or static but change over time. In simplest terms, commemoration is defined as "something that honors or preserves the memory of another." Marita Sturken argues that commemoration functions as "a narrative rather than a replica of an experience that can be retrieved and relived. It is thus an inquiry into how cultural memories are constructed as they are recollected and memory as a form of interpretation." Stephen Browne addresses the interpretive aspect of commemoration: "When remembrance is organized into acts of ritual commemoration, it becomes identifiably rhetorical, thus a means to recreate symbolically a history otherwise distant and mute." Studies on commemoration, Browne continues, "focus upon the processes of constituting the memory as well as the implications of the product for future audiences and uses."[1] For the purposes of this chapter, "commemoration" will refer to specific practices that attempt to articulate cultural memory.

As Michael Kammen notes, "There is a powerful tendency in the United States to depoliticize traditions for the sake of 'reconciliation.' Consequently the politics of culture in this country has everything to do with the process of contestation *and* with the subsequent quest for reconciliation."[2] It would seem to follow, then, that *forgetting* is as important to public memory as *remembering*. Any particular public memory is based on the choices that are made about how to construct it, and this is perhaps especially true with regard to public memories that concern race in America. Consequently, a memory will inevitably exclude or eliminate any details that don't match the present narrative of said memory. In the case of Jackie Robinson Day, much of baseball's controversial past is eliminated. The narrative that Major League Baseball constructs is one that emphasizes the present-day status of baseball but fails to include the irreparable damage wrought on the Negro Leagues as a prosperous cultural institution.

This chapter is a historical investigation into the political persona of Jackie Robinson in order to explore how Robinson's legacy could indeed embrace a dramatic change. Ultimately, Jackie Robinson Day opens a critical space that invites us to question how a particular social group comes to own a specific public memory. In this case, Jackie Robinson Day puts an "official" stamp on this version of history. Major League Baseball's Jackie Robinson Day commemoration incorporates certain strategic choices that reflect a process that minimizes controversy, privileges white America's version of baseball's integration, and invokes a public amnesia about the social consequences Robinson's historic inclusion had on the Negro Leagues and the black community in general. Furthermore, this chapter explores the ways in which Jackie Robinson Day becomes a site that may impact not only our interpretation of the past but also our subsequent behavior in the future. Major League Baseball's construction of Jackie Robinson's legacy has implications for the potential ownership of a piece of history. Ultimately, Major League Baseball's 2004 celebration of Jackie Robinson Day allows us to question how a particular memory becomes owned by an individual social group. In the case of Major League Baseball, Jackie Robinson Day is constructed as a mere token of Major League Baseball's attempts to rectify its otherwise controversial past. My argument suggests that Jackie Robinson Day serves as a way for Major League Baseball to reinforce the belief that its game is the ultimate meritocracy. Regardless of background, any player who possesses the necessary skill set and overall requisite merit is allowed to participate. Robinson's social legacy, consequently, is appropriated by Major League Baseball to serve as a symbol for a postracial space once he achieved social prominence. By failing to include any of Robinson's political endeavors in the commemoration ceremony, Jackie Robinson Day represents a convenient symbol for racial equality.

Major League Baseball: A Postracial Institution?

Before we get comfortable with Major League Baseball's construction of its own cultural legacy, we need to know how this ceremonial context frames Major League Baseball as a postracial institution. By painting itself as a contemporary space that is free from any sort of racial bias, Major League Baseball makes its exclusionary past more palatable. Jackie Robinson, the remover of baseball's color line turned political figure, has long been represented as a revered cultural icon for racial equality. And rightfully so. At the same time, Robinson's inclusion in organized baseball in 1947 reinforces the belief that sport is a meritocracy—that is, rather than being judged on one's skin color, character, or class, he or she is judged on his or her merit. That is, Selig's speeches, both in 1997 and 2004, put the lie to this myth of meritocracy because they recognize Robinson almost exclusively for breaking the color barrier. Thus, Major League Baseball's contemporary integration narrative frames baseball as a postracial institution. Furthermore, the memory of Robinson's legacy is deemed one that places racial inequality behind us and thus constitutes a more just America. However, because of the attempts to commemorate his legacy as a convenient symbol for racial equality, the collective memory of Jackie Robinson has become overly simplified.

Understanding the implications of the choices made in Major League Baseball's Jackie Robinson Day campaign, specifically Selig's commemoration speech, requires a brief examination of Major League Baseball's previous commemorative portrayals of Robinson's legacy.[3] The 2004 commemoration had important continuities with, but also differences from, previous celebrations. Throughout, of course, the dominant portrayal of Robinson is that of resilient pioneer. Again, rightfully so. And while the legacy of Jackie Robinson has taken on myriad forms, the three commemorative events that depict Robinson as the most determined of American heroes came during the twenty-fifth, fiftieth, and fifty-seventh anniversaries of Robinson's rookie campaign with the Brooklyn Dodgers.

The first commemoration came on June 4, 1972, when Robinson was invited to Dodger stadium to celebrate the quarter century that had passed since his rookie year in 1947. The celebration was primarily constructed to retire Robinson's number 42 within the Dodger organization. Spectators saw a determined yet broken-down version of Robinson's former self, suffering from high blood pressure, diabetes, blindness in his right eye, and a limp, walking to the infield to accept his jersey retirement.[4]

Robinson's number was retired that day alongside those of former teammates Sandy Koufax and Roy Campanella. Later that year, Major League Baseball commissioner Bowie Kuhn invited Robinson to appear in a pregame ceremony during Game Two of the World Series, taking place on October 15, 1972. After ending a self-imposed boycott of baseball, one in which Robinson had protested the sport's poor record in hiring minorities for managerial and front-office positions, Robinson agreed to attend. During the televised event Robinson threw out the ceremonial first pitch and then took to the microphone, voicing his disdain for Major League Baseball's unwillingness to employ black Americans in more capacities. As Robinson stated, "I'd like to live to see a black manager, I'd like to live to see the day when there's a black man coaching at third base."[5] Robinson never lived to see that day. The World Series would prove to be his final public appearance, as nine days later Robinson passed away from heart failure.

In 1997 Robinson's legacy was marked with a big celebration that included invited dignitaries, but unlike in 1972 there was substantially more media coverage. The 1997 ceremony was similar to the 1972 commemoration in that Jackie Robinson's pioneering spirit was emphasized. Understanding the details of the 1972 ceremony is important because it tells us specifically two things about the 1997 event. First, the lack of media coverage of the 1972 ceremony suggests where we were in the racial landscape of American sports at that time. While it could easily be chalked up to the fact that mainstream media coverage of baseball in 1972 wasn't what it was in the late 1990s, perhaps Jackie Robinson's social impact still hadn't been felt broadly enough across the country so that it warranted little media coverage. Second, Major League Baseball's lack of inclusion of minorities in front-office and managerial positions as of 1972 was a glaring illustration of MLB's exclusionary hiring practices, thus legitimizing Robinson's public critique. By the time the 1997 commemoration took place, Major League Baseball had at least made some strides in the hiring of minorities in positions of authority. With these two things in mind, we can look to the 1997 ceremony as to how the celebration was more robust and vigorous than the 1972 version.

The 1997 ceremony served two purposes: it publicly celebrated the fiftieth anniversary of Robinson's historic integration of the Major Leagues, and it provided a platform to retire Robinson's jersey number 42 across all of Major League Baseball.[6] The ceremony included speeches by President Clinton, Major League Baseball commissioner Bud Selig, and Robinson's widow, Rachel Robinson. In addition to the speeches, there was musical entertainment, as singer Tevin Campbell performed first, singing "The Impossible Dream." While Campbell was performing, there was black-and-white footage of Robinson's career on and off the field shown on the stadium video screens in the outfield. After the performance and video footage, President Clinton and Jackie's widow, Rachel Robinson, accompanied by Selig, took the field at Shea Stadium.[7] As the *Atlanta Journal and Constitution* reported, "Selig told the crowd that 'no single person is bigger than the game—no single person other than Jackie Robinson.' Then came Clinton, an avid sports fan, who said, 'Today, I think every American should give special thanks to Jackie Robinson, to Branch Rickey and to all of Jackie's teammates with the Dodgers for what they did. This is a better, stronger and richer country when we all work together and give everybody a chance.'"[8] Clinton also added, "Robinson's legacy didn't end with baseball. He knew that education, not sports, was the key to success in life." Clinton then addressed how the racial barrier that Robinson broke on the field should be considered as a goal off the field as well. As Clinton stated, "Despite the gains made by the civil rights movement, Robinson's message of inclusion still applies to contemporary society. We can achieve equality on the playing field, but we need to establish it in the boardrooms of America." Then, Rachel Robinson spoke, adding that Robinson's legacy "is a great tribute to a more equitable society."[9]

The contrast between Selig's and Clinton's comments about Jackie Robinson's legacy bring the heroic arc of Major League

Baseball's "official" narrative into focus. For instance, Selig mentioned that "no single person is bigger than that game . . . other than Jackie Robinson."[10] These comments isolate Robinson at the top of the racial integration narrative. This is different from Clinton's final comments, noted above, which bring attention to the collective efforts of all involved rather than highlighting Robinson's individual efforts. By stating that "this is a better, stronger and richer country when we all work together and give everybody a chance," Clinton suggests that no one, not even Jackie Robinson, can reach the top alone. It is only when given a chance by others that individual success stories can be achieved. Clinton's remarks, for instance, depict the white authority in the foreground with the memory of the African American subject in the background. By doing so, there is an emphasis on the role that white authority continues to play in the narrative about race relations. Thus, in my analysis, Selig represents the voice of Major League Baseball, and his speech clearly shows, in contrast to Clinton's, an individualistic and heroic narrative. This is part of what compels me to focus primarily on Selig's statement in the 2004 commemoration.

2004: Analysis of a New Commemoration

Because the previous Jackie Robinson commemorations took place on significant anniversaries—in 1972 for the twenty-fifth anniversary of Robinson's first start with the Dodgers, and in 1997 for the fiftieth anniversary—a special commemoration on the fifty-seventh anniversary seems not to fit the pattern. As we saw in 1972 and 1997, the anniversaries that were celebrated were those of the typical "round-number" years, so the fifty-seventh anniversary almost seems arbitrary, if not puzzling. The commemoration did coincide with a moment of crisis for Major League Baseball's public image, however. I argue that the ceremony was concocted as a way to deflect attention from this crisis. In fact, Robinson's legacy is one that tends to privilege the benefits his integration had on the larger American landscape and neglects the dire consequences his integration had on the black community. Selig's similar neglect attempts to secure a rather limited and uncomplicated legacy of Jackie Robinson. Additionally, what was the impetus for this commemoration? Major League Baseball has never officially or publicly declared the motivation behind the timing of Jackie Robinson Day. The timing of this celebration makes its purpose fuzzy and opens the door to speculation as to Major League Baseball's motivation. The dominant majority who control Major League Baseball—read: white—may have had an ulterior motive. The ceremony primarily serves the needs of predominantly white Major League Baseball.

The 2004 commemoration came on the heels of the ten-year anniversary of Major League Baseball's 1994 lockout, and rumors of another player lockout were looming as baseball's collective-bargaining agreement was being negotiated.[11] The rumors of league-wide steroid use were also emerging, resulting in potential investigations by Congress and the public threats of Senator John McCain. Thus, leading baseball officials and players were forced to confront these potential crises in their public image. Perhaps Major League Baseball felt the need to address the issue in order to forestall the possibility of waning interest in baseball from the fans. As columnist Filip Bondy wrote the following day:

> Jackie stepped to the plate in a major league game for the first time 57 years ago in Brooklyn. A new era had begun for the sport, and all the statistical achievements that came before that momentous date were rendered more or less irrelevant. . . . When we speak with justifiable skepticism about the home-run pace of today, when we worry how steroids are tearing apart bodies and skewing the record book, we should start speaking with less reverence about all the marks before 1947. That was a terrible, wrongful time as well. And maybe that era deserves a big, white asterisk of its own in the record books and at the Hall of Fame.[12]

Bondy's remarks suggest that an inevitable black eye was looming for Major League Baseball both socially and historically. Perhaps if the league could get out in front of the black eye by controlling and constructing its own social and cultural legacy regarding the praiseworthy racial integration of Jackie Robinson, a chapter in the history of Major League Baseball that almost everyone views positively, then the blow might be absorbed more easily. This strategy could be considered to have proven successful. For instance, the reaction to the ceremony was a positive one. The *Atlanta Journal and Constitution* the following day printed a story that was representative of the majority of the media responses: "For all of Robinson's athletic success, he is remembered best for becoming the man who finally integrated baseball, and in the process helped set the stage for the civil rights movement. . . . Congratulations to Major League Baseball for recognizing such a special life, and for honoring it."[13] Here, we see that Major League Baseball is being commended and congratulated for celebrating the legacy of Robinson. Because of such public praise, the steroid controversy was ensured, at least for the short term, to be relegated to the background.

The broadcast of Selig's presentation began in the late morning, at approximately eleven, one hour prior to the start of the New York Mets' season-opening game. Prior to the ceremony itself, Jackie's daughter, Sharon, rang the ceremonial opening bell at the New York Stock Exchange to honor Robinson's April 15 anniversary. Across the country thirteen Major League Baseball stadiums hosting a season-opening game had ceremonies to commemorate the inaugural Jackie Robinson Day. Jackie's wife, Rachel Robinson, officials from the Major League Baseball foundation, and officials from the Jackie Robinson Foundation were present at the ceremony at the New York Mets' Shea Stadium. At all thirteen ballparks Jackie Robinson Foundation scholars threw out the ceremonial first pitch. But the principal ceremony was in New York at Shea Stadium, which is where the visual nature of Robinson's memory is emphasized the most in the commemoration ceremony.[14] While Robinson had passed away in 1972, the concept of a commemoration is to privilege the accomplishments and impact of an individual or event. With Robinson's widow in the audience, along with members of Robinson's immediate family, friends, colleagues, and former teammates, it is clearly indicated that Selig values Jackie Robinson's contribution and legacy: "Starting this season, we have proclaimed April 15th as 'Jackie Robinson Day' in an effort to bring more exposure to the life, values and accomplishments of Jackie Robinson."[15] However, as we will see later in the chapter, Selig's valuing of Robinson's contributions and legacy is constructed in a way that, once again, provides further evidence that the controversial aspects of Robinson's legacy only disrupt the convenient legacy of an obedient Jackie Robinson. More specifically, there are three noticeable themes throughout the following analysis of Jackie Robinson Day. First, Commissioner Bud Selig assumes his authority for Jackie Robinson's legacy. Second, there is no mention of the Negro Leagues or their subsequent demise because of Robinson's integration. Finally, the racial composition, particularly regarding African Americans, of Major League Baseball had not changed much in its fifty-seven years since Robinson's breaking of the color line.

On April 15, 2004, Commissioner Bud Selig stood before the media and thirty thousand fans at Shea Stadium, home of the New York Mets, to commemorate Jackie Robinson's legacy. During his initial comments Selig was paired with Jackie's widow, Rachel Robinson, both remarking on the journey Robinson and other athletes of color had to travel to make baseball what it is today.[16] Throughout his speech there were images of Jackie Robinson posted on the stadium's digital scoreboard, all of which were juxtaposed simultaneously with Selig's words. While Selig was talking, there were various points at which the commissioner's presence at the podium was supplemented with footage of Robinson during his playing days. As Selig's speech progressed, Rachel Robinson stepped aside. About thirty seconds into the speech, on the jumbo stadium screen we see footage of Robinson walking up the dugout steps, looking out onto the playing field, seemingly overwhelmed by the landscape. This image was immediately followed by footage of Robinson and Branch Rickey sitting next to each other signing Robinson's contract, laughing and smiling so as to suggest an always affable relationship between the general manager and player. This is followed by a close-up of a newspaper headline, which reads, "Brooklyn Signs Jackie Robinson." Images of Robinson embraced by his white teammates as well as his induction into the Major League Baseball Hall of Fame were included. These images were shown while Selig urged the audience to "look back on the history of the game" so that we may remember what a powerful statement Robinson made. Selig's narration directs our interpretation of the images, providing only one version of history on which to reflect—the version that celebrates integration—leaving out other versions that question the political and economic motivations of Branch Rickey, including versions that make compelling arguments for Major League Baseball as the culprit in ruining a profitable and prosperous institution like the Negro Leagues.

Selig's role as Major League Baseball commissioner carried an authority throughout the speech, an authority that took ownership of Robinson's historical legacy, as it symbolized the relationship between those performing a public memory and the subject being remembered. As Selig proclaimed, "[Robinson's inclusion] should have happened decades earlier." Selig also positioned himself as an authority on how members of baseball circles felt about Robinson's impact, proclaiming that "baseball's proudest moment" was "when Jackie Robinson first set foot on a Major League Baseball field." Here Selig's proclamation did not allow for discussion about the ambivalence that both black and white America felt regarding Robinson's inclusion in organized baseball. That is, Selig presents Robinson's integration as baseball's proudest moment, without equivocation. By not allowing for such discussion, Selig once again is able to take ownership of Robinson's historical legacy. Also, all that was shown is Selig by himself, not joined by anyone at the podium, with the official logo of Jackie Robinson Day on the wall behind him. This depicted the white authority in the foreground with the memory of the African American subject in the background, emphasizing the role that white authority continues to play in the narrative about race relations. In this case, when whites speak out in support of a traditional and hegemonic narrative (the story of integration), there is seldom any controversy. When others invoke the sign of "race" to suggest that the narrative is something of a myth or fantasy, it is typically deemed controversial. Selig presented himself as an authority on the social significance of the subject when he stated, "When you look back on the history of our game, there's no question in my mind that Jackie Robinson's coming to Major League Baseball on April 15, 1947 . . . was the most powerful moment in baseball history. It transcended baseball. . . . It was a precursor to the civil rights movement by fifteen or sixteen years." Here Selig positioned himself as a retrospective authority, establishing the historic and catalytic moment upon which the modern civil rights movement began. Selig is reinforcing his establishment as a racialized authority, pointing out to the audience that not only does he posit Robinson's legacy as historically important, but he (Selig) has the power to denote precisely when the modern American civil rights movement commenced.

At worst Selig ignored the political challenges that constantly emerged among the American people at that time as well as the apprehension from the black community.[17] It is important to notice the ambiguity of the pronoun "we" in this instance because the phrase "*We* are further ensuring" makes a multitude of assumptions about the audience. At best Selig did not provide a space for potential political challenges to be discussed. This lack of space for potential political challenges is evident when Selig utilized the ambiguous pronoun "we" when addressing Robinson's legacy. For instance, Selig stated, "By establishing April 15 as 'Jackie Robinson Day' throughout Major League Baseball, *we* are further ensuring that the incredible contributions and sacrifices he made—for baseball and society—will not be forgotten."[18] The pronoun "we" assumes that everyone in the audience wants to remember Robinson in this particular way; it presents Selig's efforts to invite everyone to remember Jackie Robinson in this way; it assumes that Selig can speak for everyone in the audience. Again, the phrase "We are further ensuring" assumes that everyone is on board with remembering Selig's illustration of Robinson's legacy. It assumes that everyone agrees that Robinson's integration is indeed the most powerful moment in baseball's history. It also assumes that the retiring of Robinson's number will be a sufficient homage to his legacy. These assumptions further illustrate how a white authority, Selig in this case, attempts to take ownership of a particular historical narrative, especially when we can assume that the majority of the audience Selig is addressing is white.

Additionally, the notion of responsibility was foregrounded at the outset of the speech. As Selig reminded us early on, "All of you have heard me say from time to time that baseball is a social institution with what I regard as enormous social responsibilities."[19] However, Selig does not follow this statement with any discussion about what those responsibilities might be. Consequently, there is no discussion about why or how the barriers to baseball's integration were created in the first place. Selig constructs Robinson's legacy as a reminder of a celebrated past that illustrates Major League Baseball's socially just response to racial discrimination. He does this, however, while simultaneously ignoring Major League Baseball's role in the invention of those socially unjust barriers in the first place. The social responsibility of which Selig vaguely speaks, then, is left for the audience to figure out—so long as the conclusion is one that privileges a just Major League Baseball rather than an unjust one. Selig's mention of baseball's social responsibility in the process of public memory thus unveils the social function served by a specific commemorative representation. That is, Major League Baseball's commemoration of Robinson in this instance provides a narrative that paints MLB as a socially responsible institution.

In addition to Selig assuming his authority over Jackie Robinson's legacy, there is a second theme worth noting during the 2004 ceremony: the lack of reference to the Negro Leagues. In addition to Selig, others were expressing interest in the legacy of Robinson's contribution to integration. Columnist Jim

Litke of the Associated Press commented, "What no one could have known at the time was how much more lasting its effect would be on history than baseball. And perhaps Robinson's legacy will always be bigger outside the game than inside it." The *Riverside (CA) Press Enterprise* had this to contribute: "Baseball has always been a metaphor for life in America. It's been about simple joy in a carefree setting, about individual opportunity and achievement. It has been a cross-cultural field of dreams." Yet the alarming trend is that still no references to the Negro Leagues are being made. On ESPN's official website there is a tribute to Jackie Robinson Day, with the lead article titled "Jackie Changed Face of Sports." Major League Baseball included on its official website various perspectives on the 2004 commemoration, most of which focused on Robinson specifically. Again, there is sparse mention of the Negro Leagues in the text.[20] Consequently, a rhetoric of silence (of the Negro League legacy) is being foregrounded in the integration narrative. That is, Major League Baseball chooses to emphasize Robinson's legacy in an attempt to reinforce the notion that Major League Baseball is a just and invitational institution. In order to do so, Major League Baseball remains silent on the damage it did to the Negro Leagues through racial integration.

In addition to Selig's authority over Robinson's legacy and the erasure of the Negro Leagues from the narrative, there is a third prominent theme in the 2004 commemoration: that of baseball's stagnant racial composition regarding African American baseball players in today's era. There was some concern expressed by critics about the impact Robinson's legacy may or may not have had on the game despite the impression that there is a racially equal playing field. The commentary from many members of the African American community, including present and former players, journalists, and fans, expresses the fact that the alleged playing field is not so equal after all. Just after the celebration of Jackie Robinson Day had slowed down, the *Los Angeles Times* recognized that the alleged progress baseball claims to have made is not as evident as one might think: "At a time when baseball has again been celebrating the anniversary of Jackie Robinson's debut in breaking the color barrier, the numbers equate to the continuation of an alarming trend." Dave Stewart, former four-time twenty-game winner in the late 1980s and early 1990s, expressed great concern about Robinson's legacy, the state of baseball today, and the integration narrative that is passed off today. Lamented Stewart, "In Bud's [Selig] words, the game is better today than it has ever been, but I think it has taken a drastic step backward. When you look at the numbers of blacks playing the game and the numbers in decision-making positions off the field, they're way down from even three years ago." When asked about the celebrations that started in 1997 to honor Robinson, Stewart replied, "There was good progress and a feeling among black players I think that baseball was trying to do something positive. Now . . . it's as if there's been a quick turnaround. . . . Why that's happened only the people internally know, but it's not good." John Young, a veteran Major League Baseball scout, echoed a similar sentiment: "I think there [are] societal changes to which baseball was slow in responding."[21]

The concern does not stop there. The *New York Daily News* the following day was one of very few objectors to the way Robinson's legacy was constructed: "Robinson was allowed to change [the exclusion of blacks] to a degree, but he always knew he could not knock down all the barriers. To this day, disgracefully, New York baseball has never known a manager of color, despite the city's many teams and century-plus track record." A week later, the *Seattle Times* pointed out a disturbing trend not mentioned in Selig's speech: "Only one team last season could field a pitcher and catcher who were both African-American. At those positions, the game looks about the same as it did before Jackie Robinson broke into the majors in 1947. . . . The overall number of African-American players was down to 10 percent as this season opened, and blacks comprised only 3.3 percent of all starters." Furthermore, the April 18, 2004, *San Francisco Chronicle* lamented baseball's alleged success as it stated, "What has changed since Robinson's arrival? Still no black owners. Only three black general managers, one currently. What appeared to be a progression in 1975 turned out to be a peak." Something of which there is no mention in baseball's celebratory integration narrative is what the *San Francisco Chronicle* article brought to the fore: "The number of African-American big-leaguers is under 10 percent for the first time since full integration—that was 1959." In Hank Aaron's editorial in the *New York Times*, the former Negro League star and Major League Baseball Hall of Fame inductee articulated the problem correctly when he stated, "Now, 50 years later, people are saying that Jackie Robinson was an icon, a pioneer, a hero. But that's all they want to do: say it. . . . It is tragic to me that baseball has fallen so far behind . . . in terms of racial leadership. People question whether baseball is still the national pastime, and I have to wonder too." Aaron continued to lament the concerns that are invisible in the integration narrative: "Here's hoping that . . . baseball will honor him [Robinson] in a way that really matters. It could start more youth programs, give tickets to kids who can't afford them, become a social presence in the cities it depends on. It could hire more black umpires, more black doctors, more black concessionaries, more black executives. It could hire a black commissioner." Consequently, there is a large portion of the integration legacy that does not match up with its mythical proclamations. In fact, Ralph Wiley, writing for ESPN.com, argued that even Robinson himself would be unsure of what to make about the state of the playing field in contemporary sport: "If Jackie Robinson were around today, I get the uneasy feeling that he would take one look around at the wide, wide world of sports, at what's been done, and undone, and what's left to do, and for all his strength, power, versatility, and relentlessness, I believe he'd start to cry. What I don't know is whether they'd be tears of joy or pain." Even Jackie's widow, Rachel Robinson, perceived the contemporary Major League Baseball landscape as one that is in a state of ambiguity. When asked about how her husband would view baseball's present unrest, Rachel lamented, "Jack would be disappointed, obviously, and he would be fighting back, as he always did in his lifetime, and saying, 'Let's not forget what it took to get us to this point.' . . . I think there is a perception that there is a level playing field now, and that things have progressed. That is not true."[22] The erasure of the Negro League legacy can be seen as a perpetuation of the decline in current African American ballplayers. This conclusion is not definitive but certainly a primary component in the integration narrative.

These three themes, Selig's authority of Robinson's legacy, the lack of reference to the Negro Leagues demise, and the lack of progress in African American inclusion across baseball, tell us something about the 2004 celebration of Jackie Robinson Day. Primarily, Selig's authority over Robinson's legacy, and therefore the popular version of Robinson's legacy, carries much more weight when the public is not made aware of the lasting consequences Major League Baseball's endeavor in 1947 had on the black community. The mainstream narrative gains further traction as well when the celebration constructs a rosy image of baseball's equal playing field, despite statistics and a few objections to the contrary. These three themes do not work in isolation. Rather, they work together by offering a tidy, simple narrative that only reinforces the popular mainstream version of Jackie Robinson's legacy.

To this point, we have examined the ways in which the 2004 Jackie Robinson Day ceremony constructed the popular, uncontroversial version of Jackie Robinson's social impact. We have not only examined the 2004 ceremony alone but looked at the 1972 and 1997 ceremonies as well in order to see how each commemoration was both similar and different in numerous ways. We will now discuss several implications of the 2004 ceremony, including a minimizing of controversy, a perpetuation of the myth that baseball is a meritocracy, a public amnesia that results from public commemorations, a questioning of the motivation behind the construction of a public memory, an examination into the role identity politics plays on public commemorations, and a look into how public commemorations link the past to the present.

First, the choices made in Major League Baseball's Jackie Robinson Day commemoration reflect a process that minimizes controversy, privileges white America's version of baseball's integration, and invokes a public amnesia about the social consequences Robinson's historic inclusion had on the Negro Leagues and the black community in general. In most historical and popular circles Jackie Robinson is depicted synecdochically for white America's pursuit of unity. Synecdoche is one particular trope useful for rhetorical critique, as "a metaphorical perspective entails other master tropes such as irony, metonymy, and synecdoche." According to Kenneth Burke, synecdoche is a rhetorical trope that can be described as representing a "part for the whole," or "whole for the part."[23] In other words, Robinson is viewed as a symbol for unity, synecdochically reduced to serve as a sign for white America's willingness to excoriate outdated social barriers, ultimately constructing Robinson as courageous and Dodgers general manager Branch Rickey as heroic.[24] Even when Robinson can symbolize the courageous nature of black Americans in the face of extreme racial adversity, his integration can still be questioned for bringing down the profitable black institution known as the Negro Leagues.[25] Yet the preference for the solemn, reserved, and patient image among predominantly white communities marks Robinson as a symbol of accommodation and reconciliation. Selig's speech further illuminates this depiction.

Consequently, the "Jackie Robinson" that was defined for this vast audience was one that correctly portrayed a great athlete and a daring pioneer. But never once was there a mention of Jackie Robinson as a prominent, outspoken political advocate. The symbol of Jackie Robinson presented during this commemoration was incomplete, functioning more as a convenient, uncomplicated representation of racial equality in the American public landscape. Rather than complicate the ideal patriotic narrative that MLB has used Robinson to portray, Major League Baseball was content with a very limited construction of Jackie Robinson's legacy. This is not to say that the Jackie Robinson portrayed during this ceremony was a negative one. It was, however, at best narrow and apolitical.

Second, Jackie Robinson Day serves as a tokenist rhetoric in order for MLB to sustain the belief that baseball, as a significant cultural space, will always be remembered as a meritocracy. As a result, Major League Baseball's construction of Jackie Robinson's legacy has implications for the ownership of a particular piece of history. Consequently, the Jackie Robinson that was defined for the audience during Jackie Robinson Day in 2004 was one that portrayed a great athlete and a daring pioneer. Never once was there mention of Robinson as a critic of Major League Baseball's exclusion of African American baseball administrators during the 1972 commemoration ceremony. Never once was there a mention of Jackie Robinson as a prominent, outspoken political advocate. Never once do we hear any mention of Robinson as a prominent and impactful political figure who testified in front of the House Un-American Activities Committee, as a political voice that publicly clashed with Malcolm X on the front pages of the *New York Post* and the *New York Amsterdam News*, as a controversial symbol for the inevitable destruction of the Negro Leagues, as the third choice for Brooklyn Dodgers general manager Branch Rickey to integrate baseball, or as someone who, by his own admission, began his career as a baseball player strictly for the money. These specific aspects of Robinson's life will be talked about in depth throughout the remainder of this book. As the ceremony is analyzed throughout this chapter, these images or memories of Jackie Robinson are not included because they do not fit in the neat, uncomplicated univocal narrative that highlights not only Robinson's legacy but also Major League Baseball's trailblazing initiative to include African Americans in the game.

From one perspective, Major League Baseball's creation of Jackie Robinson Day may be seen as serving as nothing more than an epideictic function, celebrating the desire to remember an incomparable social icon.[26] But if we examine the discourse more closely, we might begin to see that there is much more at stake here than the ways in which we preserve a figure from the past. Marouf Hasian Jr. and Cheree Carlson argue that memories are chosen to fit the needs of a group.[27] In the case of Jackie Robinson Day, the question is: Whose needs are being served? Major League Baseball Commissioner Bud Selig's presentation attempts to secure a rather limited and uncomplicated legacy of Jackie Robinson; most important for the present analysis, it fails to address the drastic impact that Robinson's integration had on the prosperous and profitable institution known as the Negro Leagues. The lack of an explicitly stated motivation for the 2004 commemoration might contribute to the suspicion that some ulterior purpose was in play.

Third, Jackie Robinson Day allows us to see the power of "forgetting" and the subsequent public amnesia that results from "remembering" the past. The power of forgetting can take full force in many of the contested meanings implanted in the process of public memory. In the case of Jackie Robinson Day, the elimination of Robinson's role as political advocate is significant because it further perpetuates white America's convenient symbol of racial equality. The same Robinson who was outspoken against the Vietnam War and who became portrayed as a political agitator later in his life is here presented as a relatively unproblematic symbol of America's alleged triumph over racial discrimination. It will be interesting to see if future celebrations of Jackie Robinson Day will give voice to Robinson's role as a political actor. It will also allow us to see the ways in which Robinson is possibly portrayed as a passive character, one who doesn't take such an active role in the breaking of social barriers as was once thought.

Furthermore, memory both defines a culture and is the means by which its divisions and conflicting agendas are revealed. According to Cloud, "Because social systems and their prevailing ideological justifications . . . are always contested, social stability depends on the ability of the ideology to absorb and reframe challenges."[28] For Major League Baseball, any potential challenges to the integration narrative regarding Jackie Robinson must be either silenced or reframed so that the appearance of baseball as a just social institution can remain intact. Bud Selig's construction of this particular public memory speaks about the power struggle between white and black communities during Robinson's integration as well as today. However, Selig really only touches on how the white community (via Major League Baseball) utilized Robinson's integration as a way to showcase Major League Baseball's willingness to tolerate racial integration. Perhaps the most effective way for Major League Baseball to do that was to commemorate Robinson's legacy in a way that emphasized Robinson as a tolerated individual rather than as a capable, outspoken part of a collective movement.

Fourth, this particular public commemoration brings into question the true motivation behind the construction of a public memory. No one knows truly why Major League Baseball decided to construct Jackie Robinson Day in 2004. When asked, Selig stated that it was to ensure that young people know who Jackie Robinson was. But that doesn't answer the question as to why he was commemorated in 2004 rather than any other year. The motivation behind a commemoration on the fifty-seventh anniversary remains ambiguous. This ambiguity, like the use of the ambiguous pronouns Selig uses during his commemoration speech, is important because it opens up the discussion as to what Major League Baseball's true motivations for the ceremony were. The ceremony did not mark a significant anniversary of Robinson's integration like the twenty-fifth and fiftieth anniversaries did. It did, interestingly enough, however, coincide with off-the-field issues that baseball was facing at the time, issues that were gaining more and more national attention. Because of the rumors of steroid use and a looming player lockout mentioned earlier in the chapter, leading baseball officials and players were forced to confront a waning interest in baseball from the fans. With Major League Baseball confronting such adversity, what better solution than to divert attention from the negative publicity and celebrate the legacy of the remover of baseball's color line? In the midst of mayhem and division, Major League Baseball looked to the historical symbol of unity found in Robinson.

It would be easy to presume that Major League Baseball might consider the timing nothing more than a coincidence. But constructing a specific public memory requires planning and rhetorical strategy. The issues at stake are addressed by those in power, essentially the ones constructing the specific memory. Bud Selig's construction of this particular public memory speaks about the power struggle between white and black communities during Robinson's integration as well as today. Specifically, Major League Baseball—through Selig's address—articulated a simple narrative in an effort to cover over or distract from more complex issues.[29] John Bodnar reminds us that while "public memory emerges from the intersection of official and vernacular expressions," it is the official expressions that "originate in the concerns of cultural leaders or authorities at all levels of society" that promote "interpretations of past and present reality that reduce the power of competing interests that threaten the attainment of their goals." So official culture or official histories "stress the desirability of maintaining the social order . . . [and] the need to avoid disorder or dramatic change."[30] Major League Baseball's Jackie Robinson Day avoids such a dramatic change to the popular version of Robinson's legacy by constructing a univocal historical narrative regarding Robinson's inclusion in organized baseball that fits very well with the narrative already established in popular or vernacular culture.[31] Investigating the rhetoric of this commemoration as an instance of how public memory can be understood as a space for competing social perspectives is a worthwhile endeavor for anyone interested in the ways in which particular social discourse gets privileged over others. According to Roseann Mandziuk, "The examination of public memory as a rhetorical practice reveals how acts of memorializing are sites of contestation in culture."[32]

Fifth, this case study brings to the fore the role that identity politics play in public commemoration. In Robinson's case, the stakes in the politics of identity are high because supporters of his commemoration must struggle with the ways in which his legacy gets remembered. More specifically, Major League Baseball's ownership of Jackie Robinson's legacy is a microcosm of how U.S. race relations can be viewed. The destruction of the Negro Leagues is necessarily "forgotten" in order for Major League Baseball to construct Robinson's legacy as a success story of U.S. race relations. Selig's version privileges the celebratory function of baseball's racial integration, resulting in a public amnesia of what damage Major League Baseball did to its black counterpart in 1947. As a result, certain representations of Robinson's impact are remembered, while others are forgotten. The themes of imagery, authority, status, and responsibility are represented at the center of Selig's discourse, ensuring that these themes play a central role in the public memory of Jackie Robinson. The consequence is that the "official" version of Robinson's legacy could function to silence aspects of his history that could otherwise question dominant definitions of racial politics and black identity. Selig's Jackie Robinson Day speech follows the current trend of refusing to create a public space to commemorate the more radical images of Robinson, perhaps because at this moment in time we are not willing to publicize the "cultural scars of difference" that Robinson embodies.[33]

Finally, as social critics, we should not only articulate the impact public commemorations have on cultural values and meanings but also articulate the ways in which public commemorations link the past to the present. As Hasian and Carlson argue, "We should subject every . . . narrative to an exacting analysis, revealing as many facets of a story as possible, thus enlarging the repository of memory from which to construct competing narratives. In this way, we might somewhat level the field of battle in the struggle to control the interpretation of the past."[34] When the author of a new discourse controls the way a historical event gets constructed in a contemporary context, critics should raise a red flag. This is not to say that Major League Baseball's commemoration of Jackie Robinson Day in 2004 is a revisionist account of Robinson's integration. However, the discourse of the 2004 ceremony does indeed provide an account that makes us consider what is at stake when a public only gets a one-sided and privileged side of the narrative. To not question such a version of a commemorative narrative allows that version to gain only more traction and momentum in public circles. In this case, the one-sided and privileged narrative leaves Jackie Robinson's legacy without a truly robust and comprehensive depiction.

Conclusion

Taking Inventory of a Legacy

This has been a book about re-remembering the legacy of a sports and cultural icon. We have recovered historical accounts regarding the legacy of Jackie Robinson so that we may understand how his memory has been constructed, articulated, maneuvered, manipulated, and commemorated. For instance, we have seen how the National Baseball Hall of Fame and Museum, as well as Commissioner Bud Selig, has attempted to secure a rather limited and uncomplicated legacy of Jackie Robinson. Robinson's political involvement during and beyond his baseball career has made him accessible in a plethora of forms, including Robinson's own syndicated column in the *New York Post* and *New York Amsterdam News* during the 1950s and '60s, as well as the black and white press's coverage of his HUAC testimony.

This investigation into the numerous memories of Jackie Robinson has offered, hopefully, an opportunity to explore the politics of race, resistance, and community at a time when white America was, and in some circles arguably still is, the face of the national pastime. While baseball experimented with racial integration, it did so with its share of obstacles and controversies. Despite its struggle, baseball helped create yet another legacy for white America's intersection with African Americans, at least in the realm of sport. Branch Rickey's social endeavor, known as "baseball's great experiment," has often been viewed as the face and lasting legacy of the Negro Leagues. But as we have seen here, Robinson's integration was much more than that.

This book has endeavored to offer an examination into the nuanced and strategic political efforts that Major League Baseball has carried out in order to manage its own myriad power dynamics. Americans have been guided in numerous ways to remember Jackie Robinson's legacy in primarily simplistic forms. This book has utilized public memory studies as a foundation for viewing Robinson's complicated legacy. The impetus for this book was Major League Baseball's 2004 Jackie Robinson Day because that is where I began to contemplate how a privileged, white, and male perspective, such as Major League Baseball's, is able to construct a hegemonic narrative that then controls the legacy of one man. Major League Baseball is a hegemonic institution as well as a space that reinforces a narrative that celebrates a racially sensitive theme while also silencing any aspects of controversy. Major League Baseball's efforts to rejoice in its contemporary racially tolerant policies have merely perpetuated a self-congratulatory narrative that must negotiate a paradox: on the one hand, MLB has highlighted Robinson's race in order for MLB to praise itself for its willingness to include participants of any race, while, on the other hand, MLB has dismissed Robinson's race in order to emphasize the fact that merit wins out above all else, regardless of one's race. I began by examining Robinson's postbaseball career and the clashes with numerous and prominent civil rights leaders. To develop this exploration, I then examined the relationship of Robinson and Paul Robeson and its impact on perceptions of Robinson from a national perspective. I then compared the presentation of Robinson in the Major League Baseball and Negro Leagues museums and then examined Major League Baseball's contemporary version of Jackie Robinson's legacy, as well as critiquing the limitations of that version. In essence, this book has illustrated how Major League Baseball has been able to manage its credibility issues and what is at stake with that process.

The analysis of Jackie Robinson Day laid out the contemporary legacy of Jackie Robinson. Specifically, the chapter examined precisely what that legacy contains, and the previous chapters examined that which the legacy excludes. Major League Baseball commissioner Bud Selig's speech, along with the videos and images included in the 2004 Jackie Robinson Day commemoration, helped create, or in this case invent, an official legacy of Jackie Robinson. However, the invention of this contemporary legacy, or the present-day version of it, could take place only because Selig and Major League Baseball knew what controversial aspects of Robinson's life should not be included in the commemoration ceremony.

Jackie Robinson's contemporary legacy, as portrayed in the 2004 Jackie Robinson Day commemoration, is one that tends to privilege the benefits his integration had on the larger American landscape, neglects the dire consequences his integration had on black baseball more broadly, and excludes the devastating effect that his integration had on the Negro Leagues specifically. Jackie Robinson's contemporary legacy emphasizes courage, perseverance, trailblazing, and positive social change. His contemporary legacy excludes Robinson's criticisms of Major League Baseball, fellow members of the black community, and America's political and racial landscape. With an understanding of Robinson's role in the American political landscape beyond the baseball diamond, we start to see not only how sport and politics are interrelated but how such a relationship can provide a space for learning how to engage sport as a site for social resistance.

Taking into account the strategies that are utilized in the commemoration process reveals that the relationship between conflict and identity comes to the fore as the commemoration functions to minimize differences in the hopes of cultivating a unifying voice and a transcendent cultural moment.[1] Thus, the power of forgetting can take full force in many of the contested meanings implanted in the process of public memory. As Sturken argues, "A desire for coherence and continuity produces forget-

ting. . . . The desire for narrative closure thus forces upon historical events the limits of narrative form and enables forgetting."[2]

This book has provided an opportunity to see how the contemporary construction of Jackie Robinson's legacy can contribute to memory studies. For instance, how public memory can
be understood as a space for competing social perspectives is a
worthwhile endeavor for anyone interested in the ways particular social discourse gets privileged over others. As rhetorical
critics, our role in recovering and articulating cultural meaning is significant as we attempt to understand the discursive
construction of public sites of memory. The goal of studies
interested in understanding the relationship between rituals of
commemoration and cultural meaning is "to understand how
public memorializing functions as a site of cultural expression
of values, myths, and cultural knowledge."[3] In the case of Jackie
Robinson Day, we are able to see how the 2004 ceremony dis-
cursively constructs the "Jackie Robinson legacy." For instance,
the Negro Leagues, a prosperous and profitable institution on
its own terms, has often taken a backseat to Jackie Robinson
within the context of Major League Baseball's integration narrative.[4] This tension creates a commemoration that is a site of
contestation. As Stephen Browne suggests, "To read these texts,
these patriotic tokens, is to read controversy, to situate a particular performance within a broader cultural terrain of contest and competition."[5] While controversy is present in the life
of Jackie Robinson, as documented in chapters 1 and 2 specifically, the controversial aspects of Robinson's life are excluded
in the 2004 Jackie Robinson Day commemoration.

"Sport" has been a key term within this book as we have seen
how sport stretches beyond the physical playing field. Baseball
serves as the space through which this book has been analyzed,
but the physical boundaries of the baseball diamond have not
been a factor. Rather, the peripheries of the baseball diamond
have proved to be where the political, racial, and commemorative
characteristics of Jackie Robinson's legacy have taken place. As
mentioned, public gatherings for the purpose of viewing sports

competition and the celebrations that come with it make up what is described as a "culture of viewing."[6] However, the competitive on-field endeavors with which Jackie Robinson took part were not analyzed in this book. Rather, the public gathering for the purpose of viewing, and celebrating, the legacy of one particular baseball player during Jackie Robinson Day in 2004 expands the notion of a culture of viewing beyond the competitive realm.

"Race" is the final key term that has been integral to this book. As mentioned earlier, race is something that society has constructed, manipulated, and even discarded at times. The role that Jackie Robinson has played as a cultural leader is one that focuses primarily on Robinson's race. In order for Major League Baseball to reconcile any of its past racial injustices, special attention must be put on the trials and tribulations Robinson had to endure as a black man so that Major League Baseball can be viewed as racially tolerant and racially inclusive. Robinson's race has been manipulated by Major League Baseball to serve this purpose, yet simultaneously his race has been discarded in order to paint Major League Baseball as a meritocracy. Thus, Major League Baseball's contemporary legacy of Jackie Robinson has created a false paradox. On one hand, Robinson's race has to be highlighted in order to serve the best interest of Major League Baseball's racially inclusive mythos. On the other hand, Robinson's race has to be discarded in order to serve the best interest of Major League Baseball's meritocratic mythos.

Robinson's testimony in front of HUAC, as well as his public exchanges with Malcolm X and Congressman Adam Clayton Powell, were well documented. However, Major League Baseball was either oblivious to Robinson's political past or simply did not want it to complicate the neat narrative by including it in the contemporary legacy. Either way, the legacy that Major League Baseball has invented relegates racial injustices, political controversies, and public criticisms of baseball to the past. Consequently, the univocal narrative of Jackie Robinson has been perpetuated, reinforced, and ultimately invented by Major League Baseball.

To use Robinson in the ways that Major League Baseball has damages part of America's racial memory. It nourishes our appetite for national amnesia on which we depend to conveniently forget about the problems we encounter on the racial landscape. Robinson's words and actions have been relegated to the past rather than used as a way to navigate the future. By following this course of action, it is a way to keep baseball's racial progress where it is, thus stifling it and never allowing it to adapt and evolve as time goes by. For instance, Robinson's pleas for racial progress across baseball have been addressed but not entirely realized. In 1990 the percentage of African Americans filling out Major League rosters was 18 percent. Twenty years later that number was down to 8.5 percent. That translates to more than a 50 percent decrease over two decades. Granted, the percentage of players of color has increased during that time, as the number of Latino players is up to 28 percent, thus making Major League Baseball more racially diverse that in decades past. However, the number of African American or Latino team chief executives or presidents still remains at zero.[7] Major League Baseball has failed to make any sincere attempt to mention these figures in any of its public commemorations of Jackie Robinson.

Understandably, a commemoration is an exercise in celebration rather than critique. However, the fact that a team executive position within any Major League Baseball team is filled by no one of color highlights one exclusion of Major League Baseball's own narrative: that Robinson's plead for individuals of color holding such positions has yet to be fulfilled. And Major League Baseball's inability to fulfill such a vision is much easier to push to the margins and ignore when we remain fixated on the racial-progress narrative we are exposed to through Major League Baseball's commemoration of Jackie Robinson.

Perhaps many of Robinson's supporters, those of the past and present, would be uncomfortable with a close examination of the controversial and critical Jackie Robinson. And while Robinson was without question an admirable and unquestionable

American hero, we do not have to make him, nor should we try, a symbol of perfection to appreciate the enormity of his social impact. However, Robinson's contemporary legacy, as we have seen, is one that attempts to do just that.

As we saw in chapter 3, the Negro Leagues Baseball Museum did not make Jackie Robinson a focal point in the legacy of black baseball because it was understood that Robinson was only one part of that legacy. Additionally, the legacy of Negro Leagues baseball did not hinge on the status of one individual player. Major League Baseball, at least in terms of controlling the narrative and painting itself in the most positive light, did depend on the legacy of Robinson the individual. Major League Baseball made a conscious choice to exclude Robinson's political past, as well as his explicit criticisms of Major League Baseball, from this particular narrative.

As Marita Sturken argues, "A desire for coherence and continuity produces forgetting. . . . The desire for narrative closure thus forces upon historical events the limits of narrative form and enables forgetting."[8] Without forgetting there is no public remembrance. This is predicated on the fact that specific choices must be made in order to construct and articulate a particular memory. The Negro Leagues, a prosperous and profitable institution on its own terms, has often taken a backseat to Jackie Robinson within the context of Major League Baseball's integration narrative. This tension creates a commemoration that is a site of contestation.

Despite the ability of the black community to successfully push for racial integration, it rarely, if ever, acknowledged the damage it would do to such an important cultural institution like the Negro Leagues until after the fact. Some writers from the minority press knew what transgressing the color barrier meant for the Negro Leagues, but to many of them, making a political statement against discrimination outweighed the fortunes of black baseball. If they did mention the possible consequences of racial integration, like Sam Lacy of the *Baltimore Afro-American*, the emphasis was on the negative components that would continue to exist if nothing was done about it. As Lacy wrote, "The Negro Leagues [are] a symbol I [can't] live with anymore."[9]

As Mark Ribowsky reveals, "Now the Negro League leaders realized how illusory and self-defeating their dare-to-dream optimism had been, having learned the real lesson of 1947. By design and by necessity, and certainly by factors that were beyond black baseball's ability to control, when the earth parted for Jackie Robinson on April 15, 1947, it would begin to swallow up nearly a century of African-American baseball."[10] This characterizes the hierarchical nature of the American social structure when professional baseball, while slowly at first, began to decimate the existence of the Negro Leagues by signing numerous players from the league once Robinson showed it could work. After 1948, as the black press saw the writing on the wall, black newspapers reduced their coverage of the Negro Leagues significantly.[11] The irony of this is that the discursive push for racial integration ultimately is the driving force behind the Negro Leagues' demise, thus relegating the black community to the bottom of the hierarchy once again. This is significant because it allows us to see how the call for the integration of the Major Leagues was originated. The black and communist press's push for baseball's integration might seem a bit out of place in a traditional American integration narrative. But what should not be overlooked is that both camps are vying for an equal playing field. Thus, to see that both camps are not given their due credit in the integration narrative adds to the paternalistic nature of baseball's perspective on integration. None of these political or racial perspectives is addressed in the contemporary legacy of Jackie Robinson. This is further evidence supporting the idea that race is manipulated and discarded when it is convenient.

Additionally, race played a major role in the media coverage of Robinson's legacy. In addition, one omission from this book is the examination of the American Communist Party and its call for baseball's racial integration. Little, if any, presence is given to its chapter in the integration narrative. It should not be surprising, then, that communism has not been placed in the foreground of the cultural legacy of either the Negro Leagues or Major League Baseball. According to distinguished professor of politics Peter Dreier, America's collective memory of baseball's integration took place in an era, the 1950s, that was considered "more 'stable.'" For instance, "women and African-Americans 'knew their place' and the Cold War provided Americans with a clear enemy that, while threatening, was more understandable than today's Third World Terrorism and interethnic wars."[12] Consequently, to include communism as a component of baseball's integration formula would make things unstable for America's collective consciousness regarding this situation. "America's game" suddenly might not seem so American.

According to journalist D. L. Cummings, "If it weren't for the impassioned efforts of the black press, there's no telling when baseball's color barrier would have been broken."[13] There was a sentiment among the black community, boldly articulated by the black press, that the future of black baseball, for good or bad, was contingent on Robinson's success. In a sense, we can make the case that the Negro Leagues, the whole, are being set up to be represented by one part, Robinson. This synecdochical depiction of an entire culture is potentially problematic for the Negro Leagues, simply because if Robinson had failed in his social endeavor, it could have spelled failure for the entire Negro Leagues organization.

Wendell Smith, whom Rickey hired to room with Robinson during the 1947 season, wrote for the *Pittsburgh Courier* and was able to convey a personal side of Robinson not exposed in any of the other publications. Just before Robinson made his debut with the Dodgers, Smith wrote, "If Robinson fails to make the grade, it will be many years before a Negro makes the grade. This is IT! If Jackie Robinson is turned down this week, then you can look for another period of years before the question ever arises officially again."[14] The *Boston Chronicle* foregrounded the importance of Robinson's success with a headline in its April 19 edition that read, "Triumph of Whole Race Seen in Jackie's Major-League Debut in Major-League Ball."

Roy Wilkins, NAACP president, wrote in his syndicated newspaper column, "The millions who read box scores very likely have never heard of George Washington Carver. But Jackie Robinson, if he makes the grade, will be doing missionary work with these people that Carver could never do. He will be saying to them that his people should have their rights, should have jobs, decent hours and education, freedom from insult, and equality of opportunity to achieve."[15] Thus, synecdochical representations and metonymic reductions are effective for putting a legacy to a face or name. But if that face or name was to fail in some aspect, the legacy is turned on its head.

In Michael Eric Dyson's portrayal of Martin Luther King, Dyson makes it a point to recall a complex Dr. King, to examine the convenience with which we as a society have chosen to remember the civil rights leader. As Dyson proclaims,

> King's image has often suffered a sad fate. His strengths have been needlessly exaggerated, his weaknesses wildly overplayed. King's true legacy has been lost to cultural amnesia. As a nation, we have emphasized King's aspiration to save America through inspiring words and sacrificial deeds. . . . [Eventually] King stepped out of character—at least the one they had written him into. . . . This is not the King we choose to remember. . . . The King we prefer is easily absorbed into fast-food ads for his birthday celebration. Or he is touted . . . as the moral guardian of racial harmony.[16]

Dyson's depiction of King in many ways parallels the depiction of Robinson that I have tried to capture in this book. Like King, Robinson's strengths have been inflated and his weaknesses overemphasized. Robinson's legacy too has been lost in a cultural amnesia that reduces his image to one of racial harmony and to a symbol that touts the "American dream" whenever it is convenient.

If we can easily remember Robinson the baseball player, then we should just as easily remember Robinson the critic of the House Un-American Activities Committee, Robinson the opponent of Malcolm X, and Robinson the impetus for the collapse of the Negro Leagues. The focus on Robinson as one individual making a significant social difference advances the mythos of individualism, which obfuscates our view of systemic racism. Thus, if we can be convinced to take notice of examples, particularly prominent ones, of individuals who have proved to have broken through racial barriers, then it is easier to be led to believe that racism, and thus any other racial barrier, is no longer as prominent on a larger scale. If any racial barriers do still exist, then, it is easier to believe that they operate on an individual level. That is, it is easier to be convinced that our culture, in this case baseball specifically, is not a racist institution. On the contrary, if there are any racial barriers that do exist, then they are being levied by racist individuals who do not represent the culture or institution as a whole. Major League Baseball's desire to focus individually on Jackie Robinson provides the most prominent example of this perspective.

This book has examined how the past impacts the present, and thus how present memories are constructed based on past events. Contestation and the struggle over how memories get articulated are germane to understanding the past's impact on the present. As Mandziuk writes, "By their very nature as interpretive, symbolic acts, public commemorations are significant sites of struggle over the nature of the past and its meaning for the present." What does Jackie Robinson's contemporary legacy tell us about how we construct public memories? It tells us that as social critics, our role in recovering and articulating cultural meaning is significant as we attempt to understand the implications of specific memory sites. By looking at Major League Baseball's commemorative ceremonies of Robinson's playing debut, the Negro Leagues Baseball Museum, the National Baseball Hall of Fame and Museum, the black and white press's coverage of Robinson's HUAC testimony, and Robinson's open letters to Adam Clayton Powell and Malcolm X, I have hopefully recovered and articulated numerous versions of Robinson's integration narrative and the cultural meanings of those myriad versions. "What memories tell us, more than anything," Sturken attests, "is the stakes held by individuals and institutions in attributing meaning to the past." Sturken goes on to explain that the process of memory "is bound up in complex political stakes and meanings. It both defines a culture and is the means by which its divisions and conflicting agendas are revealed. To define a memory," she concludes, is "to enter into a debate about what that memory means."[17] By no means has this book attempted to tell an official version or *the* version of Robinson's legacy. It has attempted to offer, and hopefully succeeded in offering, newfound perspectives on what Jackie Robinson means to us in a contemporary context.

As we have seen, Jackie Robinson is an easy figure to recall when exploring just about anything in today's sports world that involves race, inequality, or both. Barack Obama becomes the first African American president of the United States, so consequently the comparisons to Jackie Robinson become top of mind since both men had broken significant racial and societal barriers. The movie *42* is released sixty-six years after Robinson's Major League Baseball debut, and the reminders of a presumably postracial America become the topic of the day. Jason Collins, an African American basketball player, becomes the first openly gay NBA player in history . . . Michael Sam, an African American football player, becomes the first openly gay NFL draftee in history . . . Colin Kaepernick, an African American NFL player, openly protests the American flag . . . and the first question becomes "What would Jackie Robinson say?" And perhaps most important, we can reconsider our answer whenever the question of "What would Jackie Robinson say?" arises. The fact is, we don't know what Jackie Robinson would say about anything in today's world. To pretend that we do is both shortsighted and ultimately unfair to Jackie Robinson. It presumes that Robinson's perspective would have remained static and unchanged from his final days in 1972 to nearly a half century later. Too much has changed culturally, societally, and rhetorically since his passing to presume we know what anyone would say from nearly fifty years ago. And perhaps that is the greatest legacy we can give to Jackie Robinson: that his words, thoughts, and leadership are not to be carved in stone but rather provided as an opportunity to discuss, converse, protest, and deliberate the implications of today's racial landscape not just in baseball but in society on a larger scale.

Notes

Preface

1. "Barack Obama's Speech on Race," March 18, 2008, http://www.nytimes
.com/2008/03/18/us/politics/18text-obama.html?_r=0.
2. Long, *First Class Citizenship*.
3. Dyson, *I May Not Get There with You*, ix–7.
4. Jeff Passan, "Filmmaker Ken Burns Vows True Portrait of 'Most Important Person in the History of Baseball,'" September 17, 2014, http://sports.yahoo
.com/news/filmmaker-ken-burns-vows-true-portrait-of--most-important-person
-in-the-history-of-baseball-154702667.html.

Introduction

1. Edwards, *Revolt of the Black Athlete*, xv, 58.
2. Khan, *Curt Flood in the Media*, 7.
3. "Obama = Jackie Robinson?," August 25, 2008, http://www.politico.com
/story/2008/08/obama-jackie-robinson-012798.
4. "Barack Obama Is the Jackie Robinson of American Politics," July 2,
2015, http://www.stlamerican.com/news/columnists/guest_columnists/barack
-obama-is-the-jackie-robinson-of-american-politics/article_f9dd1dee-2038–11e5
-bd09-cb3a40a0c2fb.html.
5. "Can Barack Obama Become the Jackie Robinson of the American Presidency?," May 16, 2008, http://freepress.org/columns/display/7/2008/1651.
6. "Obama and Jackie Robinson," November 27, 2008, http://www
.huffingtonpost.com/michael-dowd/obama-and-jackie-robinson_b_138292.html.
7. Sierlecki, "'Grit and Graciousness,'" 117, 120.
8. "Turner Pics Bows Starry Slate," October 16, 1995, http://variety.com
/1995/film/features/turner-pix-bows-starry-slate-99128738/.

9. "That Rookie at First Is in a New Position," April 11, 2013, http://www
.nytimes.com/2013/04/12/movies/42-with-chadwick-boseman-as-jackie-robinson
.html; "Weekend Box Office: 42 Sets Record," April 14, 2013, https://www.forbes
.com/sites/scottmendelson/2013/04/14/weekend-box-office-42-sets-record-scary
-movie-5-bombs-oblivion-launches-overseas/#7f8065f126cd; 42, May 26, 2017,
http://www.boxofficemojo.com/movies/?id=42.htm.

10. "Why NBA Center Jason Collins Is Coming Out Now," April 29, 2013,
http://www.si.com/more-sports/2013/04/29/jason-collins-gay-nba-player;
"Is Jason Collins the Jackie Robinson of 2013?," May 2, 2013, https://www
.washingtonpost.com/blogs/she-the-people/wp/2013/05/02/is-jason-collins
-the-jackie-robinson-of-2013/?utm_term=.fb8c1ea309f8.

11. "The Parable of Jackie Robinson," May 30, 2013, http://www.espn.com
/espn/story/_/id/9318975/jason-collins-coming-was-supposed-generation-jackie
-robinson-moment-espn-magazine.

12. "The Modest Heroism of Jason Collins," April 29, 2013, https://
newrepublic.com/article/113062/jason-collins-gay-announcement-nbas-jackie
-robinson-sorts; "Jason Collins Walks in Robinson's Path," last modified April
30, 2013, http://www.usatoday.com/story/opinion/2013/04/30/sports-gay-rights
-jason-collins-column/2123327/.

13. "Beware: Critics to Come for Collins," last modified April 30, 2013, http://
www.foxsports.com/nba/story/jason-collins-gay-player-critics-will-grow-after
-initial-response-043013.

14. "Missouri Defensive End Michael Sam Is Consensus All-American,"
last modified December 17, 2013, http://www.kansascity.com/sports/college
/sec/university-of-missouri/article334188/Missouri-defensive-end-Michael
-Sam-is-consensus-All-American.html; "Mizzou's Michael Sam Says He's Gay,"
last modified February 10, 2014, http://www.espn.com/espn/otl/story/_/id
/10429030/michael-sam-missouri-tigers-says-gay; "Is Michael Sam the Gay
Jackie Robinson?," last modified May 20, 2014, http://www.msnbc.com/msnbc
/michael-sam-the-gay-jackie-robinson#52247.

15. "Don't Diminish Legacies of Michael Sam, Jackie Robinson with Comparisons," last modified February 10, 2014, http://www.usatoday.com/story
/sports/nfl/columnist/bell/2014/02/19/michael-sam-jackie-robinson/5627085/.

16. "Ex–NFL LB: Michael Sam Similar to Rosa Parks, Jackie Robinson," last modified February 12, 2014, http://www.cbssports.com/nfl/news/ex-nfl-lb-michael-sam
-similar-to-rosa-parks-jackie-robinson/; "Michael Sam, Jackie Robinson, and Why
the Bigots Always Lose," last modified February 11, 2014, https://www.theatlantic
.com/business/archive/2014/02/michael-sam-jackie-robinson-and-why-the-bigots
-always-lose/283735/; "Michael Sam from an MLB Perspective," last modified February 10, 2014, http://www.espn.com/blog/buster-olney/insider/post?id=4821.

17. "Michael Sam Cut by Rams," August 31, 2014, http://www.espn.com/nfl
/story/_/id/11431047/michael-sam-cut-st-louis-rams; "Cowboys' Jerry Jones
on Michael Sam's Release: We Needed Roster Spot," October 24, 2014, http://

www.si.com/nfl/2014/10/24/michael-sam-released-dallas-cowboys-jerry-jones; "Michael Sam First Openly Gay CFL Players as He Joins Alouettes," last modified May 22, 2014, https://www.thestar.com/sports/football/2015/05/22/michael-sam-joins-alouettes-first-openly-gay-cfl-player.html.

18. "Montreal: Adopted Home of Jackie Robinson, John Carlos, and Now Michael Sam," last modified May 26, 2015, https://www.thenation.com/article/montreal-adopted-home-jackie-robinson-john-carlos-and-now-michael-sam/.

19. "Michael Sam 'Never' Wanted to Play for the Montreal Alouettes," last modified September 26, 2015, http://www.cbc.ca/news/canada/montreal/michael-sam-nfl-montreal-alouettes-1.3245323; Kahn, "Michael Sam, Jackie Robinson, and the Politics of Respectability," 3.

20. "Colin Kaepernick Explains Why He Sat during National Anthem," last modified August 27, 2016, http://www.nfl.com/news/story/0ap3000000691077/article/colin-kaepernick-explains-why-he-sat-during-national-anthem.

21. "Colin Kaepernick Is No Jackie Robinson: And Shouldn't Have to Be," last modified September 17, 2016, http://www.sportingnews.com/nfl/news/colin-kaepernick-national-anthem-protest-jackie-robinson-jason-whitlock-black-lives-matter-49ers/8cbdw598gbf212dvlp3p9ussz.

22. "Jackie Robinson: 'I Cannot Stand and Sing the Anthem. I Cannot Salute the Flag," last modified August 29, 2016, http://mlb.nbcsports.com/2016/08/29/jackie-robinson-i-cannot-stand-and-sing-the-anthem-i-cannot-salute-the-flag/.

23. "What Would Jackie Robinson Think about Colin Kaepernick's Protest?," last modified August 29, 2016, http://sports.yahoo.com/news/what-would-jackie-robinson-think-about-colin-kaepernicks-protest-223118993.html.

24. "Jackie Robinson in 1972: 'I Cannot Stand and Sing the Anthem; I Cannot Salute the Flag," last modified August 29, 2016, http://www.theroot.com/jackie-robinson-in-1972-i-cannot-stand-and-sing-the-an-1790856572.

25. "If You Hate Colin Kaepernick, You Must Also Hate Jackie Robinson," last modified August 30, 2016, http://www.nydailynews.com/news/national/king-hate-colin-kaepernick-hate-jackie-robinson-article-1.2771561.

26. "Ken Burns' *Jackie Robinson* Documentary Is a Lump-in-the-Throat Trip That Goes beyond Baseball," last modified April 11, 2016, http://www.latimes.com/entertainment/tv/la-et-st-jackie-robinson-review-20160411-column.html; *Jackie Robinson*, last accessed May 26, 2017, http://www.pbs.org/kenburns/jackie-robinson/.

27. "Ken Burns Wipes Away the Myths to Reveal the Real Jackie Robinson in His New Documentary," last modified April 11, 2016, http://www.theroot.com/ken-burns-wipes-away-the-myths-to-reveal-the-real-jacki-1790854935.

28. "Ken Burns' New *Jackie Robinson* Documentary Kills Myths of Civil Rights Legend," last modified April 12, 2016, http://www.espn.com/mlb/story/_/id/15183801/ken-burns-new-jackie-robinson-documentary-kills-myths-civil-rights-legend-mlb; "A Troubling Myth about Jackie Robinson Endures," last modified April 15, 2016, http://time.com/4294175/jackie-robinson-burns-landis-myth/.

29. "Ken Burns Says His New Jackie Robinson Documentary Is 'about Black Lives Matter,'" last modified April 10, 2016, https://thinkprogress.org/ken-burns-says-his-new-jackie-robinson-documentary-is-about-black-lives-matter-329a3b797dc2#.3cwbrqab1; "Ken Burns on His New Jackie Robinson Documentary: 'It's About Black Lives Matter,'" last modified April 10, 2016, http://www.motherjones.com/media/2016/04/jackie-robinson-ken-burns-documentary.

30. "*Jackie Robinson* Documentary Kills Myths of Civil Rights Legend."

31. "*Jackie Robinson* Documentary Kills Myths of Civil Rights Legend."

32. "Media Circus: Ken Burns on His New PBS Documentary, *Jackie Robinson*," last modified April 10, 2016, http://www.si.com/mlb/2016/04/10/media-circus-ken-burns-jackie-robinson-documentary-pbs.

33. J. Robinson, *Jackie Robinson*, 90.

34. *The Jackie Robinson Story*, last accessed May 27, 2017, http://www.tcm.com/tcmdb/title/19169/The-Jackie-Robinson-Story/articles.html.

35. J. Robinson, *Baseball Has Done It*, 220.

36. Mandziuk, "Commemorating Sojourner Truth," 273.

37. Phillips, *Framing Public Memory*, 7.

38. Casey, "Public Memory," 29.

39. Zelizer, *Remembering to Forget*, 3.

40. Araujo, *Politics of Memory*, 206.

41. Savage, *Standing Soldiers, Kneeling Slaves*, 18.

42. Saillant and Simonard, "Afro-Brazilian Heritage and Slavery," 226.

43. Sturken, *Tangled Memories*, 7–8; Dickinson, Blair, and Ott, *Places of Public Memory*, 9; Araujo, *Politics of Memory*, 206; Hamilton and Shopes, *Oral History and Public Memories*, xv.

44. Greer and Grobman, introduction to *Pedagogies of Public Memory*, 3.

45. Perelman and Olbrechts-Tyteca, *The New Rhetoric*, 116–17; Goodall and Lee, *Trauma and Public Memory*.

46. Mandziuk, "Commemorating Sojourner Truth," 273; Sturken, *Tangled Memories*, 9, 1; Bruggeman, *Born in the USA*, 5.

47. This specific book addresses the Negro Leagues, but only in the context of Jackie Robinson's legacy. However, for further reading on the demise of the Negro Leagues, see Lanctot, *Negro League Baseball*.

48. Greer and Grobman, introduction to *Pedagogies of Public Memory*, 9; Mandziuk, "Commemorating Sojourner Truth," 272.

49. Faden, "Museums and the Story of Slavery," 264.

50. Lee and Thomas, *Public Memory, Public Media, and the Politics of Justice*, 15; Grano, *Eternal Present of Sport*, Kindle ed., 787–88.

51. Miller and Wiggins, *Sport and the Color Line*, x; Miller and Wiggins, *Sport and the Color Line*, xii; Wieting, introduction to *Culture, Sport, and Society*, 1; Grano, *Eternal Present of Sport*, Kindle ed., 828–32.

52. Butterworth, introduction to *Sports and Identity*, 3; Winslow, *Sports and Identity*, 19.

53. Zirin, *What's My Name, Fool?*, 22; Oates and Furness, introduction to *The NFL*, 10, 14.

54. Winslow, *Sports and Identity*, 20–21.

55. Rader, *Baseball*, 1.

56. Rader, *Baseball*, 3.

57. Elias, *The Empire Strikes Out*, 1.

58. Elias, *The Empire Strikes Out*, 1–2; Crepeau, *Baseball: America's Diamond Mind*, x; Dreifort, *Baseball History*, xv.

59. Rader, *Baseball*, 172, 186.

60. Burke, *A Grammar of Motives*, 59.

61. Norkunas, *Politics of Public Memory*, 6.

62. Connerton, *How Societies Remember*, 1.

63. Hasian and Carlson, "Revisionism and Collective Memory," 42; Filip Bondy, "History's Stats Add Up to Doubt," *New York Daily News*, April 16, 2004, 91; Hasian and Carlson, "Revisionism and Collective Memory," 42.

64. Cloud, "Hegemony or Concordance?," 124.

1. Robinson's Postplaying Career

1. Long, *First Class Citizenship*, xiv.

2. For some of his projects, Robinson would rely on ghostwriters. For instance, Robinson's column in the *New York Post* was written by playwright William Branch, and his column in the *New York Amsterdam News* was written by public relations expert Alfred Duckett. However, these ghostwriters played the role of articulating Robinson's ideas, while Robinson made it a point to review all discourse that was published under his name before signing off on it. See Long, *First Class Citizenship*, xvii.

3. Long, *First Class Citizenship*, 163.

4. Hakim, *All the People*, 20.

5. The full text of King's speech can be found online at http://www.americanrhetoric.com/speeches/mlkihaveadream.htm.

6. Long, *First Class Citizenship*, xiv.

7. Burgchardt, "Discovering Rhetorical Imprints," 441.

2. The Robinson-Robeson Clash

1. For a full text of Robinson's testimony, see "Hearings Regarding the Communist Infiltration of Minority Groups."

2. Rampersad, *Jackie Robinson: A Biography*, 211.

3. Rampersad, *Jackie Robinson: A Biography*, 211.

4. Hartnett, *Democratic Dissent*, 6.

5. Rampersad, *Jackie Robinson: A Biography*, 211.

6. Beeching, "Robeson and the Black Press," 340; Brock, "Black America's Contradictory Inclusion of Politics," 357.

7. Smith, "Robeson-Robinson Saga," 8, 9.

8. Smith, "Robeson-Robinson Saga," 10.

9. Rampersad, *Jackie Robinson: A Biography*, 211.

10. "Paul Robeson: Son of a Slave," http://www.marcnorton.us/93588/73331.html.

11. Rampersad, *Jackie Robinson: A Biography*, 211.

12. Smith, "Robeson-Robinson Saga," 11.

13. Smith, "Robeson-Robinson Saga," 13. The eight newspapermen were John Sengstack, Negro Publishers Association president; Ira F. Lewis, writer for the *Pittsburgh Courier*; Howard H. Murphy, the *Philadelphia Afro-American* business manager; Louis E. Martin, *Michigan Chronicle* editor; Dr. C. B. Powell, *New York Amsterdam Star-News* publisher; William O. Walker, *Cleveland Call Port* publisher; Wendell Smith, *Pittsburgh Courier* city editor; and Dan Burley, *New York Amsterdam Star-News* managing editor. See Smith, "Robeson-Robinson Saga," 13, 24.

14. Smith, "Robeson-Robinson Saga," 14, 13, 14.

15. *Chicago Defender*, April 30, 1949, 1–2.

16. Smith, "Robeson-Robinson Saga," 14.

17. Smith, "Robeson-Robinson Saga," 6, 18.

18. Smythe, *Black American Reference Book*, 667.

19. *Chicago Defender*, April 30, 1949, 1.

20. Smith, "Robeson-Robinson Saga," 18.

21. Rickenbacker, "Short History of the Committee . . . ," 90–117.

22. Smith, "Robeson-Robinson Saga," 17.

23. This notion of Robinson not accomplishing his breaking of baseball's color barrier on his own is addressed in other chapters. See chapter 3's discussion on the Negro Leagues Baseball Museum addressing black baseball's legacy as one that goes beyond Jackie Robinson, as well as chapter 4's discussion of media critics disparaging Selig's comments about Robinson acting alone.

24. Mardo, "Robinson-Robeson," 101.

25. Gray, *Watching Race*, 19.

26. Smith, "Robeson-Robinson Saga," 6.

27. Burke, *A Grammar of Motives*, 508; Ivie, "Prologue to 'Democratic Dissent in America,'" 158.

28. Smith, "Robeson-Robinson Saga," 6.

29. David Hinckley, "Un-American Activities: Mr. Robinson Goes to Washington," *New York Daily News*, November 30, 2003, 37.

30. Smith, "Robeson-Robinson Saga," 20.

31. Hinckley, "Un-American Activities," 37.

32. Hinckley, "Un-American Activities," 37.

33. Hinckley, "Un-American Activities," 37.

34. Rampersad, *Jackie Robinson: A Biography*, 215.

35. Rampersad, *Jackie Robinson: A Biography*, 215.

36. Smith, "Robeson-Robinson Saga," 21.

37. Smith, "Robeson-Robinson Saga," 21.

38. Smith, "Robeson-Robinson Saga," 21, 22.

39. Ivie, "Democratic Dissent," 109.

40. Hartnett, *Democratic Dissent*, 12; Ivie, "Democratic Dissent"; Hartnett, *Democratic Dissent*, 12.

41. Mardo, "Robinson-Robeson," 98.

42. Mouffe, *The Democratic Paradox*, 13.

43. Shelly Anderson, "Shelly Anderson Says Politics and Sports Are Mixing More Often, and That's Not a Good Thing," *Pittsburgh Post-Gazette*, February 20, 2004, B2.

44. Butterworth, "Ritual in the 'Church of Baseball,'" 112.

45. Zarefsky, "Four Senses of Rhetorical History," 31.

46. Burke, *A Grammar of Motives*,14; Hartnett, *Democratic Dissent*, 7; Zarefsky, "Four Senses of Rhetorical History," 27.

3. Cooperstown and Kansas City

1. It should be noted that as of 2014, the Hubert V. Simmons Museum of Negro Leagues Baseball was opened as part of the Owings Mills Branch of the Baltimore County Public Library. While this museum is worthy of rhetorical analysis in its own right, this project focuses solely on the MLB Hall of Fame and Museum and the Negro Leagues Baseball Museum in Kansas City, primarily because of the long-standing history of the museums themselves and subsequent place they have secured in both historical and mainstream popular culture.

2. Burke, *A Grammar of Motives*, 59.

3. Blair and Michel, "Reproducing," 40.

4. "The National Baseball Hall of Fame," http://baseballhall.org.

5. The ceremony included all members of the 1936 class except for Christy Mathewson, who had died in 1925.

6. "The National Baseball Hall of Fame."

7. "Museum," http://baseballhall.org/museum/exhibits/overview.

8. "Museum."

9. "Jackie Robinson," http://web.baseballhalloffame.org/news/article.jsp?ymd=20080429&content_id=7117&vkey=hof_pr.

10. Gary Thorne, "Robinson's Role in Integration Properly Noted," http://www.usatoday.com/sports/baseball/columnist/thorne/2009–04–17-thorn-jackie-robinson_N.htm.

11. Thorne, "Robinson's Role."

12. "New Jackie Robinson Hall of Fame Plaque Unveiled in Cooperstown," http://www.wibw.com/sports/headlines/21562289.html.

13. "New Jackie Robinson Hall of Fame Plaque."

14. The official "bust" of Robinson remains the same on the new plaque. Replacing the original plaque, the new plaque is now on display in the Hall

of Fame Gallery. The old plaque will not be entirely erased, but rather it will remain a part of the museum's collections and will be used for educational purposes.

15. Ribowsky, *Josh Gibson*, 17.

16. Sullivan, *Late Innings*, 128.

17. "Visit NLBM," https://www.nlbm.com/s/visit.htm.

18. "About NLBM," http://www.nlbm.com/s/about.htm.

19. "About NLBM."

20. "About NLBM."

21. "About NLBM."

22. "About NLBM."

23. The depictions of O'Neil's statue and its placement next to the backstop are analyzed in more depth toward the end of this chapter.

4. Jackie Robinson Day

1. *American Heritage Dictionary of the English Language*, 5th ed., s.v. "commemoration"; Sturken, *Tangled Memories*, 7; Browne, "Remembering Crispus Attucks," 169.

2. Kammen, *Mystic Chords of Memory*, 13.

3. While Jackie Robinson Day has included official annual ceremonies on every April 15 since 2004, this chapter does not examine each individual ceremony. Rather, the goal is to demonstrate the clear distinctions between the two previous milestone ceremonies in 1972 and 1997 and the very first ceremony in 2004 so that we get a snapshot of Major League Baseball's *initial* attempt at memorializing Robinson's legacy.

4. "Baseball Heroes: The Jackie Robinson Story," http://www.wtv-zone.com /moe/moesboomerabilia/page16.html.

5. R. Robinson and Daniels, *Jackie Robinson*, 216.

6. Exceptions were made for active players already wearing number 42 at the time. Upon their eventual retirement, the number 42 could then no longer be worn by any player.

7. Mike Lupica, "Tribute to Hero in Jackie's Memory, No. 42 Lives Forever," *New York Daily News*, April 16, 1997, http://articles.nydailynews.com/1997–04–16 /sports/18039874_1_rachel-robinson-bud-selig-bill-clinton.

8. Terrence Moore, "Thanks, Jackie: Shea Becomes Center of National Attention," *Atlanta Journal and Constitution*, April 16, 1997, D1.

9. "Baseball Honors Jackie Robinson," http://articles.cnn.com/1997–04–15 /us/9704_15_robinson_1_robinsons-widow-jesse-sims-tribute?_s=pm:US.

10. Lupica, "Tribute to Hero."

11. The 1994 players' lockout resulted in only the second cancellation of the World Series and the first since 1904.

12. Filip Bondy, "History's Stats Add Up to Doubt," *New York Daily News*, April 16, 2004, 91.

13. "He Conquered More than a Game," *Atlanta Journal and Constitution*, April 16, 2004, A18.

14. It should be noted that I am talking about the broadcast of the speech, not just the printed transcript. The broadcast can be found online at http://mlb.mlb.com/mlb/events/jrd/index.jsp?year=04.

15. http://mlb.mlb.com/mlb/events/jrd/index.jsp?year=04.

16. http://mlb.mlb.com/mlb/events/jrd/index.jsp?year=04.

17. There was much hesitation among the black community during Robinson's integration. Many owners of Negro League teams could foresee the consequences of integration regarding the future existence of black baseball. See Lanctot, *Negro League Baseball*, for further discussion.

18. http://mlb.mlb.com/mlb/events/jrd/index.jsp?year=04.

19. http://mlb.mlb.com/mlb/events/jrd/index.jsp?year=04.

20. Jim Litke, "One Small Step in Baseball's Long Journey," *Coldwater (MI) Daily Reporter*, April 17, 2004, B1; "Jackie Robinson's Legacy," *Riverside (CA) Press Enterprise*, April 19, 2004, A8; Schwartz, "Jackie Changed Face of Sports"; Mark Newman, "Robinson Honored with Special Day," http://mlb.mlb.com/nasapp/mlb/mlb/news/mlb_news.jsp?ymd=20040415&content_id=717876&vkey=news_mlb&fext=.jsp.

21. Ross Newhan, "On Baseball: This Problem Is More than Skin Deep," *Los Angeles Times*, April 25, 2004, D6.

22. Bondy, "History's Stats," 91; T. J. Quinn, "A 'Black QB' Mentality?," *Seattle Times*, April 23, 2004, E7; John Shea, "Big Leagues a Black Hole for African Americans," *San Francisco Chronicle*, April 18, 2004, C7; Hank Aaron, "When Baseball Mattered," *New York Times*, April 13, 1997, 15; Ralph Wiley, "W. W. J. D.? [What Would Jackie Do?]," http:espn.go.com/page2/s/wiley/030303.html; Terence Moore, "Where Are Braves' Black Americans?," *Atlanta Journal and Constitution*, April 15, 2004, F1.

23. Burke, *A Grammar of Motives*, 507.

24. Branch Rickey was the owner of the Brooklyn Dodgers at the time, responsible for signing Robinson of the Kansas City Monarchs of the now defunct Negro Leagues in 1945.

25. See Lanctot, *Negro League Baseball*.

26. Epideictic rhetoric is described as a celebratory discourse, one that focuses on the present state of affairs. Among the countless sources available on classical rhetoric, see Jasinski, *Sourcebook on Rhetoric*.

27. Hasian and Carlson, "Revisionism and Collective Memory," 42.

28. Cloud, "Hegemony or Concordance?," 118.

29. Major League Baseball in this case is considered to be represented by the words of Commissioner Bud Selig. This does not suggest that Selig's words are the only representation of Major League Baseball's viewpoint, but his words offer the most visible and concrete representation of how Major League Baseball addresses Robinson's historical legacy.

30. Bodnar, *Remaking America*, 13, 246.

31. This is not to say that only one official version exists within contemporary popular culture. It does, however, suggest that the popular versions of Robinson's legacy manifest themselves in ways that are easily digested by the mainstream public.

32. Mandziuk, "Commemorating Sojourner Truth," 273. For insightful studies on public memory through a rhetorical lens, see Biesecker, "Remembering World War II"; Blair, Jeppeson, and Pucci, "Public Memorializing in Postmodernity"; Browne, "Reading, Rhetoric, and Public Memory" and "Remembering Crispus Attucks"; Ehrenhaus, "Why We Fought"; Hariman and Lucaites, "Public Identity and Collective Memory"; Hasian, "Nostalgic Longings"; Owen, "Memory, War and American Identity"; and Zelizer, "Reading the Past."

33. Mandziuk, "Commemorating Sojourner Truth," 289.

34. Hasian and Carlson, "Revisionism and Collective Memory," 60.

Conclusion

1. Mandziuk, "Commemorating Sojourner Truth," 273.

2. Sturken, *Tangled Memories*, 8.

3. Mandziuk, "Commemorating Sojourner Truth."

4. This specific book does not directly address the Negro Leagues. However, for further reading on the demise of the Negro Leagues, see Lanctot, *Negro League Baseball*.

5. Browne, "Reading, Rhetoric, and Public Memory," 245.

6. Goldhill, "Seductions of the Gaze," 108.

7. "Percentage of Black Players in Major League Baseball Drops Again," http://www.huffingtonpost.com/2011/04/21/percentage-black-players-mlb-drops _n_852085.html.

8. Sturken, *Tangled Memories*, 8.

9. Ribowsky, *Josh Gibbons*, 13.

10. Ribowsky, *Josh Gibbons*, 9.

11. Doron Levin, "Pittsburgh Recalls a Neglected Title," *New York Times*, September 12, 1988, 1.

12. Dreier, "Jackie Robinson's Legacy," 54–55.

13. D. L. Cummings, "The Key Players: Black Reporters Pressed the Issue," *New York Daily News*, April 13, 1997, 12.

14. Richard Sandomir, "Mainstream Press Gave Minor Play to Robinson Breakthrough," *New York Times*, April 13, 1997, http://www.nytimes.com/specials /baseball/robinson-0413.html.

15. Ribowsky, *Josh Gibbons*, 6, 280.

16. Dyson, *I May Not Get There with You*, 5–6.

17. Mandziuk, "Commemorating Sojourner Truth"; Sturken, *Tangled Memories*, 9, 1.

Bibliography

Araujo, Ana Lucia. *Politics of Memory: Making Slavery Visible in the Public Space.* London: Routledge Press, 2012.

Beeching, Barbara. "Paul Robeson and the Black Press: The 1950 Passport Controversy." *Journal of African American History* 87 (2002): 339–54.

Biesecker, Barbara. "Remembering World War II: The Rhetoric and Politics of National Commemoration at the Turn of the 21st Century." *Quarterly Journal of Speech* 88, no. 4 (2002): 393–409.

Blair, Carole, Marsha S. Jeppeson, and Enrico Pucci Jr. "Public Memorializing in Postmodernity: The Vietnam Veterans Memorial as Prototype." *Quarterly Journal of Speech* 77 (1991): 263–88.

Blair, Carole, and Neil Michel. "Reproducing Civil Rights Tactics: The Rhetorical Performances of the Civil Rights Memorial." *Rhetoric Society Quarterly* 30 (2000): 31–55.

Bodnar, John. *Remaking America: Public Memory, Commemoration, and Patriotism in the Twentieth Century.* Princeton NJ: Princeton University Press, 1992.

Brock, Lisa. "Black America's Contradictory Inclusion of Politics, 1898–1998." *Peace Review: Journal of Social Justice* (September 1998): 357–62.

Browne, Stephen. "Reading, Rhetoric, and the Texture of Public Memory." *Quarterly Journal of Speech* 81 (1995): 237–65.

———. "Remembering Crispus Attucks: Race, Rhetoric, and the Politics of Commemoration." *Quarterly Journal of Speech* 85 (1999): 169–87.

Bruggeman, Seth, ed. *Born in the USA: Birth, Commemoration, and American Public Memory.* Boston: University of Massachusetts Press, 2012.

Burgchardt, Carl. "Discovering Rhetorical Imprints: La Follette, 'Iago,' and the Melodramatic Scenario." *Quarterly Journal of Speech* 71 (1985): 441–56.

Burke, Kenneth. *A Grammar of Motives.* Berkeley: University of California Press, 1969.

Butterworth, Mike. *Baseball and Rhetorics of Purity: The National Pastime and American Identity during the War on Terror.* Tuscaloosa: University of Alabama Press, 2010.

———. Introduction to *Sports and Identity*, edited by Barry Brummett and Andrew Ishak. New York: Routledge Press, 2014.

———. "Ritual in the 'Church of Baseball': Suppressing the Discourse of Democracy after 9/11." *Communication and Critical/Cultural Studies* 2 (2005): 107–29.

Casey, Edward. "Public Memory in Place and Time." In *Framing Public Memory*, edited by Kendall Phillips, 17–43. Tuscaloosa: University of Alabama Press, 2004. Originally published in *Chicago Defender*, April 30, 1949, 1–2.

Cloud, Dana. "Hegemony or Concordance? The Rhetoric of Tokenism in 'Oprah' Winfrey's Rags-to-Riches Biography." *Critical Studies in Mass Communication* 13 (1996): 115–37.

Connerton, Paul. *How Societies Remember.* Cambridge: Cambridge University Press, 1984.

Crepeau, Richard. *Baseball: America's Diamond Mind.* Orlando: University Presses of Florida, 1980.

Delgado, Richard, and Jean Stefancic. *Critical Race Theory: An Introduction.* New York: New York University Press, 2001.

Dickinson, Greg, Carole Blair, and Brian L. Ott, eds., *Places of Public Memory: The Rhetoric of Museums and Memorials.* Tuscaloosa: University of Alabama Press, 2010.

Dreier, Peter. "Jackie Robinson's Legacy: Baseball, Race, and Politics." In *Baseball and the American Dream: Race, Class, Gender, and the National Pastime*, edited by Robert Elias, 43–63. London: M. E. Sharpe, 2001.

Dreifort, John. *Baseball History from Outside the Lines.* Lincoln: University of Nebraska Press, 2001.

Dyson, Michael Eric. *I May Not Get There with You.* New York: Free Press, 2000.

Edwards, Harry. *The Revolt of the Black Athlete.* New York: Free Press, 1969.

Ehrenhaus, Peter. "Why We Fought: Holocaust Memory in Spielberg's *Saving Private Ryan*." *Critical Studies in Media Communication* 18 (2001): 321–37.

Elias, Robert. *The Empire Strikes Out.* New York: New Press, 2010.

Faden, Regina. "Museums and the Story of Slavery: The Challenge of Language." In *Politics of Memory: Making Slavery Visible in the Public Space.* London: Routledge Press, 2012.

Goldhill, Simon. "The Seductions of the Gaze: Socrates and His Girlfriends." In *Kosmos: Essays in Order, Conflict, and Community in Classical Athens*, edited by Paul Cartledge, Paul Millett, and Sitta von Reden, 105–24. New York: Cambridge University Press, 1998.

Goodall, Jane, and Christopher Lee. *Trauma and Public Memory.* https://www.academia.edu/11621959/Trauma_and_Public_Memory.

Grano, Daniel, *The Eternal Present of Sport: Rethinking Sport and Religion*. Philadelphia: Temple University Press, 2017.

Gray, Herman. *Watching Race: Television and the Struggle for Blackness*. Chicago: University of Chicago Press, 2004.

Greer, Jane, and Laurie Grobman, eds. Introduction to *Pedagogies of Public Memory: Teaching Writing and Rhetoric at Museums, Memorials, and Archives*. New York: Routledge, 2016.

Hakim, Joy. *All the People: Since 1945*. Oxford: Oxford University Press, 2010.

Hamilton, Paula, and Linda Shopes, eds. *Oral History and Public Memories*. Philadelphia: Temple University Press, 2008.

Hariman, Robert, and John Louis Lucaites. "Public Identity and Collective Memory in U.S. Iconic Photography: The Image of 'Accidental Napalm.'" *Critical Studies in Media Communication* 20 (2003): 35–66.

Hartnett, Stephen. *Democratic Dissent and the Cultural Fictions of Antebellum America*. Urbana: University of Illinois Press, 2002.

Hasian, Marouf, Jr. "Nostalgic Longings, Memories of the 'Good War,' and Cinematic Representations in *Saving Private Ryan*." *Critical Studies in Media Communication* 18 (2001): 338–58.

Hasian, Marouf, Jr., and Cheree Carlson. "Revisionism and Collective Memory: The Struggle for Meaning in the *Amistad* Affair." *Communication Monographs* 67 (2000): 42–62.

Hawhee, Debra. *Bodily Arts*. Austin: University of Texas Press, 2004.

"Hearings Regarding the Communist Infiltration of Minority Groups." *Hearings Before the Committee on Un-American Activities*. House of Representatives, 81st Cong., 1st sess., July 18, 1949.

Ivie, Robert. "Democratic Dissent and the Trick of Rhetorical Critique." *Cultural Studies/Critical Methodologies* 5, no. 3 (2005): 276–93.

———. "Prologue to 'Democratic Dissent in America.'" *Public* 11, no. 2 (2004): 19–35.

Jasinski, James. *Sourcebook on Rhetoric: Key Concepts in Contemporary Rhetorical Studies*. London: Sage, 2001.

Kammen, Michael. *Mystic Chords of Memory*. New York: Vintage Books, 1991.

Katriel, Tamar. "Sites of Memory: Discourses of the Past in Israeli and Pioneering Settlement Museums." *Quarterly Journal of Speech* 80 (1994): 1–20.

Khan, Abraham. *Curt Flood in the Media: Baseball, Race, and the Demise of the Activist Athlete*. Jackson: University Press of Mississippi, 2012.

———. "Jackie Robinson, Civic Republicanism, and Black Political Culture." In *Sports and Identity*, edited by Barry Brummett and Andrew Ishak, 83–105. New York: Routledge Press, 2014.

———. "Michael Sam, Jackie Robinson, and the Politics of Respectability." *Communication and Sport* (2015): 1–21.

Kinloch, Graham. *The Dynamics of Race Relations: A Sociological Analysis*. New York: McGraw-Hill, 1974.

Lanctot, Neil. *Negro League Baseball: The Rise and Ruin of a Black Institution*. Philadelphia: University of Pennsylvania Press, 2004.

Lee, Philip, and Pradip Ninan Thomas, eds. *Public Memory, Public Media, and the Politics of Justice*. New York: Palgrave Macmillan, 2012.

Long, Michael, ed. *First Class Citizenship: The Civil Rights Letters of Jackie Robinson*. New York: Times Books, 2007.

Mandziuk, Roseann. "Commemorating Sojourner Truth: Negotiating the Politics of Race and Gender in the Spaces of Public Memory." *Western Journal of Communication* 67 (2003): 271–91.

Mardo, Bill. "Robinson-Robeson." In *Jackie Robinson*, edited by Joseph Dorinson and Joram Warmund, 98–106. Armonk NY: M. E. Sharpe, 1998.

Martin, Randy, and Toby Miller, eds. *SportCult*. Minneapolis: University of Minnesota Press, 1999.

Miller, Patrick, and David Wiggins, eds. *Sport and the Color Line*. New York: Routledge, 2004.

Mouffe, Chantal. *The Democratic Paradox*. London: Verso, 2000.

Norkunas, Martha. *The Politics of Public Memory*. Albany: State University of New York Press, 1993.

Oates, Thomas, and Zack Furness. Introduction to *The NFL: Critical and Cultural Perspectives*. Philadelphia: Temple University Press, 2014.

Owen, Susan. "Memory, War and American Identity: *Saving Private Ryan* as Cinematic Jeremiad." *Critical Studies in Media Communication* 19 (2002): 249–382.

Palacio, Frank. *Obama: The Jackie Robinson President*. N.p.: Frank Palacio, 2016.

Perelman, Chaim, and Lucie Olbrechts-Tyteca. *The New Rhetoric*. London: University of Notre Dame Press, 1969.

Phillips, Kendall, ed. *Framing Public Memory*. Tuscaloosa: University of Alabama Press, 2004.

Rader, Benjamin. *Baseball: A History of America's Game*. Urbana: University of Illinois, 2008.

Rampersad, Arnold. *Jackie Robinson: A Biography*. New York: Random House, 1997.

Ribowsky, Mark. *Josh Gibson: The Power and the Darkness*. New York: Simon and Schuster, 1996.

Rickenbacker, William. "A Short History of the Committee . . ." In *The Committee and Its Critics*, edited by William F. Buckley Jr., 90–117. New York: G. P. Putnam's Sons, 1962.

Robinson, Jackie. *Baseball Has Done It*. Brooklyn: Ig, 2005.

———. *Jackie Robinson: My Own Story*. Whitefish MT: Kessinger, 2010.

Robinson, Rachel, and Lee Daniels. *Jackie Robinson: An Intimate Portrait*. New York: Abrams, 1996.

Saillant, Francine, and Pedro Simonard. "Afro-Brazilian Heritage and Slavery in Rio de Janeiro Community Museums." In *Politics of Memory: Making Slavery Visible in the Public Space*. London: Routledge Press, 2012.

Savage, Kirk. *Standing Soldiers, Kneeling Slaves: Race, War, and Monument in Nineteenth-Century America*. Princeton NJ: Princeton University Press, 1997.

Schwartz, Larry. "Jackie Changed Face of Sports." *ESPN the Magazine*. http://espn.go.com/classic/biography/s/Robinson_Jackie.html.

Sierlecki, Bonnie. "'Grit and Graciousness': Sport, Rhetoric, and Race in Barack Obama's 2008 Presidential Campaign." In *Sports and Identity*, edited by Barry Brummett and Andrew Ishak, 106–26. New York: Routledge Press, 2014.

Smith, Ronald. "The Paul Robeson–Jackie Robinson Saga and a Political Collision." *Journal of Sport History* 6, no. 2 (1979): 5–27.

Smythe, Mabel, ed. *The Black American Reference Book*. Englewood Cliffs NJ: Prentice Hall, 1976.

Sturken, Marita. *Tangled Memories: The Vietnam War, the AIDS Epidemic, and the Politics of Remembering*. Berkeley: University of California Press, 1997.

Sullivan, Dean. *Late Innings: A Documentary History of Baseball, 1945–1972*. Lincoln: University of Nebraska Press, 2002.

Wieting, Stephen. Introduction to *Culture, Sport, and Society* 4 (1996): 1–22.

Wieting, Stephen, and Judy Polumbaum, eds. Prologue to *Sport and Memory in North America*. London: Frank Cass, 2001.

Willett, John. *Art and Politics in the Weimar Period: The New Sobriety, 1917–1933*. New York: Pantheon Books, 1978.

Winslow, Luke. *Sports and Identity*. Edited by Barry Brummett and Andrew Ishak. New York: Routledge Press, 2014.

Zarefsky, David. "Four Senses of Rhetorical History." In *Doing Rhetorical History*, edited by Kathleen Turner, 19–32. Tuscaloosa: University of Alabama Press, 1998.

Zelizer, Barbie. "Reading the Past against the Grain: The Shape of Memory Studies." *Critical Studies in Mass Communication* 12 (1995): 214–39.

———. *Remembering to Forget*. Chicago: University of Chicago Press, 1998.

Zirin, Dave. *What's My Name, Fool? Sports and Resistance in the United States*. Chicago: Haymarket Books, 2005.

Index

Aaron, Hank, 133–34, 165
Abdul-Jabbar, Kareem, 3, 137–38
African American athletes, 39; declining percentage in baseball, 163–66, 180; and social protest, 3–4
Age (New York), 91
agency, 47, 56–58; battle with Malcolm X over, 58–61; battle with Powell over, 57–58; Robinson's, 124–26
agonism, 96–97
Alcindor, Lew. *See* Abdul-Jabbar, Kareem
Alexander, Clifford, Jr., 45–46
Ali, Muhammad, 3, 4, 8
All-American Girls Professional Baseball League, 118
American Bar Association, 82
American dream, 32, 184
American Sports Annual, 92
amnesia: America's national, xii, 28, 180; cultural, xiii, 184; public, 28, 37–38, 79, 152, 166, 167, 169, 172. *See also* forgetting
Anderson, Shelly, 98
Angelou, Maya, 137–38
Araujo, Ana Lucia, 23
Ashe, Arthur, 8
Atlanta Journal and Constitution, 155, 158
Atlantic, 12
authoritative memory, 75
Ayanbadejo, Brendan, 12

baseball: and America, 31–32, 163, 165; "great experiment" in race relations by, 33, 175–76; meritocratic myths about, 120–21, 123, 129–30, 166; as social institution, 162; as space, 125–26, 128–29, 178–79. *See also* Major League Baseball (MLB); Negro Leagues
Baseball Hall of Fame and Museum: creation and history of, 104–7; desegregation narrative of, 102, 103, 129–30; honoring of Buck O'Neil by, 109; individualism as theme of, 38, 102, 103, 108, 110, 116–17, 121, 130, 141, 146, 147; as meritocratic space, 103–4, 113, 116–19, 120–23, 124, 129–30, 131–32; Negro Leagues museum as different from, 103–4, 146–48; as representative anecdote, 101–2; Robinson plaque at, 112–16, 195–96n14; Robinson portrayal at, 28, 39, 124–27, 146–48; tours of, 107–8
Baseball Hall of Fame and Museum exhibits and displays: "African American Baseball Experience," 119–20; "Autumn Glory: Postseason Celebration," 134; "The Babe Ruth Room," 117–18; "Baseball at the Movies," 111; "The Baseball Experience," 131; "Cooperstown Room," 130–31; "Diamond Dreams: Women in Baseball," 118–19;

criticisms of, x, 154, 168, 180; steroid scandal in, 42, 157–58, 170. *See also* Baseball Hall of Fame and Museum; baseball integration

Malcolm X, 2, 22, 28, 35, 46, 179, 184; battle over agency with, 58–61; battle over legitimacy with, 52–56, 67; battle over mainstream with, 63–66, 67–69; on Bunche, 35, 61; letter to Robinson by, 58–60, 64–65; and Powell, 62–63; on Rickey, 58, 59; on Robinson HUAC testimony, 60; Robinson's response to, 65–69; separatist philosophy of, 74

Mandziuk, Roseann, 26, 171, 185

Mardo, Bill, 85, 96

Margolin, Emma, 12

McCain, John, 157

media coverage: by black press, 37, 80, 91–92, 142–44, 182, 183; by mainstream press, 68, 79, 80–81, 88–90, 154, 175

memory: authoritative, 75; as choice, 25–26; collective, 29, 41, 153, 183; and commemoration, 26, 27, 39; as concept, 22; and culture, 169–70, 171; and monuments, 23–24; publicness of, 23; and social groups, 26, 152, 169. *See also* public memory

memory studies, 2, 25, 176, 178

meritocracy: Baseball Hall of Fame and Museum portrayals of, 103–4, 113, 116–19, 120–23, 124, 129–30, 131–32; Jackie Robinson Day portrayal of, 42, 152, 153, 166, 168; Major League Baseball as, 103–4, 116–17, 122, 123, 124, 129–30, 131–32, 166, 168, 176, 179; myth of, 34, 38, 40, 153, 166

Michel, Neil, 102

Miller, Patrick, 29

Mother Jones, 17–18

Mouffe, Chantal, 96–97

Moulder, Morgan, 88

MSNBC.com, 12

Muhammad, Elijah, 53, 56

National Association for the Advancement of Colored People (NAACP), 84; Robinson defense of, 51, 54, 57, 62, 72, 73

National Football League (NFL), 11–14, 82

Negro Leagues: attendance at games of, 140; Baseball Hall of Fame and Museum on, 109, 111; black press coverage of, 182; demise of, 26–27, 41, 142, 146, 159, 160, 169, 172, 177, 181–82, 184–85; erasure of, 27, 162–63, 166, 169, 172, 181–82; MLB and legacy of, 27, 160, 162–63, 181; Negro Leagues Baseball Museum on downfall of, 142; Robinson connection to, xiv, 76

Negro Leagues Baseball Museum (NLBM): baseball color bar depicted in, 140–41; Baseball Hall of Fame and Museum as different from, 103–4, 146–48; baseball integration depicted in, 102, 103; collectivist narrative of, 38–39, 102, 103, 139, 145, 146, 147–48; creation of, 136–37; educational purpose of, 138–39; Negro Leagues downfall depicted in, 142; not hall of fame, 135–36; prominent visitors at, 137–38; public memory transmission by, 39–40; as representative anecdote, 101–2; Robinson depiction by, 103–4, 141–42, 146–48, 181

Negro Leagues Baseball Museum (NLBM) exhibits and displays: "Beisbol," 141; on black press, 142–44; "Changing Times," 141–42; "Drawing the Line," 140–41; "The Early Years," 140; "The End," 142; "Heroes of the Game," 144–46; "Major Leagues," 144; "Pioneers," 140–141

Negro Publishers Association, 83

New Republic, 10

New York Amsterdam News, 48; Malcolm X letter to Robinson in, 58–60, 65–69; Robinson letters to Malcolm X in, 52–58; Robinson syndicated column for, 34–35, 45

New York Daily News, 15–16, 42, 89, 90, 164

New York Post, 34, 45, 90

New York Times, 8–9, 165

Nixon, Richard, 45, 60, 61

Oates, Thomas, 30

Obama, Barack, ix, 5–8, 186

www.ingramcontent.com/pod-product-compliance
Lightning Source LLC
Chambersburg PA
CBHW021151160426
42812CB00078B/558